Structure

Structure
Concepts, Consequences, Interactions

Howard Lasnik and Juan Uriagereka

The MIT Press
Cambridge, Massachusetts
London, England

The MIT Press would like to thank the anonymous peer reviewers who provided comments on drafts of this book. The generous work of academic experts is essential for establishing the authority and quality of our publications. We acknowledge with gratitude the contributions of these otherwise uncredited readers.

This book was set in Times New Roman by Westchester Publishing Services. Printed and bound in the United States of America.

Library of Congress Cataloging-in-Publication Data

Names: Lasnik, Howard, author. | Uriagereka, Juan, author.
Title: Structure : concepts, consequences, interactions / Howard Lasnik and Juan Uriagereka.
Description: Cambridge, Massachusetts : The MIT Press, [2022] | Includes bibliographical references and index.
Identifiers: LCCN 2021060532 (print) | LCCN 2021060533 (ebook) | ISBN 9780262544542 (paperback) | ISBN 9780262371988 (epub) | ISBN 9780262371995 (pdf)
Subjects: LCSH: Grammar, Comparative and general—Syntax. | Generative grammar.
Classification: LCC P291 .L36 2022 (print) | LCC P291 (ebook) | DDC 415—dc23/eng/20220302
LC record available at https://lccn.loc.gov/2021060532
LC ebook record available at https://lccn.loc.gov/2021060533

In memory of David Michaels,
to whom we owe more than
can be expressed in a dedication.

Contents

Preface

Mark Twain once quipped that the report of his death was an exaggeration. Generative syntax too has been systematically reported dead, or dying, for a considerable amount of time. Arguably the major contribution to linguistics from the twentieth century, syntax has somehow managed to become unpopular in the twenty-first. Some blame this on syntax's own success at describing the universal nuances of linguistic structure. The idea is that much as the chemical patterns defined in the nineteenth century became intelligible once atomic physics was developed, so too syntactic patterns should follow from underlying disciplines. This is impressive if, as in the case of physics and chemistry, the patterns in point are explained after some serious unification—not explained away. In the case of syntax, the details of such a unification have not been forthcoming.

One often finds claims to the effect that a certain pattern has been accounted for, when on closer examination one can easily see that there is a formal impossibility in the process. An analogy may help see this. One may wish to claim that absolutely *all* numbers (natural, rational, real, complex, etc.) follow from simple associations of elementary generating operations such as succession, addition, multiplication, and the like, applying on a finite set of primitives—such as the natural numbers, from applying the successor function starting on, for instance, zero identified with something like the empty set. The claim is impressive. But it has no meaning, for no generating operation can yield, for instance from an initial finite set of natural numbers as just mentioned, those numbers that result from *inverting* generating operations (precedence from succession, subtraction from addition, and so on). There simply is no way of getting negative numbers by adding positive ones. In syntax, too, certain patterns cannot follow from certain operations, no matter how often we apply them. To see this, one needs to delve into these issues, in ways that our teacher Noam Chomsky had the vision to show over half a century ago.

Chomsky came to the study of syntax in an interesting milieu, immediately after World War II, which marks the birth of our contemporary information-based society. The previous generation had produced the most impressive intellectual achievements, underlying both the massive wars and their extraordinary aftermath: relativity and quantum physics, the periodic table and chemical bonds, the geological synthesis, evolution and genetics, economy theory, anthropology, a new mathematics. . . . Among these novel approaches to old conundrums, structural linguistics was beginning to emphasize the reality of *structure* within the study of language. Chomsky saw how recursive functions could be helpful in solidifying that approach, and was lucky enough to have the shoulders of Alonzo Church, Kurt Gödel, Alan Turing, Emil Post, and John von Neuman to stand on. If structure in geology, biology, or even physics had been shown to follow from a historical sequence, it was natural to ask whether, in general, structure could be associated to a kind of history that a computation can formally reproduce. A natural arena to test such an idea was language, where scores of phenomena had been, by then, neatly classified—though where an understanding of how humans possess that very faculty was missing.

Popular at the time in psychology in the US was the Skinnerian view that operant conditioning leads to fixing behaviors in animals. In Europe, the post-*Gestalt* years had given way to Piagetian associationism within cognitive development. Then controversial or obscure studies by Karl von Frisch and Konrad Lorenz (long before their 1973 Nobel Prize in Physiology) already argued otherwise, but it took Chomsky's genius to build this case for humans and their most characteristic ability. He did it in almost complete intellectual isolation, even if with the great resources provided by UPenn, where such luminaries as Zellig Harris, Nelson Goodman, and Yehoshua Bar-Hillel, offered intellectual excitement and rigorous training. None of the early pieces that now seem revolutionary saw the light until years or sometimes decades after being produced. It was only obliquely, through the 1957 *Syntactic Structures*—in the context of an engineering program that Morris Halle had camouflaged at MIT, as related to information theory—that these ideas emerged.

We are among the children and grandchildren of this enterprise and therefore have been witnesses to how much of its story unfolded. Some might see our perspective as biased, but at the very least we think our point of view is informed, if nothing else because "we were there" when some of these notions surfaced, or got developed, or even argued (or fought) for and over. So a large part of our effort will center on rationally reconstructing syntactic structure. We do not oppose pursuing ideas that have much of what we grew up with presented in a different, hopefully deeper way. We would genuinely love to see that someday. But to get to such a Promised Land, it is capital not to throw out the proverbial clean baby with the dirty bath water that provides its context. In order not to, with such an abstract thing as structure (which can easily be confused with the very context where it exists), it is important to proceed slowly and with caution, reconstructing the essential history of what is at stake when we argue for sentence scaffolding. We will do this in the following five steps.

Chapter 1 introduces the bases for these ideas, as some of us still teach them in our classes—we may be "dinosaurs" in that regard. Still, for many generativists this chapter will be at best a reminder of ideas they may have once heard, with mostly familiar arguments. The core of the chapter was solicited long ago by Ruth Kempson, appearing in 2011 in the context of the *Handbook of the Philosophy of Science* that she coedited. If there is something novel to that portion of the chapter it is the, actually old, idea that "flat" structures are as important in language as any others, which poses intriguing puzzles for a dynamical architecture of language. In addition, we have complemented the proposal in the chapter with a discussion (first published in a festschrift for Carlos Piera) that relates to an important puzzle Ray Jackendoff posed: how certain unanalyzed (atomic) verbs do not seem to exist. If this rings a bell for some readers, harking back to generative semantics, we mean that connection unashamedly. Readers can decide whether our new twist, within the Minimalist Program and broad Evo-Devo considerations, adds anything to resolving the matter.

Chapter 2 moves us to matters of so-called structure dependence. This notion, technically proposed in the context of describing the workings of transformations, is often interpreted to mean "related to structure," or some such. This is unfortunate in two ways. First, because Chomsky's original point, and what it entailed for an understanding of the transformational devices he first systematically explored, is then missed. Second, because in thinking that they are addressing this peculiar "structure dependence," some researchers seem to be repeating philosophical errors that had already been debated back in the day. More importantly, learnability considerations touch on these debates that continue to be in the eye of the storm—why any of this is controversial. Famously, Chomsky presupposed structure dependency in the language acquisition task, raising nativist considerations in the process. We consider such matters in detail, summarizing our 2002 contribution to one of these controversies in the *Linguistic Review* and our presentation in a 2007 conference Robert Berwick organized at MIT, at a time when machine learning experts claimed that structure dependence—as they understood it—is an emergent property of their powerful algorithms.

The remaining chapters are novel, although we have mulled over the ideas underlying them for decades. Chapter 3 is our favorite: here we summarize what we take to be the best the field can offer for the incredible role of structure. One of Chomsky's greatest contributions has been to focus the energy of scores of researchers, ourselves included, so as to produce the edifice that we report on. It is, in a sense, a gradually built construction: from the foundations that chapter 1 explores to ways in which the transformational component has been constrained (and continues to expand). This may make some nervous, because the precise formalisms that chapter 1 reviews have not, yet, been unified for the phenomena in chapter 3. We do not see that as a crisis any more than lack of unification in physics, at present or ever, has been seen as a crisis. We take what we do to be empirical, with the formalism being only a tool to guide research. We want sharp tools that can be falsified and have predictive power. But we lose no sleep over whether they have the rigor of a formal edifice, much as we aspire to that goal. That said, the results in chapter 3 are firmly established on empirical grounds. Even those, in the last third of the chapter, in which we go into extremely nuanced and highly surprising global effects. That too is structure, even if it challenges overly simplistic analyses.

Chapter 4 is an attempt to reflect on a formalism that can be made to fit within present conceptions of the minimalist sort, yet going beyond so-called derivations *by phase*. Derivational phases (by whichever name one uses to describe these pockets of regularity within derivations) are very dear to our hearts. At the same time, some of our most meaningful contributions to the field have directly argued for dependencies that, to the best of our understanding, really do go beyond said phases. Some might want to rule them out on just that basis, but to us that is the equivalent of preventing the quantum behavior of electrons on the basis of God not playing dice. We have no idea what sorts of games God likes, or whether They are willing to give the two of us any insight into how long-distance relations work. But just as Saint Anselm's old truism states that not even God can make what is done undone, we feel They may not be able to make long-distance relations go away! We review that argument for readers to decide on their own, and furthermore we propose a device that, we believe, may do the job of capturing at least correlations for the core relations. Although we also hasten to add that we suspect it is worse than that: some such dependencies would seem to go beyond such relations, in ways too monstrous for us to speculate about, at least here and now.

We wrap things up in chapter 5 (and a brief chapter 6 summarizing the argument), with a couple of challenges to our colleagues in the world of machine learning. We certainly enjoy our colleagues, conferences in which we debate these matters being among the most fun we have been part of. It is in this spirit that we present our views, not as an attempt to dismiss their work, but as a way to see if we can converge. The axe we have to grind is with regard to the existence of structure itself. Anyone willing to grant us that much has our full attention, particularly if they are exploring algorithms for which structure emerges. We do not intend to be cavalier with any of this. We see this entire project as an effort to show what linguists have been doing to a wide enough audience, admittedly from our own perspective. In many ways our goals are not that different from those of so-called Bayesian and connectionist models, and we have plenty of pieces published in those areas in which our respective works have connected. But as things are getting to serious levels of sophistication, we may need one another's full focus and attention. We are willing to learn and have never shied away from a formula or a formalism, let alone an algorithm. But let's not fantasize: what we ought to be pursuing are structural matters of the sort reviewed here, at the very least. This is why we present the chapter in terms of a proto-theory of language variation: if there were no linguistic variants, there would not be anything for learners to have learned.

We would like to take the occasion to thank various individuals for help with the pages that follow—starting with Noam Chomsky, who made the field as we understand it. We probably would not have turned our ideas about these matters into a monograph were it not for Tom Bever's encouragement, which Jay Keyser found persuasive enough to consider an actual publication. Directly relevant to the manuscript were helpful comments from the reviewers and various individuals who commented on different portions, including Bob Freidin, Ángel Gallego, and Diego Krivochen. Special thanks go to Rodrigo Ranero, Aaron Doliana, and Clara Cuonzo for help with references and the index, to Justin Malčić for final preparation of the manuscript, and to Clara for proofreading.

We want to end this preface by admitting that we don't mind being charged with one thing: saying little here that is really new. Even our formalism in chapter 4 is actually nothing but cleaning up an old proposal that was central in the late 1970s, which we contributed to formulating. If we are, thus, accused of being conservative, we admit it: we do like to conserve certain things. Or to put it in Faulkner's eloquent saying that we have lived by, as willing partners to this enterprise: "the past is never dead. It's not even past." Sometimes, though, the past has to be brought back into current consciousness.

1 Investigating Structure

Structural linguistics is rooted on Ferdinand de Saussure's posthumous *Cours de linguistique générale* (1916). The *Cours* stressed the need to conceive language as separate from what we use it for. It also concentrated on how language is, not how it changes, as had been the practice in historical linguistics (the dominant approach during the nineteenth century). A system of interconnected values, language as such is first pure structure, independent even from the meaning it may convey. Now, the notion "structure" itself is hard to pin down, particularly if the set of patterns that any given system is supposed to characterize is not finite. Therein is the fundamental difference between classical structuralism and modern generative grammar. Earlier models focused on those levels of language that are finite (phonology and possibly morphology), leaving linguistic creativity to the realm of language use. Great progress, for instance, was made in terms of the paradigmatic inventory underlying phonemics and the notion of linguistic feature. However, those levels of language that deal with its recursive nature (syntax) involve a subtler conception of structure, whose understanding has consequences for many scientific disciplines. Interestingly, a treatment of structure in these terms returns to some of the fundamental results in mathematical logic (the axiomatic-deductive method). In the present review of the notion structure we will concentrate on that conception, particularly its computational version. The central challenge of generative grammar is to propose a finite system of procedures to describe an infinite output. Although the milieu within which these ideas were developed is interesting (see Kracht 2003; Tomalin 2006; and Scholz and Pullum 2007), for the most part we will concentrate only on the ideas themselves, concretely the so-called Formal Language Hierarchy (FLH).

1.1 Weak and Strong Generative Capacity

Formal languages stem from the collaboration between Noam Chomsky and Marco Schützenberger (see Chomsky and Schützenberger 1963 for essential theorems and references to earlier work). Theirs is a systematization and generalization of proposals that, through the work of Bar-Hillel (1953), connects to Ajdukiewicz (1935). The work was influenced by Rosenbloom (1950, relating to Post 1947 and Thue 1914) and Davis (1958, which circulated in manuscript form during the early 1950s). These proposals developed a version of recursive function theory based on unrestricted writing systems and progressively more intricate conditions imposed on them. Chomsky's own take on these matters in the 1950s, however, and explicitly in *Aspects of the Theory of Syntax* (1965), is uniquely linguistic, and different from both the logico-mathematical tradition just alluded to and even the structuralist approach (inherited from Harris [1952]).

Chomsky certainly benefited from all these lines of research and collaborations (as well as the search for simplicity in theorizing emphasized by Goodman [1951]), but he took a naturalistic stand that had been absent from modern linguistic studies. This is not just in terms of seeking the mental reality of linguistic structures, which is a reaction to behaviorism (as in his 1959 review of Skinner [1957]). More generally, Chomsky was ultimately interested in the neurophysiological nature of linguistic structure (a concern that only Hockett [1955] shared), and to this effect he teamed up with Eric Lenneberg, Morris Halle, George Miller, Salvatore Luria, and other colleagues at Harvard and MIT to create what was eventually to be known as the "biolinguistics" approach. This decision deeply affects what to make of the notion of structure from a linguistic perspective.

The matter can be clarified, using terminology from Chomsky (1965), in terms of distinguishing the so-called *weak* generative capacity of a computational system and its *strong* generative capacity, notions that are defined for a *formal language*. One such object consists of a finite alphabet (a set of symbols) and some combinatorial rules, typically concatenations into strings of elements of the relevant alphabet. Given a formal grammar, a well-formed formula (abbreviated wff) is a string that is derived by that formal grammar. In this view, a given grammar G is said to generate a formal language L, which is a set of expressions. We can then say that a string S is a wff (with respect to G) if S belongs to the set $L(G)$, and concomitantly that G *weakly* generates $L(G)$. While this is all quite relevant for specifying axiomatic systems in general (e.g., to describe the structure of a mathematical proof), it is an empirical matter how the notion of a formal language (and weakly generating it) relates to the biolinguistic notion of a natural language. One could certainly assume that the relevant alphabet is a mental lexicon and the corresponding rules happen to be the combinatorial procedures that determine linguistic structure in a human mind. The ensuing object in that instance, for a grammar like the one presumed relevant for a language like English, generates a set of expressions, each a wff.

Chomsky has systematically rejected the idea that what human speakers carry in their minds is aptly described that way. This is, in part, because speakers appear to have intuitions even about unacceptable expressions (e.g., they can find the subject in the ungrammatical **who did John die?*). As Chomsky (1986b:chapter 2) argued (developing points already made in Chomsky [1965:60] and elsewhere), this suggests that wffs are somewhat orthogonal to what constitutes knowledge of a language. It is senseless to declare *who did John die* a member of the set of grammatical English expressions; but assuming otherwise, from that particular viewpoint, entails denying the factuality of speakers' intuitions about this ill-formed expression. In a nutshell, native speakers do not seem to mentally store anything like this English-as-a-set-of-strings.

In a biolinguistic sense, the notion "grammaticality judgment" is as hard to pin down as the notion "sickness."[1] Several factors are involved in each instance, and it doesn't help our understanding of either grammaticality or disease to resolve it by definition. Some sentences "sound bad" to the natives, but degrees of "badness" arise:

(1) a. *Who does John love?*
  b. *Who does John love Mary?*
  c. *Who do John love Mary?*
  d. *Who John love Mary?*
  e. *Who John Mary love?*

The expressions in (1) intuitively degrade as we go down the list, and declaring them (or not) part of "the set called English" doesn't help us characterize this fact. All objects in (1) except (1a) are not in the relevant set. However, speakers have robust intuitions about many structural aspects of all of these expressions. None of that real knowledge can be characterized by an "extensional" view of English. The analogy with a sick animal again drives the point home: declaring it sick, and therefore not a member of some (healthy) species, may help improve, for example, breeding methods—but it hardly tells us anything about the structure of the sick animal and, ultimately, its species.

One may be tempted to object that, if we are to proceed in biolinguistic fashion, it is pointless to use a computational system to describe human language; after all, classical computational systems do work with wffs. Even if that were true, nothing in the biolinguistics program would collapse: all it would mean is that the characterization of the relevant structure is to be sought beyond (that form of) computation.[2] But given our present understanding, there is no powerful reason to abandon a computational approach to linguistics. All that seems necessary is a slight shift in perspective. Intuitively, in (1b) fewer "grammatical features" are violated than in (1c). But then we need a computational system that generates not just the "terminal strings" corresponding to the sentences in (1), but all the nuanced properties of those strings (e.g., their configurational relations, agreement marks, construal conditions). In technical parlance, again from Chomsky (1965), we need to mind the *strong* generative capacity of the system (the set of strings generated *and* the structure assigned to those strings).

That distinction is central. In mathematics, it doesn't make a difference whether we generate, say, the set of negative numbers by inverting addition operations in the set of natural numbers or, rather, by multiplying natural numbers by −1. The relevant set is (weakly) generated both ways. However, in human language the most basic distinctions are captured only if close attention is paid not just to the output string, but also to the process that took us there. Consider, for example, Groucho Marx's famous comment: "I shot an elephant in my pajamas—what it was doing in my pajamas, I'll never know." Close analysis of this "structurally ambiguous" sentence clarifies the joke. The structures in (2) are identical at the terminal string. However, the structures also differ when we realize that in (2a) the prepositional phrase (PP) *in my pajamas* is attached to the verb phrase (VP) (thereby modifying the event of shooting denoted by the verbal expression), while in (2b) the same phrase is attached to the direct object noun phrase (NP) (entailing modification of the elephant referred to by that nominal expression).

(2) *I shot an elephant in my pajamas.*

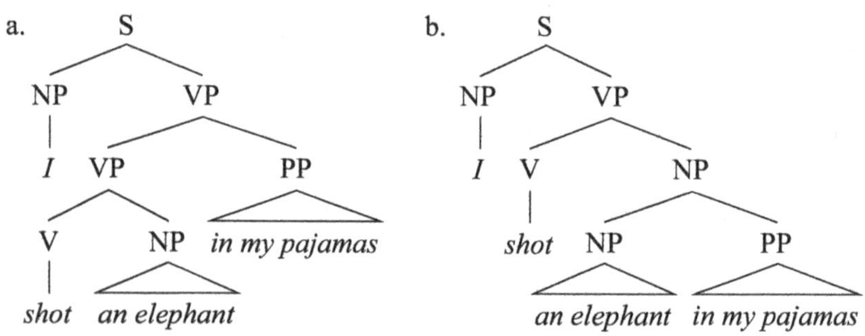

So there are two ways of strongly generating the output string, which underlies the approach linguists give to this kind of ambiguity.[3] The sentence *I shot an elephant in my pajamas* is structurally ambiguous if it can be generated in nonequivalent ways, as in (2). This basically entails that phrasal relations are not "associative," for it matters much whether *in my pajamas* is associated to *an elephant* or to *shot*.[4] Groucho's joke works because pragmatic considerations favor the structuring in (2a), but deadpanning that the elephant had managed to enter his pajamas forces the unexpected reading.

We may consider a "generative procedure" to be not just the results of a derivation (its terminal string) but also the process that took the system there. The complex system constituting the generative procedure may be technically called an I-language, in which the "I" stands for "intensional" or "internal."[5] In a naturalistic program, the only thing that is taken to exist within the mind/brain is the generative procedure itself, which yields structured expressions as in (2) and more intricate ones. If structureless strings turn out also to play a role (see section 1.3.2), it is interesting how that can be, with the grammar yielding structured strings.

Somewhat analogously, if physical forces result in structured atoms, it is interesting to know whether subatomic dependencies are also possible. In the linguistic instance, the issue boils down to whether, and if so how, associativity (in the sense of note 4) is ever recovered for some grammatical dependencies, contrary to what we witness in (2). More generally, from a biolinguistic or I-language perspective, the results in Formal Language Theory that matter most are those that pertain to strong generative capacity—and these are actually rather hard to come by in such purely formal terms.

All of that said, we feel it is important not to throw the baby out with the bath water: we show in the following why we find reason for optimism in the study of the formal structures that underlie language, even if much work lies ahead. Our approach in this review can largely be seen in this light, as we know of no worked-out alternative to the computational theory of language, even when it comes to I-language as just described.

1.2 The Formal Language Hierarchy

Structural linguistics showed us how such phenomena as "a phrase" or even "a phoneme" are far from simple-minded, directly observable conditions that one could abstract from, say, a synthesized speech stream. The problem starts with a drastic oversimplification that this very sentence highlights. It has twelve words. This is easy to ascertain in our familiar writing system. Such a system appears so natural to us that we are bound to forget that it involves several theoretical abstractions, including one at the level of words and another at the level of the letters that compose the orthographic representations. While both of these are important, neither has a privileged status in syntactic theory.

Any student of linguistics knows that words group themselves into constituents. While such nuances are part of the training of linguists, no writing system fully represents them. What gets written as words and letters is already a folk theoretical proposal about language. English reminds us how limited that proposal is in the case of letters. If one wanted to remain close to observables, one would have to turn to a phonetic transcription;[6] then the very first issue would be to identify (abstract) words out of such a speech stream. Writing gives us a shorthand method to achieve this task, although it has little to say about phrases, and literally nothing to contribute regarding more complex structural conditions of the sort we discuss in what follows. These ideas were clearly overlooked in the logical tradition alluded to in the previous section, which still informs mainstream computational linguistics through the very notion of a formal language.

To see the centrality of structure to language, recall how Chomsky began the discussion of grammar in *Syntactic Structures* (1957) by presenting "an elementary linguistic theory" consisting solely of finite-state Markov processes (used often in thermodynamics and statistical mechanics, mathematical biology, economics, and more). These are mathematical models for a system's progress, for which a given state depends solely on itself (or a finite collection of preceding states). In other words, Markovian systems are devoid of "memory." Chomsky offered an often-cited argument for the inadequacy of these processes as general models of human languages: (portions of) such languages have non-Markovian properties.[7] As presented, the argument was expressed in terms of sets of wffs and the (weak) generative capacity of the grammars generating them. But between the lines of Chomsky (1965:60–61) is another, equally powerful and more straightforward, argument: sentences of human languages are highly structured objects, whereas Markov processes can be seen as providing strings of symbols only.[8]

1.2.1 The Upper Limits of Finite-State Description

For illustrative purposes, we begin with some simple examples of finite-state formal languages (the first finite, the second infinite), from Chomsky (1957), and graphic representations of the finite-state Markov processes generating them:

(3) a. *The man comes / The men come*

b.

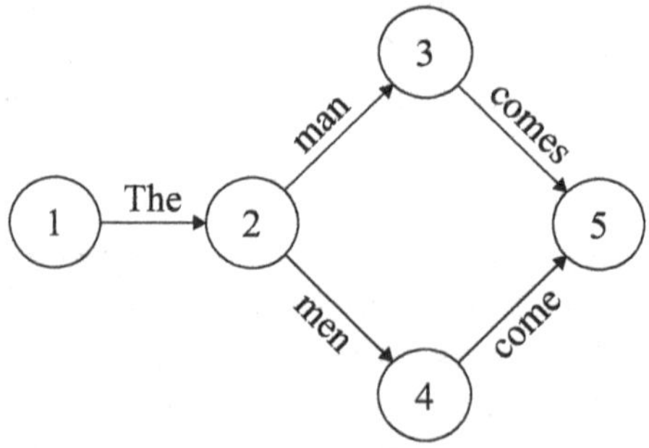

(4) a. *The man comes / The old man comes / The old old man comes / . . .*
a′. *The men come / The old men come / The old old men come / . . .*
b.

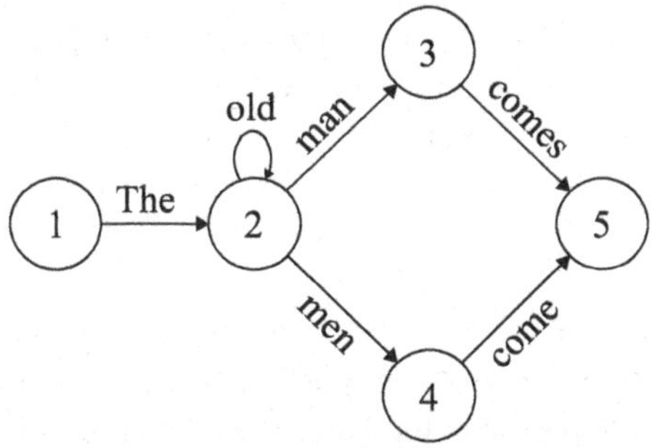

It should be easy to see that the adjective *old* in (4) can iterate as many times as the loop in the graph is invoked. This type of iteration is characteristic of finite-state Markov processes, and it can be introduced indefinitely many times, as follows:

(5) a. *The man comes / The* (*old*) *man* (*always*) *comes / . . .*
b.

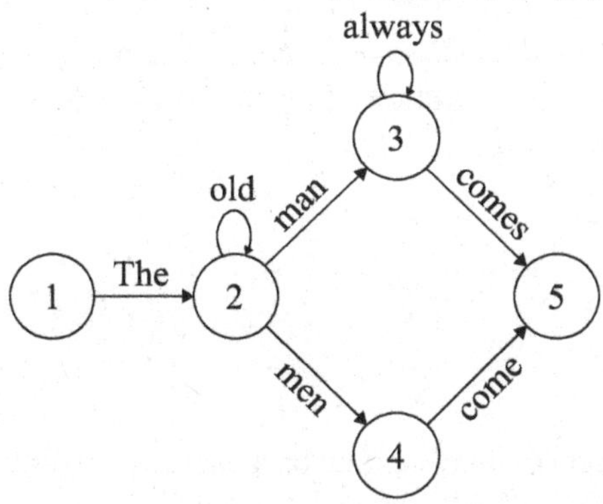

Bear in mind, however, a limitation of the situation in (5). The second loop in the upper part of the graph has no bearing on the lower part. So according to (5b) we cannot generate *the* (*old* . . .) *men always* (*always* . . .) *come*, only the singular version of that sentence, as only in that version have we made the loop explicit. In a sense, the iteration that the loop introduces is only relevant with regard to whatever structure has been generated up to the point in which it appears—and it ceases to be relevant thereafter. We can see that by noting that although we can iterate the *old* adjective and the *always* adverb, there is no way of guaranteeing that the number of iterations of the first coincides with the number of iterations of the second. They are independent processes.

Alongside those, Chomsky introduces some non-finite-state context-free languages. Now we present these and the context-free grammars generating them. Chomsky calls these [Σ, F] grammars, as Σ is a finite set of initial strings and F a finite set of Post-style instruction formulas, each rewriting a single symbol (rewrite rules):[9]

(6) *ab, aabb, aaabbb, . . .* , and in general, all sentences consisting of n occurrences of a followed by n occurrences of b and only these.

(7) $\Sigma : S$
$F : S \rightarrow aSb$
$S \rightarrow ab$

Even such a simple system is capable of a form of recursion more powerful than the iterations discussed thus far. Note, in particular, that (7) generates languages of the form $a^n b^n$ (the superscript indicates the number of token repetitions of a or b). Can we guarantee that the number of repetitions is the very same for a and b? Readers can easily verify that this is indeed the case, contrary to what we saw for the independent loops in (5b), which only yield $a^n b^m$ languages instead.[10] Chomsky goes on to show other types of interesting languages that rewrite systems allow. For instance:

(8) *aa, bb, abba, baab, aaaa, bbbb, aabbaa, abbbba, . . .* , and in general, all sentences consisting of a string X followed by the "mirror image" of X (i.e., X in reverse), and only these.

(9) $\Sigma : S$
$F : S \rightarrow aSa$
$S \rightarrow bSb$
$S \rightarrow aa$
$S \rightarrow bb$

Chomsky then shows sentences that cannot be generated in finite-state terms:

(10) a. If S_1, then S_2
b. Either S_3, or S_4
c. The man who said that S_5, is arriving today

The crucial property of these real-life examples is not merely that there can be a string of unlimited length between the dependent items (*if-then*, *either-or*, *man-is*). There can also be a string of unlimited length between *the* and *man* in the finite-state language (4b). But in (10) we have genuine recursion, while in (4b) we merely had iteration.[11] As Chomsky puts it:

In [(10)a], we cannot have 'or' in place of 'then'; in [(10)b], we cannot have 'then' in place of 'or'; in [(10)c], we cannot have 'are' instead of 'is'. In each of these cases there is a dependency between words on opposite sides of the comma (i.e., 'if'-'then', 'either'-'or', 'man'-'is'). But between the interdependent words, in each case, we can insert a declarative sentence S_1, S_3, S_5, and this declarative sentence may in fact be one of [(10)a–c]. . . . It is clear, then, that in English we can find a sequence $a+S_1+b$, where there is a dependency between a and b, and we can select as S_1 another sequence containing $c+S_2+d$, where there is a dependency between c and d, then select as S_2 another sequence of this form, etc. A set of sentences that is constructed in this way . . . will have all of the mirror image properties of [(8)] which exclude [(8)] from the set of finite state languages. (22)

[Σ, F] grammars are capable of handling languages with the properties of those in (6) and (8). Furthermore, they can easily generate all finite-state (formal) languages as well. For example, the language that (4b) generates can also be generated as follows:

(11) Σ : S

$$
\begin{aligned}
F: & S \rightarrow NP_1 V_1, \\
& S \rightarrow NP_2 V_2, \\
& NP_1 \rightarrow DET \bar{N}_1, \\
& \bar{N}_1 \rightarrow ADJ \bar{N}_1, \\
& NP_2 \rightarrow DET \bar{N}_2, \\
& \bar{N}_2 \rightarrow ADJ \bar{N}_2, \\
& \bar{N}_1 \rightarrow N_1, \\
& \bar{N}_2 \rightarrow N_2, \\
& V_1 \rightarrow \textit{comes}, \\
& V_2 \rightarrow \textit{come}, \\
& N_1 \rightarrow \textit{man}, \\
& N_2 \rightarrow \textit{men}, \\
& ADJ \rightarrow \textit{old}
\end{aligned}
$$

Therefore, this state of affairs yields a set-theoretic picture as in figure 1.1. At this point in his presentation, Chomsky simply abandons finite-state description.

Abandoning a description because an alternative is *more inclusive* (in the sense of figure 1.1) is an argument about the system's weak generative capacity, that is, an extensional set-theoretic characterization. Chomsky (1986b:chapter 2.2) coined the term E-language (where the E stands for "extensional" and "external") to denote this conception of language—implying that there is no utility to this notion. For him the concept contrasts with the linguistically more relevant I-language, mentioned in section 1.1. From the biolinguistic perspective, the linguist's task is to formulate feasible hypotheses about I-language and to test them against reality (by describing acceptable expressions, how children acquire variants, the specifics of language use, how brains may represent them, etc.). It is then an empirical question whether, in I-language terms, a "more inclusive" description entails abandoning a "less inclusive" one. To start with, the meaning of "inclusiveness" is far less clear in terms of a generative procedure, as compared to a set-theoretic notion.[12]

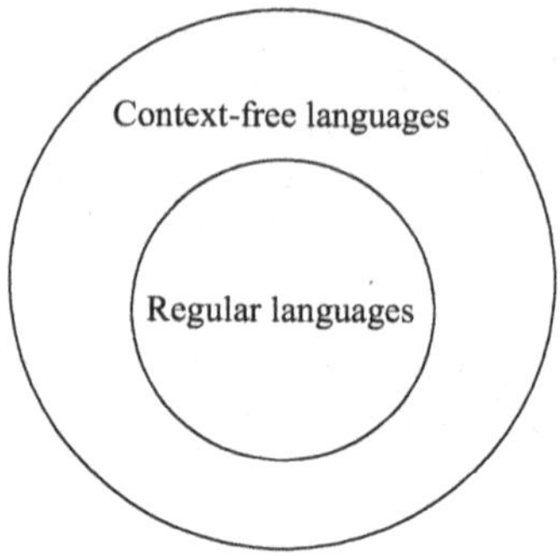

Figure 1.1
FLH up to context-free languages

The descriptive advantage of Post-style phrase structure (PS) grammars, as compared to finite-state grammars, is that PS grammars can pair up things that are indefinitely far apart and separated by dependencies without limit (see note 10). The way they do that is by introducing symbols that are never physically manifested: the nonterminals. That is, PS grammars introduce structure, as graphically represented in the tree diagram of a sentence from language (6), *aaabbb*, where *a*, *b* are terminals and *S* is a nonterminal symbol:

(12)

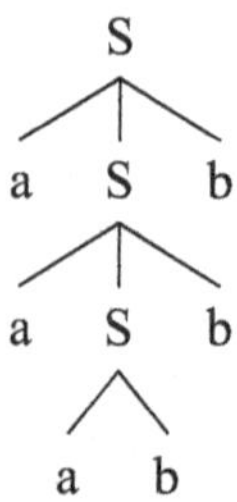

Although we return to this fundamental consideration, we want to emphasize that there is no dispute within generative grammar with regard to the significance of this sort of structure, and arguments abound to demonstrate its reality. We will review just four.

1.2.2 Basic Constituency Tests

Consider, first, the contrasts in (13):

(13) a. *(Usually,) cats chase mice.*
b. *Cats chase mice(, usually).*
c. *Cats (usually) chase mice.*
d. *Cats chase (*usually) mice.*

The question is why adverbs can be placed in all the positions in (13) except between the verb and the direct object. An account of the contrasts is possible if an adverb must associate to a phrasal constituent. If there is a constituent formed by *chase* and *mice* (a VP), then the modification in (13c) is as straightforward as in (13a) or (13b), involving even more complex constituents that get modified. Example (13d) fails because no constituent is formed by *cats* and *chased*, so the adverb has nothing it can associate to.

Confirmation of the reality of the abstract VP structure stems from the fact that it can be displaced as a unit, which the following facts directly show:

(14) a. *They say cats chase mice, and chase mice I've surely seen them do!*
b. *They say cats chase mice, *and cats chase I've surely seen* (*do*) *mice!*

So-called VP fronting is a colloquial way of emphasizing this sort of expression, as in (14a), where the entire constituent *chase mice* is displaced. A parallel fronting, involving the subject *cats* and the verb *can*—though logically imaginable as a source of emphasis of the semantic dependency between cats and their abilities—is unavailable, as (14b) shows. This follows if only phrases can displace and *cats can* is not a phrase. The issue is purely structural. Had language presented "subject phrases" (including the subject and the verb) as opposed to VPs, the preceding distributions would reverse.

Asymmetries between subjects and predicates and what they contain are easy to find, and they provide yet another argument for structure. Thus consider (15), which involves an anaphor such as *each other*:[13]

(15) a. *Jack and Jill* [*kissed each other*].
b. **Each other* [*kissed Jack and Jill*].

Whereas an anaphor in object position can take the subject as its antecedent, the reverse is not true. This is not just a fact about anaphors; asymmetries remain with pronouns:

(16) a. *Jack and Jill said that* [*someone* [*kissed them*]].
b. *They said that* [*someone* [*kissed Jack and Jill*]].

In (16a) the object pronoun can take the names in subject position as antecedent. In contrast, in (16b), with the reverse order, *they* (now in subject position) must not refer to Jack and Jill in object position. The matter cannot be one of simple precedence in the presentation of names, pronouns, and anaphors, for (17), which is very similar to (16b), is fine with *their* referring (forward) to Jack and Jill (see note 12):

(17) [*Their teacher*] *said that* [*someone* [*kissed Jack and Jill*]].

The difference between these two sentences is standardly described in terms of structure too: *their* is buried inside the phrase *their teacher* in (17), the subject of the main clause, while this is not true for *they* in (16b), which is itself the subject of the sentence. As it turns out, anaphors, pronouns, and names are sensitive to whether there is a direct phrasal path between them and their antecedent, which goes by the name of c-command.[14] That notion is totally dependent on a precise phrasal description.

Although the divide between subject and predicate is fundamental in determining phrasal asymmetries, it is not the only one. Anaphoric facts of the abstract sort discussed in Barss and Lasnik (1986) directly show asymmetries internal to the VP:

(18) a. *Jack [showed Jill to herself (in the mirror)].*
b. **Jack [showed herself to Jill (in the mirror)].*

Such asymmetries are prevalent and become manifest in all sorts of circumstances. For example, while compounds are possible involving a direct object and a verb, as in (20a), whose import is that of (19), they are generally impossible with any other verbal dependent (indirect object, subject, etc.) or with so-called (circumstantial) adjuncts:[15]

(19) Mailmen carry letters (for people) (on weekdays).

(20) a. *Mailmen are letter-carriers (for people) (on weekdays).*
b. **Mailmen are people-carriers (letters).*
c. **Letters are mailman-carrier/carried (for people).*
d. **Mailmen are weekday-carriers (letters) (for people).*

1.3 Beyond Phrasal Description

Next, we want to acknowledge that traditional phrasal description, useful as it has been in understanding linguistic correlations, presents some interesting limitations too. Understanding these has been a central area of discussion and debate within generative grammar—and it continues to be a fruitful area of research.

1.3.1 Upper and Lower Limits of Phrasal Description

Having shown the centrality of phrasal description in language, we want to signal a certain irony that arises at this point. While human language fragments abstractly like those shown in (6) and (8) were presented by Chomsky as motivating the move from finite-state description to [Σ, F] description, he did not actually use the crucial relevant property of these grammars in his linguistic work at the time. The property in point is unbounded self-embedding. However, the Logical Structure of Linguistic Theory of Chomsky (1955), assumed in Chomsky (1957), has no self-embedding. The [Σ, F]

module of that grammar generates only a finite number of structures. It is, instead, a module of the grammar containing more powerful rules (which can alter a phrase structure representation) that introduces recursion in the system. This so-called transformational component is what embeds one sentence within another, thus accounting for the infinitude of language. This point is only hinted at in Chomsky (1957:80), but had been fully developed in Chomsky (1955:518, 526).

Chomsky (1957) proceeded to develop a [*Σ*, *F*] grammar for a small fragment of English, and then he used the English auxiliary verb system as part of a demonstration of the inadequacy of even [*Σ*, *F*] description. In a nutshell, he showed that basic parts of the system have "cross-serial" dependencies, as in the partial structure of *have been writing*:[16]

(21)

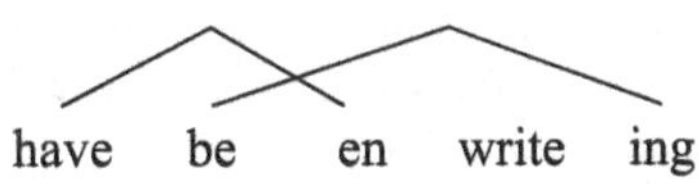

Phrase structure rules cannot in general deal with these sorts of dependencies; they work at characterizing *nested* dependencies, as we saw in (8), but not cross-serial ones. This is one of Chomsky's arguments for a more powerful device—so-called transformations.

The new sort of structuring can be said to have the quality of being "context-sensitive," as opposed to "context-free."[17] This is because of the way transformations are supposed to work. Contrary to what we saw for Post-style rewrite rules (which only care about rewriting a given nonterminal symbol regardless of the context in which it appears), context-sensitive operations do care about the neighborhood in which a given symbol has been generated. *Context* here simply means a (partial) record of the derivational history. Context-free operations have no use for such a record, but context-sensitive operations are a modification of preexisting representations and therefore must keep track of what sort of object to manipulate (the "structural description") to produce a related, but different, output (called the "structural change").

Now the auxiliary portion of English is finite, so strictly speaking that fragment of English is not beyond the bounds of [*Σ*, *F*]—or even finite-state description. A list, after all, can be essentially represented as a finite-state grammar. But that is really beside the point. A lower level account would be clumsy and uninformative. As Chomsky (1957:41) put it, "we see that significant simplification of the grammar is possible if we are permitted to formulate rules of a more complex type than those that correspond to a system of immediate constituent analysis". We emphasize that this simplification is not just a formal matter, the sort of concern that Chomsky inherited from Goodman

(1951). As noted, Chomsky was already deeply interested in biolinguistic issues, as is apparent on the very first page of chapter 1 of Chomsky (1955 [1975]:61):

A speaker of a language has observed a certain limited set of utterances in his language. On the basis of this finite linguistic experience he can produce an indefinite number of new utterances which are immediately acceptable to other members of his speech community. He can also distinguish a certain set of "grammatical" utterances, among utterances that he has never heard and might never produce. He thus projects his past linguistic experience to include certain new strings while excluding others.

Syntactic Structures (Chomsky 1957:15) also briefly summarizes this point of view:

a grammar mirrors the behavior of the speaker who, on the basis of a finite and accidental experience with language, can produce or understand an indefinite number of new sentences. Indeed, any explication of the notion "grammatical in *L*" (i.e., any characterization of "grammatical in *L*" in terms of "observed utterance of *L*") can be thought of as offering an explanation for this fundamental aspect of linguistic behavior.

Interestingly, Chomsky's conclusion in the case of cross-serial dependencies differs deeply from his conclusion for the inadequacy of finite-state description. In the latter case, he rejected the lower level description, constructing a theory in which Markov processes play no role. But in the one now under discussion, his proposal was to keep both the lower level ([Σ, F] description) and a higher level (transformations):

The notions of phrase structure are quite adequate for a small part of the language and . . . the rest of the language can be derived by repeated application of a rather simple set of transformations to the strings given by the phrase structure grammar. If we were to attempt to extend phrase structure grammar to cover the entire language directly, we would lose the simplicity of the limited phrase structure grammar and of the transformational development. (41–42, note 6)

We speculate that the different kinds of rejection of the two lower level modes of description stem from the fact that human language sentences are clearly structured, while Markov productions are best seen as "flat" under associative conditions. It may have seemed at the time that there was no role at all in the grammar for Markov processes. Be that as it may, Chomsky's reasoning makes sense only if the strong generative capacity of the system is at stake. This is because, as we saw in the related situation in figure 1.1—for the relation between regular and context-free conditions—in set-theoretic terms, a new and more inclusive set has now been added. In terms of the system's weak generative capacity, one could ask why the context-free conditions should be identified if the system is already at the more inclusive context-sensitive level. Nonetheless, from the point of view of the strong generative capacity, the way structuring

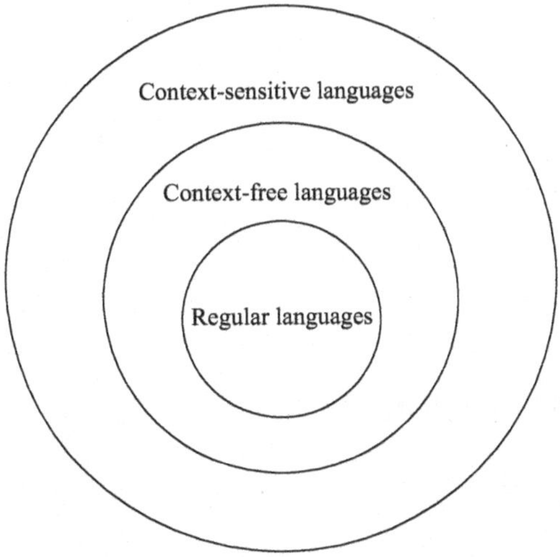

Figure 1.2
FLH up to context-sensitive languages

happens at a "more inclusive" level is radically different from how it happens at a "less inclusive" one, which we return to. While mechanisms of the context-sensitive sort *presuppose* those of the context-free sort, it is not true that context-sensitivity makes context-freeness superfluous.[18] A biological analogy with locomotion may clarify this: running possibly presupposes walking, but even if so, the more difficult condition wouldn't make the simpler one superfluous (even if the distances a runner runs span over those a walker walks).

There are certain language phenomena that plausibly involve a degree of flatness, as discussed by Chomsky (1961a:15), Chomsky and Miller (1963:298), and Chomsky (1965:196, note 7). This is curious because such structures suggest that context-freeness does not make the simpler, presupposed Markovian representations superfluous either. One such phenomenon is what Chomsky called "true coordination" as in (4a):

(22) *The man comes / The old man comes / The old old man comes/ . . .*

Chomsky (1961a:15) states, for this and similar cases, that "immediate constituent analysis has been sharply and, I think, correctly criticized as in general imposing too much structure on sentences." That is, there is no evident motivation for a structure in which, say, each *old* modifies the remaining sequence of *old*s plus *man*, as in (23), or some such.

(23)

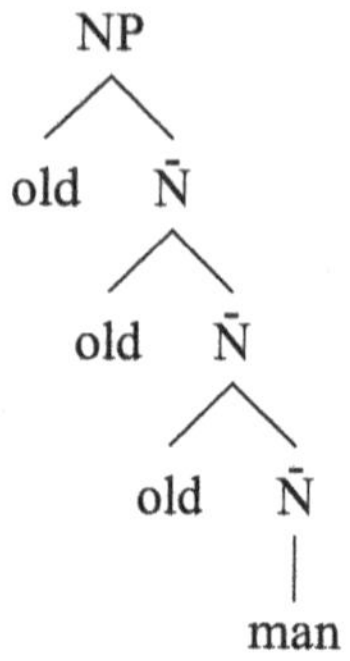

Preferable might be something like:[19]

(24)

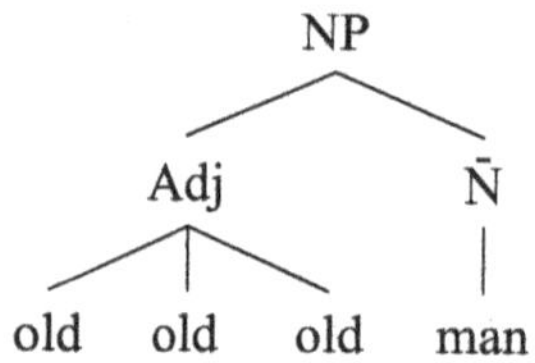

Chomsky mentions (25) and says: "The only correct P-marker would assign no internal structure at all within the sequence of coordinated items. But a constituent structure grammar can accommodate this possibility only with an infinite number of rules; that is, it must necessarily impose further structure, in quite an arbitrary way" (15).

(25) *The man was old, tired, tall . . . , but friendly.*

Chomsky and Miller (1963:298) present a very similar argument: "a constituent-structure grammar necessarily imposes too rich an analysis on sentences because of features inherent in the way *P*[*hrase*]-markers are defined for such sentences." With respect to an example identical to (25) in all relevant respects, they say:[20]

> To generate such strings, a constituent-structure grammar must either impose some arbitrary structure (e.g., using a right recursive rule), in which case an incorrect structural description is generated, or it must contain an infinite number of rules. Clearly, in the case of true coordination . . . no internal structure should be assigned at all within the sequence of coordinate items.

1.3.2 On the Inadequacy of Powerful Solutions to Simple Structuring

The conclusion of Chomsky (1961a) and of Chomsky and Miller (1963) about the issue in the previous section was that we need to go beyond the power of [Σ, F] description to adequately describe natural languages. In particular, the model is augmented by a transformational component. We would like to show next that this particular approach does not ultimately address the concern raised in the previous section. Chomsky (1955, 1957) had already shown how transformations can provide natural accounts of phenomena that can only be described in cumbersome and unrevealing ways by [Σ, F] grammars. But he had little to say there about the "too much structure" problem we are now considering. Chomsky (1961a) and Chomsky and Miller (1963) do not have much to say either beyond the implication that transformations will somehow solve the problem. That is, we need to move up the power hierarchy as in figure 1.2. As mentioned, Chomsky 1955 had already claimed that there is no recursion in the [Σ, F] component, only the transformational component (generalized transformations [GTs]) being responsible for linguistic infinitude.[21]

Chomsky discussed several aspects of the coordination process, though without giving a formulation of the relevant transformation(s). It is interesting to note that all the examples discussed in Chomsky (1955) involve coordination of two items, as in (26).

(26) *John was sad and tired.*

For such cases, it is straightforward to formulate a GT, even if, as claimed by Chomsky (1961a:21-22), these are strictly binary operations (see note 20). As an example, he gives *John is old and sad* from *John is old, John is sad* with resulting structure (27) (and see note 18).

(27)

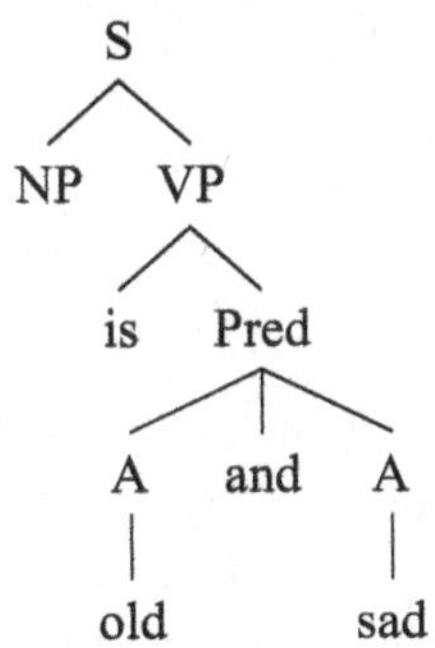

Chomsky and Miller also seem to assume binarity, at least in one place in their discussion: "The basic recursive devices in the grammar are the generalized transformations that produce a string from a *pair* of underlying strings" (304, emphasis added). It is not entirely clear, however, what is supposed to happen when we have multiple items coordinated, as in the phenomena under discussion here, or in (28), for example:

(28) *John was old and sad and tired.*

One possibility is that we would preserve the structure of *old and sad* in (28) and create a higher structure incorporating *and tired*—or, somewhat revising (27), as in (30).

(29)

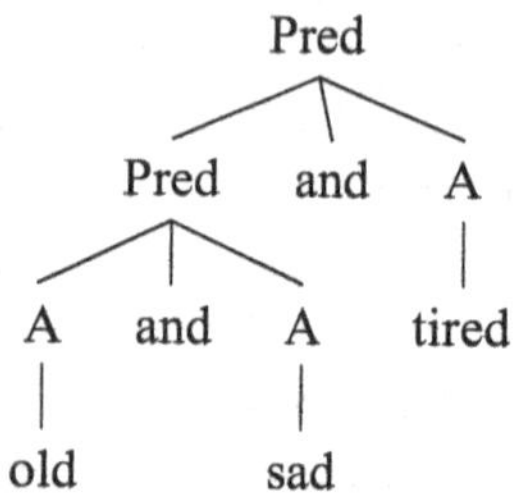

(30)

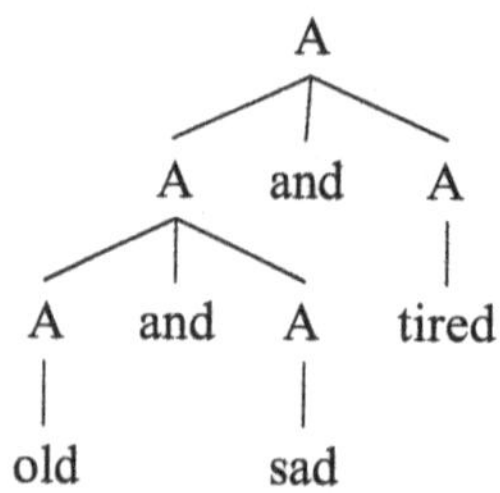

Another possibility is surely a right-branching analogue:

(31)

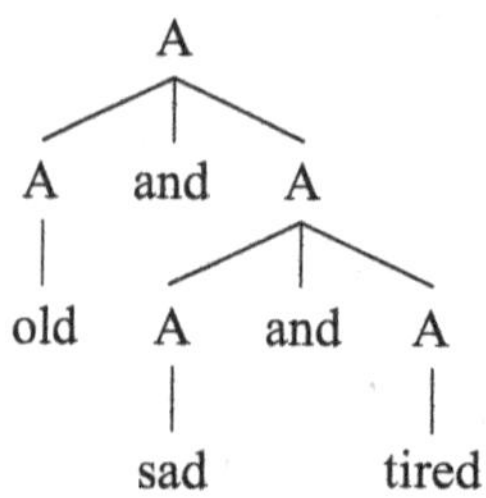

But any of these would run afoul of Chomsky's and Chomsky and Miller's arguments. We do not always even want that extra structure. That is not to say the extra structure should never be available. Rather, we must be able to distinguish between the situations where the structure is motivated and those where it is not. For example, a person who is tired for someone being old and sad (with a compositional structure plausibly corresponding to (30)) may not be the same as a person who is old for someone who is sad and tired (31).[22] And both of these might differ from someone who merely has all three properties with no particular relations among one another. But we are lacking a representation for this final case.

Reciprocals bring that lack out even more clearly. Consider:

(32) *John and Mary and Susan criticized each other.*

Relevantly different structures for (32) may be as in (33) and (34):

(33)

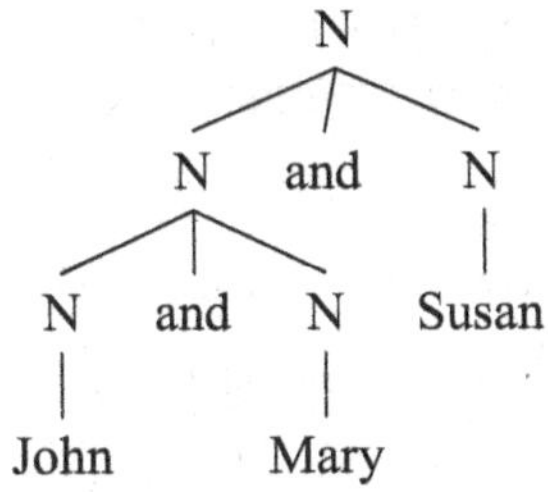

(34)

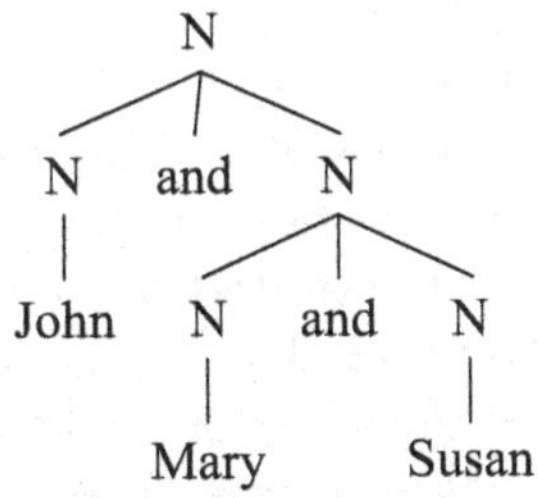

A situation making (32) true might involve John and Mary criticizing Susan, and vice versa, which is naturally expressed as in (33). But (32) would come out true, also, if John criticized Mary and Susan, and vice versa, because its compositional structure is more natural than in (34). Here is the crucial situation now: What if *each of the three criticized each of the others*? This is also a possible scenario that would make (32) true. The most natural structure to correspond to such a semantics would seem to be a totally flat structure.

A formal possibility that might yield the desired result arises if we relax the binarity requirement for GTs altogether. Chomsky and Miller seemingly countenance this option in at least one place in their discussion: "We now add to the grammar a set of operations called *grammatical transformations*, each of which maps an *n-tuple* [emphasis added] of *P*-markers ($n \geq 1$) into a new *P*-marker" (299). Then a GT could be formulated to coordinate three items (alongside the GT coordinating two items). But there really is no limit on the number of items that can be coordinated, which is Chomsky's original point. So this solution merely replaces one untenable situation with another: in place of an infinite number of phrase structure rules, one for each number of coordinated items, we now have an infinite number of GTs.[23]

Thus, moving up the power hierarchy ultimately does not help in this instance. What we really want to do is move *down* the hierarchy, so that, at least in relevant instances, we give ourselves the possibility of dealing with "flat" structures. Finite-state Markov processes, assuming associativity for the relations they represent (see note 3), yield effectively flat objects. But unfortunately without further qualifications that cannot be quite the answer either. While it would work fine for coordination of terminal symbols, phrases can also be coordinated, and, again, with no upper bound. Compare:

(35) *John and Mary and Susan criticized each other.*

(36) *The old man and the young man and the little boy criticized each other.*

So we need a "higher order" flatness to handle this simple structure in full generality.

1.3.3 Regaining Flatness without Losing Structuring

That last sentence can hardly be meaningful if one's notion of language is insensitive to structure. It is only if one attempts to capture the nuances of linguistic phenomena via structural dependencies that such abstractions make sense. To start with, the situation in (36) highlights the need for "cyclic" computations, in the sense of Chomsky et al. (1956).[24] Otherwise, it would make little sense to have chunks of structure that have achieved phrasal status (e.g., *the old man*) concatenate one to the next as if they were words. So what we would need, as it were, is "dynamic flatness." But this is the sort of concept that sounds incomprehensible in a classical computational view, while making sense to those for whom syntactic computations are psychologically real.

The traditional FLH is presented in terms of concentric diagrams of the sort in figure 1.3, indicating proper subset relations as already discussed, which extends to the entire class of denumerable formal languages. Now while we find this concept insightful, it is necessary to be cautious in any attempt to compare any of those diagrams to one another as models of human language competence.

First, again, the proper subsets concern solely weak generative capacity—languages as sets of symbol strings, or E-languages in current parlance. Yet, as already discussed and observed by Chomsky (1965:60), "the study of weak generative capacity is of rather marginal linguistic interest. . . . Presumably, discussion of weak generative capacity marks only a very early and primitive stage of the study of generative grammar."[25]

Second, all of the sets in the hierarchy include finite languages, trivially (in fact, *all* finite languages). But human languages seem to be invariably infinite,[26] so much of what these diagrams describe squarely falls outside of the language faculty of humans (though it is possible that other animals' cognition or communication systems can be thus described; see Berwick et al. [2012] in this regard).

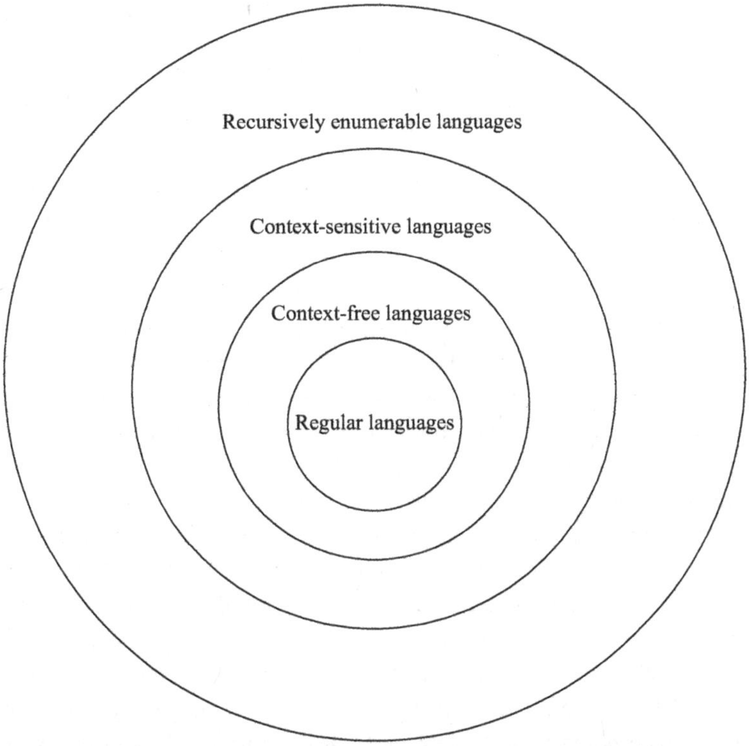

Figure 1.3
FLH (classical formulation)

Related to that concern is a third that has been implicit up to now: going up in the hierarchy does not entail that simpler types of structures should be discarded. If human language were some simple formal object, a more powerful description carrying the system to a domain where it can describe both the complex *and simpler* wffs should indeed make us discard the less powerful description as redundant. But the very ways of generating word strings is what seems central to human language. In the case discussed, the same string may have different derivational histories and corresponding phonological or semantic properties. That said, the systems used to generate the observables—say, in finite-state or phrase structure terms—are no longer redundant.

For example, (33) and (34) and a hypothetical flat structure with the very same words simply do not constitute a natural class. The good news is that formal languages, in the traditional sense, are systems whose mathematical properties are well understood, at the level of their weak generative capacity. The bad news, that for the most part this is somewhat irrelevant to biolinguistic concerns. But, although the task ahead seems formally daunting, we find no reason to doubt that the FLH is still real in a broad sense.

1.4 Toward a Better Understanding of Complex Structuring

A constituent is different from a "discontinuous constituent" (which is usually the result of a *displacement*) or for that matter a flatter dependency. That much is generally agreed on by every linguist, even if different schools of thought build complexity in different fashions: For some, the syntactic structures themselves yield the relevant structural abstractions needed to yield observable patterns. For others, abstraction should be built into the system's semantics by allowing for formal objects of a sort that do not seek their dependencies in more or less local and standard terms, but instead satisfy such needs at a distance, for example. However, at the level of abstraction that we are talking about these are probably notational variants, though this is hard to formally prove.[27]

Much current work relates to ideas introduced by Joshi (1985), which explored so-called *mild* context-sensitive (MCS) languages. Although Joshi himself was careful enough (225) not to treat this notion as formal, it is useful in that MCS grammars are meant to generate all context-free languages, while satisfying three externally imposed conditions: (i) to capture cross-serial dependencies of the sort in (21), (ii) to present constant growth,[28] and (iii) to allow polynomial parsing.[29] Joshi noted how the first and third conditions depend on the grammars, while second condition depends on the languages, so this is a "mixed" (and not formal) statement. Still, Stabler (2013a) observes how:

> a computational consensus was identified by Joshi (1985) in his hypothesis that human languages are both strongly and weakly mildly context sensitive (MCS).... [T]he claim is so fundamental that it can be connected to many diverse traditions in grammar. To say that language is "strongly and weakly" MCS is to say that MCS grammars can both define the sentences of human languages (weak adequacy) and also provide the structures of those languages (strong adequacy). Joshi's original definition of MCS grammars was partly informal, so there are now various precise versions of his claim. One is that human languages are defined by tree adjoining grammars (TAGs) or closely related grammars, and another theoretically weaker (and hence empirically stronger) position is that human language are definable by the more expressive (set local) multi-component TAGs or closely related grammars. (318)

According to Stabler, the phrase "or closely related grammars" carries within a profound insight, given that various formalisms fall under that description:[30]

> Tree adjoining grammar (TAG); a certain kind of combinatory categorial grammar (CCG); set-local multi-component (MCTAG); a certain kind of abstract categorial grammar (ACG); multiple context free grammar (MCFG)...; minimalist grammar (MG).... [Plus] a convergence [within MG]: MG with head movement (MGH); MG

with head parameters specifying whether complements are to the left or right (DMG); MG in which the features triggering (external) merge can also trigger move (internal merge) (CMG); MG in which phases constrain extraction (PMG); MG with sideward movement (SMMG); MG within which relativized minimality constrains extraction (RMG). (319)

As Stabler puts things, "across traditions," the following inclusion relations hold among the languages formally defined by different grammars:

(37)
$$\boldsymbol{CFG \subset TAG = CCG} \subset$$
$$\subset MCTAG = ACG = MCFG = MG = MGH = DMG$$
$$= CMG = PMG = SMMG = RMG \subset \boldsymbol{CSG}$$

If we set aside the first three (traditional CFGs, Joshi's [1985] original TAG model, and Steedman's [2000] CCGs), and totally unrestricted context-sensitive grammars as in the last line, there remains an equivalent class of objects that are more complex than the (extended) context-free domain but less so than the unrestricted context-sensitive domain. As Stabler observes, "these grammars were not designed to mimic each other. On the contrary, these various ideas come from sometimes fiercely opposed grammatical traditions, and yet they converged on grammars that are weakly equivalent in the sense that they define exactly the same sets of sentences." Which suggests there is something right to the idea that human language exists in the space between context-free and -sensitive grammars (CFGs and CSGs)—wherever that turns out to be.

Thus conceived, much work lies ahead, beyond the need for detailed formulations. For example, pursuing ideas that go back to Berwick and Weinberg (1984), Boeckx and Uriagereka (2012) observe that core linguistic structures are extensions of binary constructs, albeit at various levels within the FLH. They argue that most finite-state structures (of the infinitely many that could exist) are extensions of reduplicative patterns of the *da-da* sort (as in *very very simple*). In turn, they suggest that projections along phrasal stems are, in some sense, super-reduplicative patterns, stated on nonterminal expressions, not words (so a path going from X to XP is a relation between two X-X labels likened to *da-da* at the morphological level).[31] They finally extend this idea from abstract projections to abstract "subjacent" domains, understood as super-projections among systemic phases within the derivation.[32] In all these instances, infinitely many other abstract dependencies would be formally possible, but in fact natural language restricts itself to extensions of a trivial reduplicative sort at various levels of formal complexity. This sort of move makes sense only if the FLH is taken seriously by making generalizations about abstract structures as opposed to observable symbols (like pronounced words).

1.5 Structure at the Bottom

Up to this point we have discussed syntagmatic relations, one word after the next. But a classical structuralist concern was also to understand what it may mean to have (and ultimately acquire) paradigmatic relations among words. Early generative grammar provided a way to deal with syntagmatic dependencies, and it also had something to say about paradigmaticity, as exemplified in Lees (1960). Lexically related words were transformationally related—so paradigmaticity was reduced to syntagmaticity. For example, only a verb (such as *destroy*) would be listed in the lexicon; then, through idiosyncratic transformations, one could obtain lexically related items (*destruction*, *destructive*, etc.). This approach led to the Generative Semantics program.

1.5.1 Is There Room at the Bottom?

An important point to recall regarding the alphabet in a generative grammar is that both the set of terminals and the set of nonterminals are finite. Formal systems of this sort are designed to capture Wilhelm von Humboldt's insight that language "makes infinite use of finite means" (Chomsky 1965:8–9). Chomsky's use of Post's ideas about recursion was an explicit attempt to deal with the Cartesian problem of creativity, which is based on generating unbounded behavior, albeit from finite means.[33] That said, just what should the alphabet be? Linguists know enough not to work with written typographical conventions, but should the system bottom out on a finite set of words or a finite set of even smaller units? 'Word' is an elusive notion, defined in various ways in different cultural traditions. Even scientifically defined words (e.g., in terms of accentual units or units of atomic semantic values) change from language to language, as was noted by Humboldt himself.[34]

These sorts of considerations, plus the desire to give a unified account for how systems bottom out in all languages, led generative semanticists in the mid-1960s to propose that lexical access is a late, or surface, phenomenon in a syntactic derivation. The computational system, in this view, works with more basic units, ideally the sorts of morphemes one sees in languages where a decomposition of words into morphemes is more or less straightforward, such as in Japanese. In this perspective, a possible paradigm (a class of viable words) is a structure derived by the computational system.

For expository reasons, we illustrate the idea with an English example—even though this language is not transparent to these sorts of considerations. Take, for instance, (38c), which has the (rough) semantic import of paraphrases as in (38b) or even (38a):[35]

(38) a. *The president has caused [that the Organization of American States (OAS) become rational].*
b. *The president has caused to become rational the OAS.*
c. *The president has rationalized the OAS.*

It is easy to show that a comparable correspondence as in (39) does not obtain:

(39) a. [*That the OAS* (*has/should*) *become rational*] *has caused quite a stir.*
b. **The OAS to become rational caused quite a stir.*
c. **The OAS rationalized quite a stir.*

While (39a) is a sensible thought, it doesn't have a grammatical paraphrase as in (39b) nor is there a meaning for *rationalize* as in (39c) with the semantic import of something like (39a). We would like to explain why the latter is important, developing a sort of argument that was first proposed—in different forms but along the same general lines—by McCawley (1968), Lakoff (1971), and Postal (1970).

We can provide an explanation for why (38b) can be transformationally related to (38a), in a way that (39b) cannot be related to (39a). Consider the representations for (38a) and (39a), in simplified format. Assume the causative expression *cause to become* is generated via a transformational process, by relating an initial phrase marker of the form in (40a) to a derived phrase marker of the form in (41a).

(40) a.

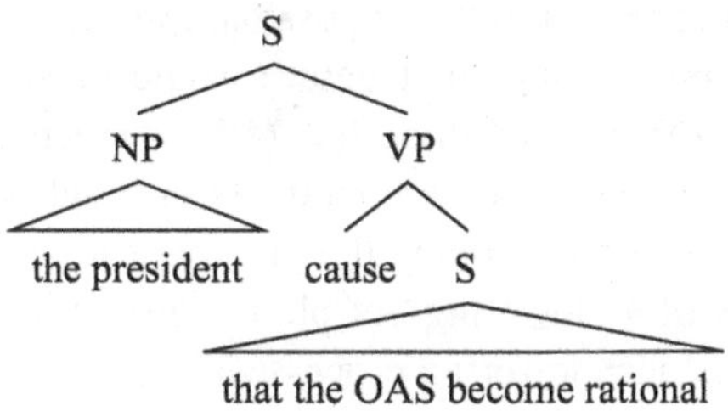

b.

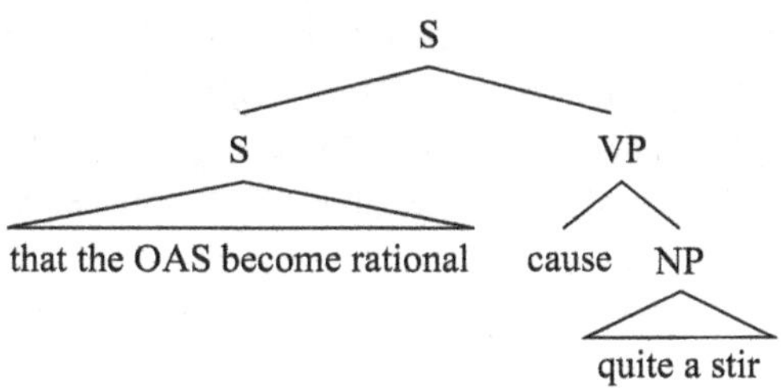

(41) a.

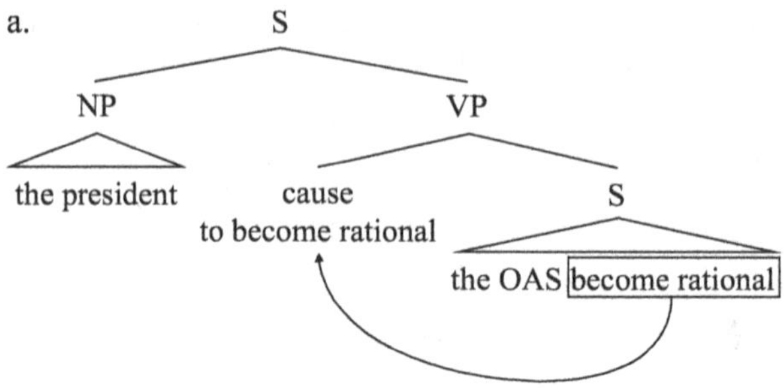

b.

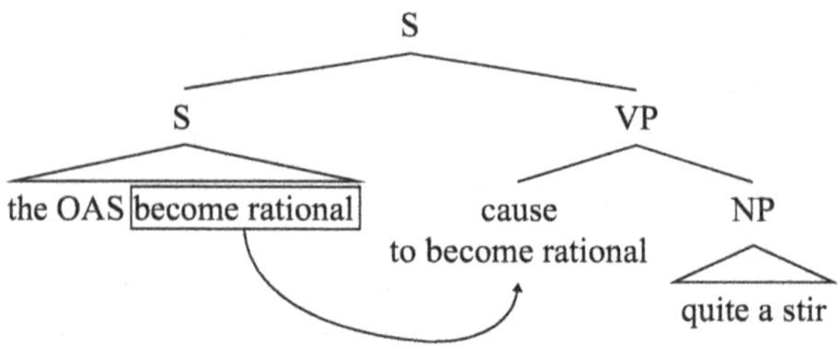

As we saw, transformations were developed by Chomsky (1955) to capture the relatedness among sets of sentences that native speakers detect. Once these devices are part of the system, it becomes an empirical question whether they should be used to relate the periphrastic (38a) to its causative version in (38b). If the answer is affirmative, an approach to the impossible causative in (39c) stems from the fact that its transformational structure would have to be a mapping from something like (40b) to something like (41b)—which is problematic. In (41a) the "displaced" element c-commands its original position. The same is not true for (41b), where intuitively the putative causative construction is generated in terms of a "lowering" of phrasal information (see Baker [1988] on a way to prevent such lowering processes).

It does not matter now what the ultimate explanation is for this state of affairs—call it condition X. The key to Generative Semantics was that (syntactic) condition X should hold also *in the formation of words*. The idea is to model the impossibility of (39c) (vis-à-vis (38c)) on the impossibility of (39b) as analyzed in (41b), as compared to the possible (38b), and analyzed as in (41a). Graphically:

(42) a.

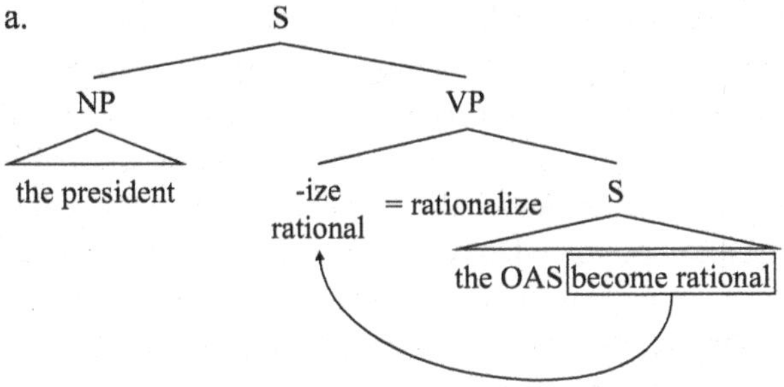

b.

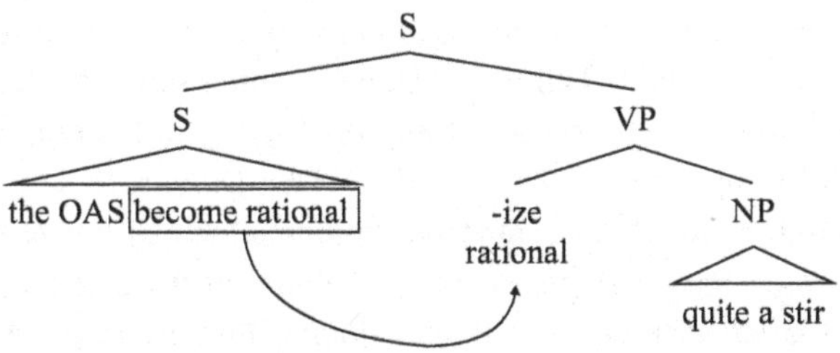

Crucially, if this sort of analysis is generally correct, terminal elements in derivations can be formatives such as the "causative" morpheme *-ize* in *rationalize.* This is the stuff that makes "agglutinative" languages look agglutinative.

From this perspective, one cannot simply assume that the generative system bottoms out in a finite lexicon, giving meaning to the classical intuition that a language is "a grammar and a dictionary." Rather, the lexicon itself is a generalization of surface syntax. An arbitrary decision akin to compiling the words *kick* and *bucket* into the idiom *kick the bucket* (to mean "die") is responsible for lexicalizing processes as in (42a). The task of the grammarian, then, is to find out what those primitive atomic units are, whose relational dependencies yield not just phrases, but also words—in much the same way that early structural linguists had to find out what the units of phonetics were. The grammarian is then seeking thoughts of some sort, as they materialize into words.

1.5.2 Lexicalism Strikes Back

The proposal just discussed created quite a stir in the 1960s. It is hard to argue with its elegance: the same sorts of conditions that rule over syntagmatic relations decide on paradigmatic ones. A skeptic, however, may want to ask just how one proposes to study thoughts, if not materialized through words in their usual syntagmatic format (within sentences). One may also bear in mind that a computational theory ought to have three intuitive properties. If a pocket calculator works, this is because when we type one number it *systematically* is what it is regardless of the context in which this happens. Also, if we have a recursive procedure within the calculator such as addition, it continues to apply *productively* regardless of how many times we try it. Finally, we could *transparently* unpack our accounting in such a way as to follow it with pencil and paper. When we apply those three computational criteria of systematicity, productivity, and transparency, it can be argued that words may be playing a more central role than the discussion in section 1.5.1 assigns them. This was essentially what Chomsky (1970) argued[36] on empirical grounds that we review next.

Note 35 already discussed that the paraphrases in section 1.5.1 are not as clean as one would want if all these structures truly had the same underlying representation.[37] That is, does one really *rationalize* an entity when one simply causes it to become rational? Famously, Don Quixote's death causes him to finally become rational, tragically accepting the futility of his plight. But we can't meaningfully say that *Death rationalized Don Quixote* (it's not even clear what that would mean). This is far from unique. One can *hospitalize* a patient but not **clinicize* them, *enlighten* but not **endarken* an audience, or be a great admirer of *electricity* but not of **eclecticity*. Plainly, in many languages this unsystematicity has to be learned one lexical item at a time. But if that is the case, we wonder: What good does it do to say that these structures are generated by a computational system? After all, the point of the generative enterprise is to address creativity. But is there something creative in learning one word at a time?

Skepticism over a derivational treatment of these paradigmatic matters is justified by lexical meanings being highly idiosyncratic. A *decent* X contrasts with an *indecent* Y, but a *flammable* X surely doesn't contrast with an *inflammable* Y. Our biological fathers have *fathered* us, but our mother may not have *mothered* us, and one doesn't get **cousined* or **grandmothered* (plus *to grandfather a proposal* has little to do with kinship of any kind). The same holds, again, for *rationalize*, which can certainly mean something like "downsize" or "decrease," a meaning that does not seem obviously related to anything being (just) rational. Idiosyncrasies of this sort are to be added to the unsystematicity noted in the previous paragraph, making one wonder whether a genuinely computational treatment is in order here, because the way in which a computer yields unbounded output from limited resources is precisely in terms of it being *regular* and *systematic*, which is the whole point behind recursion.

But there is still a third reason to doubt that yielding *rationalize* from *cause to be rational* is the right way to go. The argument that follows was provided, in slightly different form, in Fodor (1970). Observe (43), where we have added adverbial modifications to the sorts of examples we discussed in (39):

(43) a. *This year the president has caused [that the OAS become rational next year].*
b. ?*This year the president has caused the OAS to become rational next year.*
c. **This year the president has rationalized the OAS next year.*

While (43a) is sensible, though slightly degraded, (43b) is much better than (43c), which sounds senseless. This must mean that the word boundary around #rational-ize# is opaque enough not to allow modification into the word's parts. But why should this be the case if the word is just the result of syntactic incorporation of *rational* into *-ize*?

After having noted difficulties with the systematicity and productivity of the allegedly syntactic output of these sorts of putative rule processes, the fact that their outputs should not even be structurally *transparent* is yet another serious concern. If one wants to equate *rationalize* with something like *cause to become rational,* the null hypothesis is that the resulting object should be every bit as transparent, systematic, and productive as the standard syntactic object is. Otherwise we would not be witnessing a genuine instance of a recursive structuring process at work.

1.5.3 Structural Complexity within the Lexicon?

The issues just noted, while creating a lengthy debate in the 1960s, never really got resolved, becoming live again within Minimalism. The concern was raised already by Ray Jackendoff during Chomsky's 1987 seminar, just as Chomsky was beginning to sketch the basis of what was later to become an entire research program.

Jackendoff noted that, just as an example like (39c) is impossible—and Chomsky was providing a syntactic analysis of this impossibility, along the lines discussed—so too a *lexical* version of this sort of verb is unattested. One could stipulate that, while in English (and setting aside the scruples shown in section 1.5.2), a verb like *rationalize* means "for *x* to cause *y* to become rational," it just doesn't have the meaning "[that *y* become rational] causes *z*" in this language. Unfortunately, such a verb does not exist in any language anyone has studied, and the question is whether such a systematic gap is significant.[38]

That sort of consideration has been behind much recent work, attempting to decompose lexical items in much the ways seen herein.[39] One can decompose them into smaller units without claiming that such components have the form of words (e.g., that *-ize* means the same as the word *cause*). One can also argue that the rules of dependency holding among morphemes are different from those obtaining in standard syntax for regular syntagmatic dependencies.

But is that a better, or even different, theory than Generative Semantics? From that perspective the assumption would be that the system doesn't bottom out in words and that the behavior of elements within words is every bit as structural as it is above words—and every bit as computational. These are the assumptions that lexicalist arguments were produced against in the late 1960s: sublexical paradigmatic relations are idiosyncratic and nonproductive, and the word acts as a kind of "barrier" or "derivational phase" shielding information within from interactions with supra-lexical information. Attempts to deviate from the Generative Semantics line, in addition to still facing these difficulties, have to show why whatever rule-governed behavior they invoke (i) does not exist within the same set of conditions as syntagmatic relations and (ii) is not fully predictive (systematic and productive). At that point, it seems to us that the Generative Semantics line is the null hypothesis, if only because, while facing the same empirical difficulties as its more recent alternatives, it does not have to duplicate structuring conditions.[40]

For that special syntax either will or will not predict all lexical relations. If it is taken to predict only the existing ones, theorists ought to show what, other than a list of exceptions, rules out those words that, while apparently following paradigmatic patterns, are nonetheless impossible (why are verbs like **to daughter/son/cousin/uncle* . . . impossible with the rough import of "to act like a daughter/son/cousin/uncle . . ." on analogy with *to mother* with the rough import of "to act like a mother"). Theorists ought to show, also, what yields the fact that words that are apparently formed by the same relational conditions nonetheless yield different meanings (*to mother* vs. *to father*). In the absence of explanations for these simple facts, it is fair to assume that a syntagmatic treatment of paradigmatic relations, whether it is with the exact same procedures or some variant that is still a recursive system, simply overgenerates. Effectively, that is the criticism that Fodor and Lepore (1998) present to much current work within the "decompositionalist" tradition, as we discuss next.[41]

1.5.4 Toward a Biolinguistic Solution Embracing Complexity?

Fodor and Lepore couched their criticism of lexical decomposition in a logico-philosophical fashion: there is no exhaustive way to characterize a word in terms of other words.[42] In fairness to the decomposition tradition, however, one doesn't have to argue for such a version of "analyticity." If sublexical elements exist and they combine, they are what they are; there is no more reason for them to be words than there is for the components of syllables (phonemes, features, etc.) to be, well, syllables. So the real issue is not whether analyticity is a doomed logico-philosophical project; the question is where the recursive system bottoms out, regardless of the ultimate nature of the building blocks.

However, as far as we can tell, things happen with the syntactic/computational logic of genuine productivity, systematicity, and transparency only when words are the minimal units of analysis. This fact seems unavoidable to us, quite aside from whether one believes in or is skeptical about classical decomposition (of words into lesser words). An equally unavoidable fact, however, is that if one suspends one's scruples with regard to the syntactic nature of whatever rules the conditions inside words, one can predict certain paradigmatic relations among words. That's the force of Jackendoff's argument.

Uriagereka (2008) sketched a logical way to address this impasse, by assuming that the language faculty—if it is to be understood in genuine biolinguistic terms—ought to be seen in the rich developmental light that the so-called Evo-Devo paradigm in biology assumes.[43] While we cannot go into the details of this approach here, because we have no other direction to point toward to resolve the tension, we will mention its essentials.

From that perspective, the language faculty is taken to go from a decompositionalist to an atomist stage, effectively a *metamorphosis* in the course of its development (see note 42). Language learners prior to the critical age (when they stop being able to acquire language the way children do) are *decompositionalists*. In contrast, language users (after the critical age) are *atomists*.[44] The intuition is that the systematicities of standard syntax are an excellent way to help in the acquisition of lexical concepts, as argued for in Lasnik (1981, 1989) and Gleitman (1990). The claim that children are, in point of fact, Generative Semanticists of sorts is consistent with the lexical overgeneralizations that they display (Pinker 1984): a child who says something like (*I'm*) *sistering* (*my doll*) or who takes *inflammable* to mean *not flammable* is growing normally into adult language use. The question is then why the latter, in fully adult form, involves fixing lexical meanings in atomic fashion, often reversing earlier decisions (e.g., *inflammable* means the same as *flammable*, *sister* is not a verb).[45]

That possibly relates to information stabilization: fixed atoms, once acquired, do not allow further structural drifts. Interestingly, the acceptance of idiomatic expressions seems roughly to correlate with this transition: children resist idioms well into their school years (Lodge and Leach 1975), often getting their idiomatic import only after explicit training from peer tutors.[46] When they finally get the point of idiomatic expressions, they are effectively adult atomists, and after that they no longer acquire lexical concepts with the ease of the toddler years—nor do they say "funny things" anymore, regularizing paradigmatic dependencies in syntagmatic fashion.

This view presupposes a scaffolding that, as the structure develops, becomes virtually unusable (except for general presuppositions about paradigmatic information). That scaffolding may in the end be quite similar to whatever syntax builds, as the Generative Semantics project suspected. Then again, it may be a less articulated syntax, as is assumed in more current models. The logic of this proposal has nothing to say about that particular issue, thereby not deciding whether, in the end, paradigmaticity fully reduces to syntagmaticity, or rather they involve different structuring mechanisms.

Lest this could be confusing, we distinguish two types of lexical gap: (i) lexical items that cannot be derived without violating (e.g., locality) constraints (such as **The OAS rationalized quite a stir*—(39c)), and (ii) random gaps in the lexicon (e.g., a verbal *sister* on analogy with the verbal *mother*). The present exercise (for that matter, Postal's original argument or Jackendoff's version) has no bearing on random gaps. By the overarching argument we are entertaining here, at some point in their lives humans stop being "generative semanticists" and start acting as "atomists." So at no point in our lives will we learn a word *schmationalize*, such that X *schmationalizes* Y means "[X BECOME rational] CAUSE Y." However, a reviewer raises the question of whether our argument needs to involve a "critical age." The reviewer then goes on to suggest two alternative ways of interpreting our hypothesis. One is based on the possibility that principles like those invoked here are not syntactic. As they point out, this may be the view that Jackendoff himself would take, following ideas expressed in Jackendoff (2002): locality (and other) constraints are to be deployed over Conceptual Structure representations, assuming appropriate decompositions. We have issues with this approach, but they are irrelevant to the logic of the present piece, so the first possibility the reviewer raises is worth pursuing.[47] In our view, a more intriguing possibility is that the transition from decomposition to atomism takes place "in the development of a(n individual's) lexical entry," as the reviewer puts it. Then atomism would not be so much a developmental process as an effect of "familiarity" with a lexical item, perhaps a consequence of how lexical memory ultimately works. Uriagereka (2008) raises this possibility too. This work also notes that, given present understanding, it is hard to tell whether the systemic transition that our logic implies is developmental (in an individual) or a side effect.

In other words, the challenge is to distinguish two hypotheses regarding our "behaving as Postal wants us to throughout our lives," in the reviewer's words. (i) Is it because we are attempting to generate—and failing—a syntactically impossible construct? Or (ii) at a later stage in life do we simply lack a generative device to acquire new words, and to the extent that we do, we utilize heuristics that have little to do with the syntactic engine, but "do the job" because most of the lexicon is already learned by then? We will not attempt to decide between these alternatives and simply thank the reviewer for the thoughtful discussion, which we expect future research will help clarify.[48]

1.6 Concluding Remarks on "Mixed" Systems

We realize that structure, broadly construed, has to be more than (standard Turing) computation, or there would be no structure to nondenumerable spaces within mathematics. It is unclear whether that has a bearing on specifically linguistic structuring, though, and in any case we have little to offer about anything other than computational structuring—the scientific paradigm we work with and we consider productive. Strictly within the confines of computational structuring, generative grammar has provided an interesting hypothesis about the human language faculty as a biological capacity. In this regard, it is important not to confuse the (technically) weak and strong generative capacities of a grammar, which is understood as a computational procedure. Somewhat surprisingly, human language appears to be sensitive to the richer notion of structure, to the extent that it seems to deploy radically different forms of structuring the same superficial observables, and to make use of these differences in nuanced semantic ways. In our view the system is, in that regard, "mixed" in three different ways.

First, we have argued that the various levels of the FLH—at least up to some "mildly" context-sensitive dependencies—play a role in linguistic representation. Just as long-range correlations of the agreement sort coexist with purely configurational phrasal dependencies, so too in our view do the latter coexist with "flat" structures, in list or conjunctive relations. That is, the fact that the more complex way of structuring is possible doesn't preclude use of the simpler forms; we have offered some arguments that the grammar capitalizes on those structural differences to map corresponding semantic dependencies of the appropriate sort. Just as too much baggage can be detrimental to traveling, too much structure can be irrelevant to meaning. For instance, we see nothing compositional (phrasal) in describing a virus as *tiny, tiny, tiny* or in *never, never, never* surrendering to the unethical: the literal addition of adjectival or adverbial occurrences of this sort seems to us purely Markovian, resulting in a flat portion of structure. We see no bad consequences with such an assumption, any more than we have any issues with phrases coexisting with chains (resulting from transformations). These complexities are expected in biolinguistic systems, which systematically and simultaneously present organs, tissues, cells, cell organelles, and so on—plus interactions across domains.

Second, our system is "mixed," also, in that characterizing it accurately takes stock from whichever realm of theorizing seems relevant. Joshi's (1985) notion of "mild" context-sensitivity is paradigmatic in that regard, as it admittedly mixes notions from formal grammars and formal languages. A pure formalist may wish to disregard the notion because of that. We want to show, instead, how precise formalizations from different, even opposing, traditions converge on the same mild context-sensitive space, as Stabler (2013a) aptly noted. We admit that much work is still needed to find a serious unification in this area, but that should not preclude researchers from continuing the search, otherwise such a unification will never emerge. We offer some suggestions later in this monograph. In our view, because we are doing biolinguistics, the formal tools are merely that: instruments to achieve a descriptive purpose. Some tools will be sharper than others, but it is important not to confuse the analytical purpose they serve with their very existence as formal objects. Just as we do not think it is productive to ignore the strictures that such entities suggest ought to be part of the language faculty, it seems equally fruitless to insist on such precision for the tool that if it cannot be formally defined yet, then it is to be banned. That hinders progress.

Third, it is intriguing to unearth the intricacies of lexical paradigms by considering whether to apply the same computational devices that helped generative grammar account for syntagmatic dependencies, or at least similar ones. For that to be fairly evaluated, any computational proposal needs to consider whether what it models presents the productivity, transparency, and systematicity that should be the hallmark of a computational outcome, which was at center stage in the demise of Generative Semantics. That said, Ray Jackendoff observed how that paradigm was designed to capture logically possible though syntactically impossible gaps in lexical paradigms. We discussed how Jackendoff's puzzle has not been resolved and speculated that an Evo-Devo treatment might be possible if we think of the problem in two stages: at a language acquisition phase that lasts up to roughly puberty and at a consolidation phase that ensues thereafter. Obviously that proposal of ours is as "mixed" as it gets, although what mixes in this instance is the role given to the atomization of phrasal outputs of the computational system into vocabulary units with prelexicalist stages where such a compilation has not taken place yet. We see no reason not to treat organisms as presenting "before" and "after" stages that we clearly witness elsewhere in development. The main issue is whether linguistic structuring itself also partakes of such stages.[49]

The task ahead for a biolinguistic project is to test the ensuing "mixed" hypotheses in terms of the findings stemming from neurobiological, evolutionary, sociopsychological, and related treatments, as relevant in each instance. If the notion of mixed structure investigated in this chapter is even remotely on track, a concrete program lies ahead, in terms of what it might mean for pertinent representations to ultimately be embodied in the human brain. To us, this is the most exciting aspect of the generative enterprise.

Future understanding, in empirical and formal terms, may bring us closer to a viable characterization of linguistic structure within a human mind. But when this structure is postulated as explicitly and flexibly as we have attempted to depict it here, the question of whether its essentials (primitive features, symbols, processes, memory capacity, mixed interactions, etc.) have a concrete place in the neurobiology of brains—while certainly a difficult physiological inquiry—does not seems senseless at all.

2 Learnability Matters

In chapter 1 we presented general ways to approach the notion structure that is familiar from Chomsky's classical work. In this chapter we want to discuss linguistic notions that presuppose structure and argue for its reality. The central such notion involves what is commonly referred to in linguistics and cognitive psychology as "poverty of the stimulus" (POS). That term is explicitly used in Chomsky (1980b), although the idea is much older, particularly along the lines expressed in Goodman (1946). In its linguistic guise, POS was central to Chomsky's skepticism regarding Skinner's behaviorism or Piaget's associationism. As we saw in chapter 1 already, linguistic representations seem far richer than anything human children are exposed to, that being "the stimulus." POS arguments push the logic of the situation toward the need to conclude that aspects of what humans know about the language(s) they speak cannot have been induced from the data they encounter. Most papers published on the elaborate syntax of a given language (some of which will be summarized in the ensuing chapters) can be seen as further POS evidence, because such pieces typically present structural correlations that have not been induced. At the very least, skeptics of the POS approach ought to try and give an analysis of such paradigms in the literature to show how they are learnable without the kinds of innate priors we're willing to assume.

We emphasize the latter point because, among scores of POS arguments that have appeared in the linguistic literature, the most widely discussed is relatively exotic to syntacticians, based on "structure dependence" (SD). As we hinted in chapter 1, Chomsky characterized a property of transformations that demand these operations rely on analysis into constituent structural units and not on, say, linear sequences of words or morphemes. There is no logical necessity in Chomsky's idea: it could have been that transformations did rely on linear sequences—perhaps an alien language could work that way. But Chomsky argued that human transformations simply do not depend on linear notions and, instead, care about structure, in the sense we have examined already. Moreover, he argued that this interesting property must be part of the initial state of the acquisition mechanism because, according to him, two important situations arise: (i) human languages invariably conform to this kind of SD, and (ii) the input to the learner is too impoverished to provide the data to induce the learning of said structure from the data alone. Both aspects of the argument are important. Situation (ii) is POS, this time touching on the specific (alleged) nature of syntactic transformations; in turn (i) is a claim about the universality of the system, and thus a plausibility argument for the relevant knowledge being innate, in whatever sense we care to give to that notion.[1] If only *some* languages present SD transformations, it couldn't be true that a hypothetical systemic property guarantees anything as a consequence of human nature.

In what follows we quote Chomsky's work extensively, if nothing else to show readers how these general concerns are quite explicit and also very old within the generative enterprise.

2.1 The POS Classic Argument

The instance Chomsky originally discussed (one among many that he could have used as illustrations) involves the relation in English between declaratives and corresponding simple interrogatives. The familiar core paradigm is exemplified in (1).

(1) a. *John would like it.* a′. *Would John like it?*
b. *John has seen it.* b′. *Has John seen it?*
c. *John is reading it.* c′. *Is John reading it?*
d. *John has been writing it.* d′. *Has John been writing it?*
e. *John could be swimming.* e′. *Could John be swimming?*
f. *John could have laughed.* f′. *Could John have laughed?*
g. *John could have been sleeping.* g′. *Could John have been sleeping?*
h. *John likes it.* h′. *Does John like it?*

Descriptively, these pairs of sentences "feel related" (the second element typically is interpreted as a question version of the first). Example (1h) is somewhat puzzling, in that the relevant sentence in the second column introduces a new element: *does*. It is also interesting to ask which of the verbal elements in the first column (and note that in all but (1h) there are several) is the one that starts the sentence in the second column. Clearly, that is not random. For example, the "main verb" never starts the sentence (at least in modern English).

These are the sorts of facts that syntacticians hope to capture in terms of elegant mechanisms and their interactions.

The core of Chomsky's (1955, 1957) analysis is as follows. First, he presupposed context-free rewrite rules that allow us to build a phrase marker that we can schematize as in (2), in addition to something like the phrase structure rule in (3):

(2)

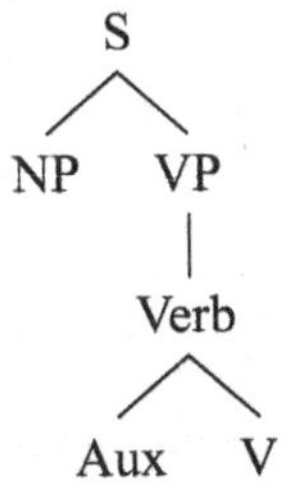

(3) *Aux* → *C* (*Modal*) (*have en*) (*be ing*)

Example (3) may seem strange inasmuch as it does not generate anything like a grammatical sentence. Readers can see that the system, as presented so far, generates nothing like (1g) and instead allows abominations like **John C can have en be ing sleep.* This is not bad just in English: it does not work as a "surface form" in any language. But key to Chomsky's reasoning is that he intends (3) to be a very abstract rule that is adjusted into what comes out of speakers' mouths by way of transformational operations.

It should be obvious from chapter 1 that the novel mechanisms in Chomsky's analysis are the transformations, for which phrasal context is central. Thus, in the optional rule (4), the so-called *structural analysis* (also known as *structural description*) is, first of all, centered around precisely locating (types of) the C element in a given phrase-marker—in terms of the morphemes that go with C and what phrases, if any, happen to be right and left adjacent to it.[2] Then the *structural change* executes a rearrangement of these key elements, thereby implementing the actual transformation of the structure (in (4) this is a subject-auxiliary inversion).

(4) T_q – optional
Structural analysis:

$$\left\{ \begin{array}{l} NP - C - V \ldots \\ NP - C + M - \ldots \\ NP - C + have - \ldots \\ NP - C + be - \ldots \end{array} \right\}$$

Structural change:

$X_1 - X_2 - X_3 \rightarrow X_2 - X_1 - X_3$

[intended as permutation of the first and second terms.]

Chomsky's classical analysis also involved obligatory transformational rules intended to determine the right morphological shape of verbs, as follows:[3]

(5) "Affix Hopping" (informal statement)
Right adjoin affix (S, ∅, past, en, ing) to v (V, M, have, be) to its immediate right.

(6) "*Do*-Support" (informal statement)
Left adjoin *do* to an affix that failed to hop.

Finally, the system presents morphophonemic specifications of the situations arising for C after the transformations are applied, instantiating concord configurations of the subject-verb sort:

(7)
$$C \rightarrow \begin{Bmatrix} S \text{ in the context } NP_{sing} \\ \varnothing \text{ in other contexts} \\ past \text{ in any context} \end{Bmatrix}$$

After (7) applies to the contexts generated by (5) or (6), which in turn result from the permutation in (4), the abstractness of (3) is concretized into the various situations in (1).

That sort of analysis directly captures the felt-relatedness among the pairs in (1). It also provides a natural description of the examples in the second column of (1) and succeeds in using the same mechanism for the superficially very different (1h). Ultimately, the entire discussion in which this account is embedded is part of Chomsky's elaborate argument for transformations. The general point is seen in the following passages from Chomsky (1957):

> there are languages (in our general sense) that cannot be described in terms of phrase structure, but I do not know whether or not English is itself literally outside the range of such analysis. However, I think that there are other grounds for rejecting the theory of phrase structure as inadequate for the purposes of linguistic description. The strongest possible proof of the inadequacy of a linguistic theory is to show that it literally cannot apply to some natural language. A weaker [demonstration is] to show that any grammar that can be constructed in terms of this theory will be extremely complex, ad hoc, and 'unrevealing', that certain very simple ways of describing grammatical sentences cannot be accommodated within the associated forms of grammar, and that certain fundamental formal properties of natural language cannot be utilized to simplify grammars. (34)

> We can greatly simplify the description of English and gain new and important insight into its formal structure if we limit the direct description in terms of phrase structure

to a kernel of basic sentences (simple, declarative, active, with no complex verb or noun phrases), deriving all other sentences from these (more properly, from the strings that underlie them) by transformation, possibly repeated. (106–107)

Chomsky's argument for his account of the examples in (1) is not that a context-free phrase-structure grammar couldn't generate those data. Rather, his point is that coming up with as many phrase structure rules to describe the data in (1) as types of examples are presented there is not a satisfying analysis of the phenomenon. Intuitively, he expects grammatical devices to be able to accommodate "simple ways of describing grammatical sentences" (like the permutations that a Subject/Auxiliary Inversion presupposes)—so as to "simplify grammars." This is even if, to implement the simplification, the theorist must assume abstract notions like "a kernel of basic sentences," so that some structures (e.g., passives, questions) are derived from more basic ones.[4]

The more explicit and comprehensive Chomsky (1955) added the following about the particulars of the transformational analysis of auxiliary verb phenomena:[5]

The simplest class of sentences not included in our grammatical sketch . . . is the [yes/no] class of interrogative sentences. . . . For any sentence of the form $NP - VP_A - VP_1$ . . . we can form a corresponding question by inverting the *NP* and an initial segment of the VP_A (auxiliary verb phrase). Thus such a question will be of the form $X^\wedge NP^\wedge Y^\wedge VP_1$ where $X^\wedge Y$ is the VP_A of the corresponding declarative. (418)

Later, Chomsky insists on the simplicity consideration as an argument for the transformational analysis. For that purpose, another concomitant abstract move is that the grammar needs central elements of the analysis for unrelated phenomena:

The transformational analysis . . . is clearly somewhat simpler than the extension of the kernel grammar . . . even in absolute terms as these analyses now stand. Thus we must accept the transformational analysis of yes-or-no questions, and drop them from the kernel. The difference in complexity between these two analyses would become more compelling if we could show that [the crucial parts of the analysis] are needed anyway, for other transformations. But this is in fact the case [as seen in (8), his 12]. (423)

(8) a. *I saw the play and so did he.*
b. *I will see the play and so will he.*
c. *I have seen the play and so has he.*
d. *I have been seeing the play and so has he.*

The key here, given the transformational analysis of yes/no questions, is for sentences of this general form to be introduced transformationally

with no independent characterization necessary. . . . In other words, we have found that two phenomena which on the level of phrase structure are distinct and complex become, in transformational terms, instances of a single generalization. But this naturally leads us to choose the transformational analysis in this case and, in particular, to drop yes-or-no questions from the kernel. (425)

Chomsky then indicates how sentences like (9) (his 22) provide support for the analysis:

(9) *I saw the play and he did too.*

2.2 The POS Angle

These are hardly ad hoc considerations. The following passage a decade later provided the foundation for much further discussion in subsequent years, regarding the notion of SD. It is useful to reflect on why it is relevant to POS considerations and the innatist philosophy underlying a putative approach to the puzzle:

A theory that attributes possession of certain linguistic universals to a language-acquisition system, as a property to be realized under appropriate external conditions, implies that *only certain kinds of symbolic systems can be acquired and used* as languages by this device. Others should be beyond its language-acquisition capacity. . . . In principle, one might try to determine whether invented systems that fail these conditions do pose inordinately difficult problems for language learning, and do fall beyond the domain for which the language acquisition system is designed. As a concrete example, consider the fact that, according to the theory of transformational grammar, only certain kinds of formal operations on strings can appear in grammars—operations that, furthermore, have no a priori justification. For example, the permitted operations cannot be shown in any sense to be the most "simple" or "elementary" ones that might be invented. In fact, what might in general be considered "elementary operations" on strings do not qualify as grammatical transformations at all, while many of the operations that do qualify are far from elementary, in any general sense. Specifically, *grammatical transformations are necessarily "structure dependent" in that they manipulate substrings only in terms of their assignment to categories.* (Chomsky 1965:55–56, emphasis added)

This is the SD notion that concerns us in the present chapter. We want to comment on the currency of the approach too: Chomsky is squarely speaking of artificial algorithms to check the properties found within natural languages. For a generative grammar, it is as important to describe what the system generates as it is to understand what it does not. This may seem obvious, but one should bear it in mind when considering alternatives to the proposal we are examining. In particular, we see immediately how many imaginable alternatives fail.

Chomsky goes on to illustrate his point with rule (4):

a transformation that can insert all or part of the Auxiliary Verb to the left of a Noun Phrase that precedes it, independently of what the length or internal complexity of the strings belonging to these categories may be. It is impossible, however, to formulate as a transformation such a simple operation as reflection of an arbitrary string (that is, replacement of any string $a_1 \ldots a_n$, where each a_i is a single symbol, by $a_n \ldots a_1$), or interchange of the $(2n-1)^{th}$ word with the $2n^{th}$ word throughout a string of arbitrary length, or insertion of a symbol in the middle of a string of even length. [Such a theory would] predict that although a language might form interrogatives, for example, by interchanging the order of certain categories (as in English), it could *not form interrogatives by reflection, or interchange of odd and even words, or insertion of a marker in the middle of the sentence.* Many other such predictions, none of them at all obvious in any a priori sense, can be deduced from any sufficiently explicit theory of linguistic universals that is attributed to a language-acquisition device as an intrinsic property. (56, emphasis added)

Here the key is that SD prevents certain logically possible processes (italicized in the quote), which thus are not even entertained by a human learner who happens to be sensitive to SD. Again it is logically possible that an alien learner would have been capable of postulating transformations that are sensitive, say, to making an interrogative "by reflection," so that a sentence like *John has seen Mary* in that straightforward hypothetical would become a question of the form *Mary seen has John?* (meaning the same as our *Has Mary seen John?*).

That is the origin of the English auxiliary-fronting phenomenon as a way to illustrate, by a clear and accessible example, the general idea behind SD. Chomsky (1968) continued to use this very example in other contexts, for instance reminding us how grammatical transformations

are invariably *structure-dependent* in the sense that they apply to a string of words[6] by virtue of the organization of these words into phrases. It is easy to imagine structure-independent operations that apply to a string of elements quite independently of its abstract structure as a system of phrases. For example, the rule that forms the interrogatives of [(10), his 71] from the corresponding declaratives of [(11), his 72] . . . [7] is a structure-dependent rule interchanging a noun phrase with the first element of the auxiliary.

(10) a. *Will the members of the audience who enjoyed the play stand?*
b. *Has Mary lived in Princeton?*
c. *Will the subjects who will act as controls be paid?*

(11) a. *The members of the audience who enjoyed the play will stand.*
b. *Mary has lived in Princeton.*
c. *The subjects who will act as controls will be paid.*

In contrast, consider the operation that inverts the first and last words of a sentence, or that arranges the words of a sentence in increasing length in terms of phonetic segments ("alphabetizing" in some specified way for items of the same length), or that moves the left-most occurrence of the word "will" to the extreme left—call these O_1, O_2, and O_3, respectively. Applying O_1 to [(11a)], we derive [(12a)]; applying O_2 to [(11b)], we derive [(12b)]; applying O_3 to [(11c)], we derive [(12c)] [his 72 and 73 examples]:

(12) a. *stand the members of the audience who enjoyed the play will*
b. *in has lived Mary Princeton*
c. *will the subjects who act as controls will be paid*

The operations O_1, O_2, and O_3 are *structure-independent.* Innumerable other operations of this sort can be specified. (52, emphasis added)

Chomsky goes on to argue that there are no a priori reasons why human language should make use of SD operations, instead of other operations like O_1. He then suggests that those sorts of structure *in*dependent processes are in no obvious sense harmful to the human species (e.g., in terms of communicative efficiency), yet they are simply not part of what English (or any other known language) allows as grammatical processes. For reasons hard to rationalize—beyond arguably innatist considerations—language learners just happen to know that SD transformations such as (4) and the like are possible within a grammar, whereas O_1 and the like are not even considered.

If we establish the proper "psychic distance" from such elementary and commonplace phenomena as these, we will see that they really pose some nontrivial problems for human psychology. We can speculate about the reason for the reliance on structure-dependent operations . . . but we must recognize that any such speculation must involve assumptions regarding human cognitive capacities that are by no means obvious or necessary. And it is difficult to avoid the conclusion that whatever its function may be, *the reliance on structure-dependent operations must be predetermined for the language-learner by a restrictive initial schematism* of some sort that directs his attempts to acquire linguistic competence. (52, emphasis added)

The POS argument based on the SD of Subject/Auxiliary Inversion as in (4) reappears in Chomsky (1971:27–28):

Notice further that we have very little evidence, in our normal experience, that the structure dependent operation is the correct one. It is quite possible for a person to *go through life without having heard any relevant examples that would choose between the two principles.* It is, however, safe to predict that a child who has had no such evidence would unerringly apply the structure-dependent operation the first time he attempts to form the question corresponding to the assertion "The dog that is in the corner is hungry." Though children make certain kinds of errors in the course of language learning, I am sure that *none make the error of forming the question* "Is the dog that in the corner is hungry?" despite the slim evidence of experience and the simplicity of the structure-independent rule. Furthermore, all known formal operations in the grammar of English, or of any other language, are structure-dependent. This is a very simple example of an invariant principle of language, what might be called a formal linguistic universal or a principle of universal grammar. (emphasis added)

Chomsky (1971:26–28) develops the point further, from the perspective of linguists who encounter a sentence like *The dog in the corner is hungry,* whose relevance they want to understand vis-à-vis the question *Is the dog in the corner hungry?*—by way of fronting *is*. Chomsky invites his readers to imagine two proposals [1] and [2] that such linguists may make:

> [1] states that to form a question, we first identify the subject noun phrase of the sentence, and we then move the occurrence of "is" following this noun phrase to the beginning of the sentence. Thus in the example in question, the subject noun phrase is "the dog in the corner;" we form the question by [1] *moving the occurrence of "is" that follows* [*this subject*] *to the front of the sentence*. Let us call this operation a "structure-dependent operation," meaning by this that the operation considers not merely the sequence of elements that constitute the sentence but also their structure; in this case, the fact that the sequence "the dog in the corner" is a phrase, furthermore a noun phrase. For the case in question, we might also have proposed a "structure-independent operation": namely, [2] *take the leftmost occurrence of "is" and move it to the front* of the sentence. We can easily determine that the correct rule is the structure-dependent operation. Thus if we have the sentence "The dog that is in the corner is hungry," we do not apply the proposed structure-independent operation, forming the question "Is the dog that __ in the corner is hungry?" Rather, we apply the structure-dependent operation, first locating the noun-phrase subject "the dog that is in the corner," then inverting the occurrence of "is" that follows it, forming: "Is the dog that is in the corner __ hungry?" (emphasis added)

Curiously enough, Chomsky does not make much of this example as such. He states:

> Though *the example is trivial*, the result is nonetheless surprising, from a certain point of view. Notice that the structure-dependent operation has no advantages from the point of view of communicative efficiency or "simplicity." If we were, let us say, designing a language for formal manipulations by a computer, we would certainly prefer structure-independent operations. These are far simpler to carry out, since it is only necessary to scan the words of the sentence, *paying no attention to the structures into which they enter*, structures that are not marked physically in the sentence at all. Mathematicians have studied structure-independent operations on strings (inversion, shuffling, etc.), but it has occurred to no one to investigate the curious and complex notion of "structure-dependent operation," in the relevant sense. (emphasis added)

Unfortunately, despite Chomsky's insistence on there not being any particular significance, as such, to an auxillary-fronting paradigm that he describes as trivial, other scholars have been misled into taking one particular aspect of the pedagogical analysis as the principal (or even the only) SD claim. Moreover, some took this as the principal (or even only) POS claim within generative grammar. We consider this next to clarify its relative relevance.

2.3 A "Sane Person" at Work

Among the many interesting interchanges in the October 1975 Royaumont encounter (which was edited into Piattelli-Palmarini [1980]), there is one between Chomsky and Hilary Putnam that concerns the POS argument.

Chomsky, as we have just seen in other forms, formulates two reasonable, informal, versions of auxiliary fronting, calling H_1 structure-independent and H_2 structure-dependent:

(13) a. H_1: Process the declarative from beginning to end (left to right), word by word, until reaching the first occurrence of the words *is*, *will*, etc.; transpose this occurrence to the beginning (left), forming the associated interrogative.
b. H_2: same as H_1, but select the first occurrence of *is*, *will*, etc., following the first noun phrase of the declarative.

Chomsky then observes how the following data directly refute H_1 but are predicted by H_2:

(14) a. *The man who is here is tall.—Is the man who is here tall?*
b. *The man who is tall will leave.—Will the man who is tall leave?*

(15) a. **Is the man who here is tall?*
b. **Is the man who tall will leave?*

Chomsky then, predictably, asks how a child knows that H_1 is false (see section 2.2). It is surely not the case that the child first hits on H_1 (as a neutral scientist might) and then is forced to reject this hypothesis on the basis of data such as (14). Plainly, no child is ever taught the relevant facts. Children make many interesting errors in language learning, but none like (15), prior to appropriate training or evidence. In Chomsky's view:

> A person might go through much or all his life without ever having been exposed to relevant evidence, but he will nevertheless unerringly employ H_2, never H_1 on the first relevant occasion (assuming that he can handle the structures at all). . . . If humans were differently designed [like aliens insensitive to SD considerations], they would acquire a grammar that incorporates H_1 and would be none the worse for that. In fact, it would be difficult to know, by mere passive observation of a person's total linguistic performance, whether he was using H_1 or H_2. . . . Such observations suggest that it is a property of S_0 [the initial state of the language faculty] that rules (or rules of some specific category, identifiable on quite general grounds by some genetically determined mechanism) are structure-dependent. The child need not consider H_1; it is ruled out by properties of his initial mental state, S_0. (Piattelli-Palamarini 1980:40, emphasis added)

Interestingly for our purposes, Hilary Putnam rejected Chomsky's conclusion, responding, in part that "H_1 has never been 'put forth' by anyone, nor would any sane person put it forth" (287). One should consider why no "sane person" would entertain Chomsky's H_1—despite the fact that we (and we suspect Chomsky)—would be willing to entertain the possibility of a "sane *alien*" (not a human) reasonably entertaining H_1 or other structure-independent hypotheses about a formal language to acquire.

Chomsky's counter-response is as follows:

> Putnam considers my two hypotheses H_1 and H_2, advanced to explain the formation of yes-or-no questions in English. He observes that the structure-independent rule H_1 would *not be put forth by any "sane person," which is quite true*, but merely constitutes part of the problem to be solved. The question is: Why? The answer that I suggest is *that the general principles of transformational grammar belong to* S_0^L *as part of a schematism that characterizes possible human languages.* (311, emphasis added)

In other words, while it is true that humans do not even entertain non-SD hypotheses like H_1, concentrating, instead, on SD ones like H_2, what needs to be scientifically explained is the reason for this fact of human nature. Chomsky's answer is that the particular formalism that he argued for since his early work on the topic (the transformational mapping) happens to be narrowed down to SD considerations, thus ipso facto limiting the class of hypotheses that a human mind even entertains. One might not like Chomsky's answer, but we agree with him that an answer is necessary, just as it is necessary to provide a reason, for instance, for why humans do not bother to explore the (humanly) nonvisible part of the spectrum, while we clearly experience infrared radiation as heat and a bee visually processes ultraviolet radiation.

Many psychologists, philosophers, and cognitive scientists, are troubled by Chomsky's innatist position that SD is part of the "initial state" of humans. In Piattelli-Palmarini (1980:293), Putnam offers an argument against Chomsky's view, based on the linguistic abilities of Washoe, a chimpanzee who was carefully and explicitly taught to use a certain amount of American Sign Language by Alan and Beatrice Gardner (Gardner et al. 1989). Putnam recalls how Washoe presents the ability to coordinate nouns and to coordinate sentences. He then goes on to claim that "these are *structure dependent* rules which Washoe has learned without benefit of an innate template for language." However, as Chomsky points out, this argument is based on a misunderstanding of the concept SD. Chomsky notes that

> H_1 and H_2, present rules that [affect] internal structure in some way (to be precise, the rules apply to the abstract structures underlying sentences, but we may put this refinement aside [see note 4]). Both the structure-independent rule H_1 and the structure-dependent rule H_2 make use of the concepts 'sentence', 'word', 'first' and others; they differ in that H_2 requires in addition an analysis of the sentence into abstract phrases. *A rule that does not modify the internal structure of a sentence is neither structure-dependent nor structure independent.* For example, a phrase structure rule, part of a phrase structure grammar in the technical sense of the term, is neither structure-dependent nor structure-independent. (Piattelli-Palmarini 1980:315)

In other words, by definition of the very notion SD, this arises *for rules modifying structures*, which we described in chapter 1 and section 2.1 as (broadly) context-sensitive. One can ask whether a (structure modifying, in that sense context-sensitive) rule is, in itself, structure dependent. But it is meaningless to ask whether a (structure building, context-free) rule is structure dependent.[8] As Chomsky puts it:

> The rule for conjunction that Putnam discusses in his Washoe comments takes two sentences *p* and *q* and combines them to form *pq*; in the framework of my discussion, *it is a phrase structure rule rather than a transformational rule.* It is neither structure-dependent nor structure-independent in my sense of these terms, since *it does not require an internal analysis of the sentences to which it applies* as a sequence of words or as a system of phrases. The rule does nothing to the internal structure of the sentences, and thus lies outside the bounds of the present discussion." (ibid., emphasis added)[9]

2.4 Bayesian Rationality

Complaints against this particular POS argument of Chomsky's are abundant, and some are even recent. Perfors et al. (2006), for example, present one such case that we would like to examine in detail. As they put it, the POS argument holds that human children

> do not receive enough evidence to infer the existence of core aspects of language, such as the dependence of linguistic rules on hierarchical phrase structure. We reevaluate one version of this argument with a Bayesian model of grammar induction, and show that *a rational learner without any initial language-specific biases could learn this dependency given typical child-directed input.* This choice enables the learner to master aspects of syntax, such as the auxiliary fronting rule in interrogative formation, even without having heard directly relevant data (e.g., interrogatives containing an auxiliary in a relative clause in the subject NP). (663, emphasis added)

For readers unfamiliar with Bayesian inference, this is a kind of dynamical statistical inference, based on Rev. Thomas Bayes's famous theorem giving the probability of an event based on prior knowledge of possibly related conditions.[10] This theorem is typically used to update the probability of particular hypotheses as information surfaces. Bayesian updating and inference is relevant to a variety of human activities, from legal considerations to matters of interest here, involving learning as information becomes available and can be updated. Evidently, if one such model allows us to entirely induce grammars without any language-specific biases of the sort Chomsky claimed were necessary, this would be big news—so it is important to evaluate such news.

For perspective, to test the significance of such an important claim, we would next expect a model that learns a (fragment of a) transformational grammar of the sort Chomsky gave us to treat paradims as in (1). Moreover, we would expect a model without a SD predisposition. This reasonable expectation is reinforced by the next passage, where we find a nice summary of what we have presented in the preceding sections:

> The phenomenon of auxiliary fronting in interrogative sentences is *one example of the PoS argument*; here, the argument states that children must be innately biased to favor structure-dependent rules that operate using grammatical constructs like phrases and clauses over structure-independent rules that operate only on the sequence of words. *English interrogatives are formed from declaratives by fronting the main clause auxiliary.* Given a declarative sentence like "The dog in the corner is hungry," the interrogative is formed by moving the *is* to make the sentence "Is the dog in the corner hungry?" Chomsky considered two types of operation that can explain auxiliary fronting (Chomsky 1965, 1971). The simplest (linear) rule is independent of the hierarchical phrase structure of the sentence: take the leftmost (first) occurrence of the auxiliary in the sentence and move it to the beginning. *The structure-dependent (hierarchical) rule*—move the auxiliary from the main clause of the sentence—*is more complex since it operates over a sentence's phrasal structure* and not just its sequence of elements. (663, emphasis added)

They continue (and we emphasize some details to continue evaluating the approach):

> In this work we present a Bayesian account of linguistic structure learning in order to engage with the PoS argument on its own terms—taking *the existence of structure seriously* and asking *whether and to what extent knowledge of that structure can be inferred by a rational statistical learner.* This is an ideal learnability analysis: our question is not whether a learner without innate language-specific biases must be able infer that linguistic structure is hierarchical, but rather *whether it is possible to make that inference.* (664, emphasis added)

So far, so good. If it is possible to make such an inference, Chomsky's conclusion may be wrong—or at least not one to be cornered into—because the learner in point would need no particular innate assumptions. Moreover, Perfors et al. claim to demonstrate that a learner

> [I] . . . equipped with the capacity to explicitly represent both hierarchical and linear grammars—but *without any initial biases*—could *infer that the hierarchical grammar is a better fit to typical child-directed input.* [II] We show that inferring this hierarchical grammar results in the *mastery of aspects of auxiliary fronting*, even if no direct evidence is available. [III] Our approach provides a *clear and objectively sensible metric of simplicity*, as well as a way to explore *what sort of data and how much is required to make these hierarchical generalizations.* (664 emphasis added)

Regretably, if we have understood their argument, Perfors et al. wind up doing no such thing as claimed in [I] through [III], nor do they even seem to attempt it.

In a nutshell, when presented with a context-free language of the right sort, the system in Perfors et al. (2006) learns a context-free language of that sort. It could have been worse: their system may not have learned that much. That said, in their approach, the relation between declaratives and interrogatives in English—the entire raison d'être behind Chomsky's initial postulation of transformations to address regularities as seen in (1)—is not even addressed. All of the grammars presented as targets of the learning are particular phrase structure grammars (again, a formalism shown by Chomsky [1955, 1957] to be *inadequate* for capturing the relevant generalizations). So in effect they wind up repeating, two decades after it was first made, one of Putnam's errors, as reviewed in section 2.3. Thus, as Chomsky observed in discussing Putnam's argument, to talk of SD in such conditions is to make a category mistake. SD (and structure independence) are properties of *transformations*. One could define a different notion of SD, have it apply to other processes (e.g., context-free phrases, Turing-computable structures of any kind, or for that matter imaginary creatures) and see whether it holds. But it is hard to see how any of that would have a bearing on Chomsky's original POS argument, once the target has been moved.[11] It is as if these authors wish to take the technical notions of being "structure dependent" to mean "related to structure." About that we have little to say, beyond emphasizing that Chomsky never discussed a conceit along those lines.

It is instructive to see a representative sample of the grammars that Perfors et al.'s (2006) learning procedure considers their least (16) and most comprehensive ones (17):[12]

(16) *Level 1 CFG*

$S \rightarrow whC$	$I2 \rightarrow AP$
$S \rightarrow whI$	$AP \rightarrow adj$
$S \rightarrow NPI$	$NP \rightarrow detN$
$S \rightarrow I2$	$NP \rightarrow N$
$S \rightarrow wh$	$NP \rightarrow NPC$
$S \rightarrow co$	$NP \rightarrow pro$
$C \rightarrow auxI2$	$NP \rightarrow adjN$
$I \rightarrow auxI2$	$N \rightarrow n$
	$I2 \rightarrow NP$

(17) *Level 6 CFG*

S → *whAP*
S → *whPP*
S → *whNP*
S → *whIP*
S → *whC*
S → *whI*
S → *auxIP*
S → *auxVI*
S → *NPV*
S → *NPI*
S → *I*
S → I_2
S → *V*
S → *CP*
S → *wh*
S → *T*
S → *co*
CP → *compC*
IP → *NPI2*
IP → *NPC*
IP → *APC*
C → *auxIP*
C → *auxI2*
C → *V*
C → *NPV*
C → *NPI*
I → *auxI2*
I → *aux*
I2 → *I2PP*
I2 → *T*
I2 → *NP*
I2 → *VI*
I2 → *VP*
I2 → *AP*
I2 → *PP*
AP → *adjT*
AP → *T*
V → *VNP*
V → *VPP*
V → *VT*
V → *VAP*
V → *v*
VI → *vi*
VI → *VINP*
VI → *VIPP*
VI → *VIT*
VI → *VIAP*
VP → *part*
VP → *VPNP*
VP → *VPPP*
VP → *VPAP*
VP → *VPT*
T → *toVI*
T → *to*
NP → *NPT*
NP → *NPPP*
NP → *detN*
NP → *N*
NP → *NPCP*
NP → *NPVP*
NP → *NPC*
NP → *pro*
NP → *prop*
N → *adjN*
N → *n*
PP → *prepPP*
PP → *prepVP*
PP → *prep*
PP → *prepNP*

When we introduced Chomsky's original data set, of the sort in (1), we already pointed out that one can certainly generate the relevant data with a list, as large as one cares to produce, of phrasal combinations. We quoted Chomsky (1957:34), presenting a "demonstration of inadequacy" for a theory in terms of its applying to a data set only clumsily, showing how "any grammar that can be constructed in terms of this theory will be extremely complex, ad hoc, and 'unrevealing' [and] certain very simple ways of describing grammatical sentences cannot be accommodated within the associated forms of grammar." Perfors et al. (2006) go a long way toward illustrating this critical point. It is unclear to us what in these sets of rules provides any insight into the simple Subject/Auxiliary Inversion process illustrated in (1), or how any particular formal property of a system along these lines could be utilized to simplify our grammatical description of the phenomenon in point—assuming that is one of the goals of grammatical theory.

Unfortunately, the discussion by Perfors et al. does not ease our concerns. Witness:

> Because this work is motivated by the distinction between rules operating over linear and hierarchical representations, we would like to compare grammars that differ structurally. The hierarchical grammar is context-free, since CFGs generate parse trees with hierarchical structure and are accepted as a reasonable "first approximation" to the grammars of natural language (Chomsky 1959).

Once again, because target grammars in the paper are not transformational, their results have no bearing on SD, and thus, a fortiori, on any POS arguments based on SD. The way they put it:

> All grammars are probabilistic, meaning that each production is associated with a probability and the probability of any given parse is the product of the probabilities of the productions involved in the derivation. *The probabilistic context-free grammar (PCFG) is the most linguistically accurate grammar we could devise that could parse all of the forms in the corpus*: as such, it contains the syntactic structures that modern linguists employ, such as noun and verb phrases. (665, emphasis added)

Whatever the import of arguments and results in this paper, they really have no bearing on the initial question: How does the learner come to know that *transformations* (in particular, the one for English interrogatives) *are invariably structure dependent?* Curiously, they take themselves to

> use a Bayesian framework for grammar induction to address a version of this argument and show that, given typical child-directed speech and certain innate domain-general capacities, an ideal learner could recognize the hierarchical phrase structure of language without having this knowledge innately specified as part of the language faculty. (Perfors et al. 2011:306)

There is, indeed, overwhelming reason to believe that sentences of human language are hierarchically structured, and it is of interest to determine whether that property could be learned, under reasonable assumptions about data and learning procedures (which Perfors et al. articulate). But while the attribution of said hierarchical structure is clearly *necessary* if we are to account for the demonstrated properties of the declarative-interrogative alternation, it is surely not *sufficient*. Now at least this time, while Perfors et al. mention the alternation several times, they do not claim to have dealt with it. Rather, they merely state their focus to be "on the more basic question of how a learner can come to know that language should be represented in terms of hierarchical phrase structure" (310). So Chomsky's original question remains, and we have still seen no argument that the SD property *of transformations* could be learned. Once again, one may wish to deny the existence of a transformation like (4) to be coupled with an abstract rewrite rule like (3) and propose instead systems like those summarized in (16) and (17). No one ever claimed this is formally impossible, only whether it is scientifically tenable, given Occam's Razor (let alone ontologically more ambitious considerations as in the Minimalist Program). That said, Bayesian exercises so far have not, in any sense, addressed the SD aspect of a transformational system. At best, they address a different claim: that there is a descriptively equivalent, nontransformational, grammar that can be abstracted away from a finite amount of selected data of the relevant sort. In section 2.6, we will return to the issue of how that data ever got to possess that amount of structure to start with, which the Bayesian approach presupposes. But it should be clear that an approach of this sort cannot be addressing the SD aspect, literally by definition (as the original argument was based on a specifically structural limitation on transformations required to provide an elegant explanation of the data).

It may be worse. Suppose one does find a reasonable nontransformational way to relate rules of the sort in (16) or (17), with the intention of capturing generalizations across rules, for example, in terms of Subject/Auxiliary Inversion applying when there is an auxiliary verb—otherwise, the *Do*-Support rule taking over (as opposed to, say, the main verb displacing, as is possible in other languages).[13] As far as generative grammarians can tell, such mechanisms are dependent on structural nuances, as their specificities become concrete enough to be meaningful. In other words, while SD has been accurately and productively stated in terms of transformations, any device that ends up covering the same data range (e.g., the paradigm in (1)) will end up being equally dependent on SD considerations. We may be accused of "moving the target" by such a claim, but the opposite is intended: Even if the target as traditionally (transformationally) specified turned out to be one among a class of such (then more abstract) structural conditions, we are willing to conjecture that the resulting process will present a nuanced SD-like condition over the manipulation of the relevant structures.[14] In other words, we do think that, among those we have seen, the transformational analyses provide us with the most accurate and learnable representations of the data. However, to the best of our understanding, even reasonable, nontransformational, alternative ways of capturing the relevant long-range correlations will present SD-like conditions once they are explicitly worked out. Nothing in Perfors et al. (2006) appears to address the significance of such conditions, either narrowly applied to classic transformations or to extended phrasal systems enriched so as to align with long-range dependencies that, in effect, are still under SD strictures in the manipulation of structures in that range, which appears never to be over linearly expressed dependencies, as opposed to phrasally articulated ones.

2.5 On the Poverty of the Challenge

We turn next to a small reaction to Pullum and Scholz's (2002) extensive critical discussion of POS arguments, so as to show that misunderstandings continue to be broad, this time around in relation to data exposure. Calling the auxiliary-fronting argument "the apparently strongest case of alleged learning from crucially inadequate evidence discussed in the literature, and certainly the most celebrated" (36), they reject Chomsky's claim of unavailability of relevant evidence for the learner. They say in particular that, to date, it has not at all been established that children are not exposed to interrogative sentences where the subject contains an auxiliary verb and where that auxiliary is not what has been fronted. To make their case, they furthermore present several occurring examples of the relevant sort as found in various computational searches. They also state that "Chomsky's assertion that you can go over a vast amount of data of experience without ever finding such a case is unfounded hyperbole. We have found relevant cases in every corpus we have looked in" (44). On that empirical basis, they conclude:

> Our preliminary investigations suggest the percentage of relevant cases is not lower than 1 percent of the interrogatives in a typical corpus. By these numbers, even a welfare child would be likely to hear about 7,500 questions that crucially falsify the structure-independent auxiliary-fronting generalization, before reaching the age of 3. But assume we are wrong by a whole order of magnitude on this, so there are really only 750. Would exposure to 750 crucial examples falsifying the structure-independent generalization not be enough to support data-driven learning? (45)

This data-oriented argument misses two essential points. First, in our view it is simply not correct, empirically. The corpora that Pullum and Scholz examined were all newspaper databases that seem far from representative of speech directed toward children. When corpora of child-directed speech were examined (e.g., in Legate and Yang 2002), the relevant disambiguating data occurred at rates of less than 0.07% of all utterances—a number two orders of magnitude smaller than that of other constructions that children acquire by or at age 3.[15]

Second, as Lasnik and Uriagereka (2002) observe, the number of relevant sentences is beside the point. That is, while one might read Chomsky as implying that the availability of the relevant grammatical questions in the child's data would undermine the poverty argument, that is actually not the case. For suppose the child is presented with data like:

(18) *Is the dog that is in the corner hungry?*

Although this does seem to indicate the incorrectness of a rule *demanding* that the first auxiliary be fronted to form an interrogative (19a), and the relative superiority of (19b), it provides no basis for excluding a rule like (20a), or others like (20b)—(20d), and so on.

(19) a. Front the first auxiliary.
b. Front the matrix auxiliary

(20) a. Front any auxiliary.
b. Front any finite auxiliary.
c. Front the last auxiliary.
d. Front either the first or last auxiliary.

The way Lasnik and Uriagereka (2002:149) put it:

> [Pullum and Scholz] are missing Freidin's [1991] point: [(18)] is not direct evidence for anything with the effects of hypothesis [(19b)]. At best, [(18)] is evidence for something with the logical structure of [(19a)] or X, but certainly not for anything having to do with [(19b)]."

In other words, the very few examples illustrating auxiliary fronting that children actually seem to be receiving (something like one of every ten thousand utterances)[16] are not sufficient, in and of themselves, to discard non-SD hypotheses, which children could come up with more or less randomly instead of the correct hypothesis they manage to rapidly converge into. We know of no way to explain this simple fact other than by assuming that certain crucial priors to the acquisition task (such as the notions subject or auxiliary) are in some sense or another innate.

2.6 Where Does Structure Come From?

We want to finish this chapter with a reflection on the presence of structure in data sets, which any proposal hoping to induce the data from the data set presupposes. There simply would be no way to induce the relevant rule, be it (4) or any other, if patterns such as those in (1) did not exist. Truth is that finding such patterns "out there," in nature, has not been easy. More generally, it is implicit in the discussion of any "emergent computational systems" that structure "is there," in the data sets, so that learners may induce it. But how did it "get there"?

One possibility may stem from the nature of information itself. For example, Berwick (1982) argued that a CFG may be seen as an effective way to compress information that would be only clumsily describable in finite-state terms. One could then imagine an evolutionary scenario suggesting that data coevolved (perhaps in the sense of Dennett [1995]) with human cognition in such a way that, once a certain criticality (e.g., in group, and consequently data, size) was reached, a version coalescing into a data set that a CFG can describe is easier to learn. So if humans evolved to learn language easily, language had to coevolve to be easily learned.[17]

There is some hand-waving in that reasoning. We know what it means for a species *S* to evolve: (i) *S* must exist in time so as to transform; (ii) *S* must have descended from some ancestor;[18] (iii) *S* must be able to produce diverse offspring; (iv) *S* must be able to gradually change; and finally (v) natural selection must affect *S* and its competitors. If all those conditions obtain (and possibly others), under certain specific metrics of fit to an environment, we may say that *S* has evolved. But there is no such specific meaning *for a language* to literally evolve, as emphasized in Berwick and Chomsky (2015). While a language *L* does (i) exist in time and (ii) generally descend from some ancestor, it is doubtful that any of the other conditions obtain for *L*. Individuals produce offspring, languages do not; the sense in which languages change is across generations: for an individual speaker, languages effectively remain stable;[19] and there is no obvious sense in which the conditions of natural selection would result in a language being fit(ter) to any given environment. This is all to be kept in mind when one takes data sets to be organized, so that learners can putatively induce that organization (or any organization compatible with the data) from statistical generalization. Once again: how did the structure *get there*? Coevolution is a meaningful concept for competing species, but unless we are missing key components that we cannot apprehend in standard evolutionary terms, it is less so for the relation between humans and their language. Something else might result in the attested complexity in the data (of the sort in (1)), but theorists need to provide that. Chomsky's argument that the complexity comes from the human mind is, if nothing else, concrete enough to be tested.

To up the complexity ante, it was already known to structuralists that constituent analysis does not suffice to describe language (recall note 2). Chomsky turned that problem into a theory, by way of his transformational analysis (see section 2.1). It does not much matter now whether, in the end, what that amounts to is something like a CFG plus some extra.[20] Call that a CFG+. The relevant point is that, whatever that is, formally, it is not a CFG with standard first-order symbolic manipulation.[21] The question is where that kind of (CFG+) complexity is coming from.

There are natural phenomena that arguably fit a CFG description. For example, Lindenmayer (1968) famously used so-called L-systems to describe the behavior of plant cells, thus modeling plant development.[22] Such systems have also been used (e.g., by Rozenberg and Salomaa 1976) to model growth and more in other organisms; these systems can also be used to generate self-similar fractals.[23] Evidently, organic morphology or population dynamics could be at right angles with information structures as needed to describe linguistic phenomena (and see note 20). Perhaps more relevantly, Roeske et al. (2018) have argued, by a multifractal analysis of certain bird songs, that such rhythms reveal music-like dynamic structure. If such results hold and generalize, and furthermore the algorithm to describe such structures is of the L-system sort or some equivalent, it is at least arguable that these kinds of behaviors may be in the league that should be relevant to cognitive scientists analyzing elaborate behaviors (see note 23).[24]

Gallistel and King (2009) present elaborate behaviors in nonhuman animals that arguably go beyond finite-state terms, into the realm of CFGs. More recently, Kheifets et al. (2017) studied probability estimation in mice that can store event probabilities in ways that would seem to require something like constituent structure.[25] As such, none of that is of the CFG+ sort, although one could keep pushing this agenda to try and find out whether any such (more complex) behaviors also exist in the animal world. Perhaps we should clarify that this work pertains to animal conducts in general (e.g., foraging or navigation systems), not just to communication schemes. We know of no uncontroversial instances involving communication that require CFGs (see note 21), although this may be a matter of time with the relevant research agenda. In the case of humans, several familiar behaviors would seem to be of the right sort, for example, exhibiting "cross-serial" dependencies (discussed in section 1.3.1) (e.g., in the construction of knots and other forms of weaving, traditional dwellings, elaborate hunting, rituals, art). It is not at all obvious that any of these are present even in closely related apes.

It may turn out that no animal behavior exhibits CFG+ conditions—except the human language faculty. It is possible that other complex cognitive behaviors one can witness associated with humans are directly or indirectly associated with language too. There have been arguments (e.g., Searls 1992) that CFG+ conditions exist in natural phenomena at molecular levels (in particular in the formation of RNA pseudo-knots or protein foldings), where cross-serial dependencies are systematically encountered. That being said, molecular biology is even more removed from communication than navigation or foraging systems are, so such long-range correlations, in themselves, may be of moderate relevance to information-theoretic dependencies.

This is all to say that postulating hypothetical computational devices that succeed in recognizing already existing structures still leaves the question of how said structures got coopted into linguistic systems. The task, per Berwick's

(1982) argument, may perhaps relate to information packaging—at least if what one is after is a CFG system. In turn, per Gallistel and King (2009), one could grant the presence of such systems beyond communicative circumstances. Then the issue boils down to some sort of neurophysiological transfer from CFG systems, in a cognitive area for which there is evidence beyond language, to one in which such an import becomes relevant, perhaps with selective pressure imposed by information packaging. Berwick and Chomsky's (2015) proposal is of roughly that sort.[26] Then again, if the relevant linguistic system is, instead, of a CFG+ sort, even that story would not suffice. It is certainly possible that, just as a CFG effectively compresses information whose finite-state description is clumsy, so too a CFG+ device follows suit with compressing information whose CFG description is clumsy. In a sense, that was Chomsky's (1955, 1957) original argument (see section 2.1). But while Berwick's (1982) argument had the character of a proof, similar results have not yet arisen for the more complex algorithms, particularly assuming the transition from E- to I-languages. This may mean nothing as such, particularly given Stabler's (2013a) discussion of the various independently proposed formalisms, all of which appear to converge into something of the same formal sort. While a plausibility argument is not a proof, we are willing to grant the benefit of the doubt to this kind of approach, because its logic and direction are straightforward.

But it is worth pointing out another caveat, regarding the formulation of computational analysis in other species, particularly when it comes to spatial grounding. It is unclear how one would use the machinery of formal languages, as discussed in chapter 1, to build a cognitive map (e.g., so as to look up on it information whose coordinates are presupposed).[27] Even for insects, navigation results show several species possessing something like an address-addressable memory system and sophisticated ways of manipulating relevant representations. Part of the problem here is that the original machinery that Chomsky either revamped or proposed anew is based on strings. Movement from E-language to I-language already pushed linguists in a direction where the role of strings is less obvious, a topic that we will return to in subsequent chapters. The bottom line for other species, at least in terms of navigation conditions, seems to be that something like a vector space (and a corresponding linear algebra) is the sort of formalism that matters, but the conditions of which are still unclear. By chapter 4, we speculate about one such possibility in the case of language too, so as to capture otherwise recalcitrant phenomena. But much specificity is still wanting, so extrapolation with relevance to the matter considered in this section becomes virtually impossible. We want to be clear about it in case others can clarify the matter further.

One last thought may be in order. Famously and controversially, Hauser et al. (2002) argue that the phenomenon of recursion is what is unique to human language (see Berwick and Chomsky [2015] for a more recent reflection on that argument). If an animal has enough memory to invoke constituency, it is hard to see what would prevent such a constituent structure from presenting recursion. Of course, a formal stipulation could.[28] But the issue is why such a stipulation would make sense within the CFG equivalent. An alternative possibility is that recursion as such is ancient (as argued in Jackendoff and Pinker [2005] in a different context), and perhaps the novelty of human language, instead, has to do with whatever the "plus extra" is in what we are calling CFG+.

This leaves the possibility open that CFG+ conditions only made it to human cognition, or to be fair and specific, to human language (the rest of relevant cognition is essentially parasitic on language or its underlying syntax). If this is true, it is unclear what gain there is in saying that language coevolved these properties with human learners (assuming that a postulate could be made concrete enough to be testable). Then the question becomes why language (co)evolved those particular properties as opposed to others—and why this evolutionary track did not emerge for other creatures. The way to diffuse this argument would be to show us unmistakable CFG+ conditions in other animal behaviors, which is just what Chomsky did in the 1950s for language.

2.7 Conclusions

In this chapter we have examined learnability considerations as they pertain to the POS argument. While there have been many attempts to undermine the argument through analysis of auxiliary-fronting rules, these miss several points. First, while this argument is a prominent and popular one, in no sense does it represent the strongest case; indeed, when Chomsky (1975:30) discussed this particular scenario, he called it "the simplest one that is not entirely trivial." Second, the argument is about the *relation* between sentences and their structures; it is not about the grammaticality of particular yes/no questions, but about the relation between these questions and the corresponding declaratives (which is what motivates elaborate analysis arguing, in particular, for transformational processes). Third, the argument based on structural dependence is not meant as hand-waving in the direction of syntactic structures; it is a precise statement about a very precise statement: that transformational processes relating structures are characterized over structural fragments, not any weaker notion. Finally, bear in mind that any POS argument is based on a comparison of hypotheses. But, as noted, any bounded data set is compatible with a potentially unbounded number of grammars. So, even if there is evidence in speech to children that favors the correct analysis over one explicit alternative (unclear), this does not decide the question against the poverty argument. To do so it would be necessary to show that the available evidence also excludes all other logically possible reformulations of the rule.

One other aspect that makes the present chapter interesting is that it touches on state-of-the-art machine learning algorithms of the sort we return to in chapter 5. In our view, such devices have at best shown so far how if structure is already presupposed in a data set, said structure can be generalized by the algorithm. Unfortunately, that as such has no bearing on the issue of transformational approaches to the data sets in point. Finally, we conclude by reflecting on how structure may have gotten into the data sets, if not because of how the humans think/speak, those who create such data. It is worth wrapping up by pointing out something that is obvious to any working linguist: the most powerful arguments for structure are not of the sort reviewed in this chapter. There are dozens of explicit and hundreds of implicit POS arguments in the literature, all of the same general sort, but using different structures and paradigms routinely presupposing transformations. We will be seeing many of these in chapter 3. Alternative analyses are always possible in science, but they cannot be routinely presupposed, let alone ignored, for the simple reason that the Devil is always in such specific details. If nothing else, we invite skeptics to read on, so as to enjoy the complexity that, by now, linguists know language presents. If we had to bet, we would be gambling on this complexity not going away any time soon, even when the emphasis in recent years has been on seeking streamlined computational conditions and resulting representations. This is to be expected with progress, but much of what has emerged from serious study is the realization that the structural subtlety of language is even more surprising than perhaps was initially fathomed.

3 Locality and Beyond

In this chapter we present more sophisticated arguments for structure. These come in two guises, depending on whether they implement "locality" conditions or patterns that seem irreducible to those. We first introduce locality effects as classically understood, showing how the notion evolved over the years. This will take us into current locality conceptions, which are often uncritically assumed to describe syntax as a whole. But there are plenty of nonlocal phenomena in the technical literature. While some of those might break down into component parts that could have an analysis based on locality considerations, we are skeptical that this is true for all such instances. This matter has been central to linguistic theorizing since at least Chomsky (1973), which we will be presenting in its essentials. We will review that history, concluding that some processes are necessarily long-distance. But both local and nonlocal relations argue for the central role of structure. For local ones, this is because the domains in which relevant syntactic relations need to be stated are themselves purely structural, typically phrases presenting some characteristic that the computational system must keep track of. For long-range syntactic correlations, as we will see, the key is that they happen in a narrow set of circumstances, for example, when exhibiting c-command strictures. In other words, the confines for their occurrence are structural though not reducible, we believe, to short-range correlations. This is to say that the structural nature of syntactic dependencies may go up high within the hierarchy discussed in chapter 1.

It is worth bearing in mind that, as one delves deeper into that hierarchy, matters structural become more intricate. At the lowest level, all one can really say with regard to a list is whether this comes before that or some sequence loops around. Already at the next, phrasal, level, conditions gain complexity, allowing us to tell apart chunks of structure on the basis of typing associated with some abstract label; different such types and corresponding configurations have a bearing on interface conditions of the external (e.g., stress, intonation) or internal sort (e.g., thematic relations, information structure). Complexity thrives beyond that domain, as we move into transformations. The pieces we will review in this chapter stem from a tradition studying structural constraints on variables in syntax, transformations themselves, the rules of grammar more generally, or even derivations as a whole. It is on the basis of said constraints that the edifice of generative grammar was built, all the way to the current Minimalist Program. Each of them, in its own right, presents an argument for elaborate structure. To be sure, because of that very complexity, much debate has gone into the ultimate shape or even relevance of each such condition. This is to be expected in any science. But let that not hinder the rich case for structure that this collective effort outlines. Indeed, it is *because* we see very significant common threads that have survived twists and fashions that we are willing to rationally reconstruct the history of some such constraints, with an eye on what they tell us about the elaborate structures that their very existence limits.

3.1 Classic Locality Effects

One interesting argument for structure stems from the study of locality conditions in the statement or operation of a transformation. In early generative grammar, transformations were far more specific than in later developments factoring properties out of specific transformations. Relevant examples stem from locality, of which there is virtually no discussion in Chomsky (1955). The only hint is in the analysis (437) of a certain restriction on the Wh-transformation, as in unacceptable examples of the following sort:

(1) **Whom did my interest in _ seem to you so strange?*

Surprisingly from a contemporary perspective, Chomsky suggested incorporating whatever constraint is responsible for the impossibility of (1) into the transformation itself that relates *whom* to its thematic position after *in*. It is in Chomsky (1964a) that one can first find the idea of formulating *general constraints* on the operation of transformations. There, we find a relatively modern-looking Wh-movement transformation, whose statement is simple and general. Basically:

(2) $Y - Wh + X - Z \rightarrow Wh + X - Y - Z$

As Chomsky notes, this generality raises potential problems of overgeneration. Some of these are addressed by constraints on movement, of the following sort:

> although several Noun Phrases in a sentence may have Wh attached to them, the operation [(2)] must be limited to a single application to each underlying terminal string. Thus we can have "who saw what?," "you met the man who saw what?," "you read the book that who saw?," "you saw the book which was next to what?," etc., but not "who what

saw?", "you saw the book which was next to" (as a declarative), and so on, as could arise from *multiple applications of this rule*. These examples show that [(2)] cannot apply twice to a given string. (43, emphasis added)

Chomsky provides several additional arguments that this constraint is necessary; notably the following, an instance of what came to be called the Wh-Island Condition:

(3) *What did Mary wonder where John put?*

Again foreshadowing modern concerns, Chomsky raises important conceptual questions:

The constraint that [(2)] may not reapply to a given string is thus necessary if the grammar is to achieve descriptive adequacy. Once again, to achieve the level of explanatory adequacy, we must find a principled basis, a general condition on the structure of any grammar, that will require that in the case of English the rule [(2)] must be so constrained. Various suggestions come to mind, but I am unable to formulate a general condition that seems to me entirely satisfying. (45)

In later developments, Subjacency or Superiority conditions were proposed as general constraints from which these specific subcases follow. The A-over-A Constraint (though not by that name) was also first suggested in Chomsky (1964b), along these lines:

(4) *A-over-A Constraint*
When phrase X of category A (i.e., $[X]_A$) is embedded within a phrase ZXW of category A (i.e., $[Z[X]_A W]_A$), no rule R applying to A applies to $[X]_A$ (R only applies to $[ZXW]_A$).

Example (4) is meant to predict the ungrammaticality of examples of the general form in (5c):

(5) a. *Caesar died* [*on the steps* [*of the Senate*]$_A$]$_A$
b. $_A$[*On what steps*] *did Caesar die* __ ?
c. *$_A$[*Of what building*] *did Caesar die* [*on the steps* __]$_A$

Chomsky's original examples were actually as in (6), with (6b) degrading:

(6) a. *What would it be difficult for me to understand* __ ?
b. **What would for me to understand* __ *be difficult?*

If subjects are always NPs, Chomsky (1964b:46) notes how "the Noun Phrase to be preposed is contained within a Noun Phrase, while in the legitimate case, it is not."

Chomsky (1964b) already exhibited some discomfort with (4), as discussed by Ross (1967), where many more counterexamples were pointed out. The matter becomes important in Chomsky (1977), where he considered what he took to be grammatical examples like

(7) *Who did you see a picture of __?*

As such, (7) is clearly a violation of the A-over-A Condition. In turn, Ross (1967) argued against the A-over-A and other initial conditions that Chomsky suggested, proposing, in their place, a set of what he called "island constraints on movement."[1]

Some of Ross's constraints are as follows, with relevant example sentences:

(8) *Complex NP Constraint*
(modified version of a constraint attributed to Ed Klima)
No element contained in a sentence dominated by a noun phrase with a lexical head noun may be moved out of that noun phrase by a transformation.

(9) a. **The man who I read a statement which was about __ is sick.*
b. *The man who I read a statement about __ is sick.*

(10) *Coordinate Structure Constraint*
In a coordinate structure, no conjunct or element within may be moved out.

(11) a. **What sofa will he put the chair between some table and __?*
b. **Whose tax did the nurse polish her trombone and the plumber compute __?*

(12) *Left Branch Condition*
No leftmost constituent of an NP can be transformationally reordered out of it.

(13) a. *The boy whose guardian's employer we elected president __ ratted on us.*
b. **The boy whose guardian's we elected __ employer president ratted on us.*
c. **The boy whose we elected __ guardian's employer president ratted on us.*

(14) *Sentential Subject Constraint*
No element dominated by an S may be moved out of that S if that node S is dominated by an NP which itself is immediately dominated by S.

(15) a. *The teacher who the reporters expected the principal would fire __ is an old fizzlebotch.*
b. **The teacher who that the principal would fire __ was expected is an old fizzlebotch.*
c. *The teacher who it was expected that the principal would fire __ is an old fizzlebotch.*

While Ross's thesis was prolific in discovering entirely new phenomena, Chomsky felt there should be a general way to unify these conditions, by exploring constraints on the operation of transformations. Thus in 1973 he proposed a Subjacency Condition as in (17), in an attempt to unify some of Ross's island constraints:

(16) Definition of *Subjacent*
If *X* is superior to *Y* in a phrase marker *P*,[2] then *Y* is "subjacent" to *X* if there is at most one cyclic category *C* . . . *Y* such that *C* contains *Y* and not *X*. (Chomsky 1973:247)

(17) *Subjacency Condition*
No [movement] rule can involve *X*, *Y* (*X* superior to *Y*) if *Y* is not subjacent to *X*.

The "subjacent" intuition is seen in contrast to cycle adjacency: for instance, in coordinate structures *XY*, the cycle of transformations happening within *X* is adjacent to the one for transformations within *Y*; for such categories, rule applications are parallel and, thus, unaffected by their respective orders. In contrast, two subjacent cycles *X* and *Y* structured in the form $[_X Y]$ are in the immediate derivational space of one another, in such a way that ending the transformational cycle for *Y* leads to the beginning of the next transformational cycle for *X*. More technically, if *Y* is subjacent to *X*, *Y* is contained in all the same cyclic categories as *X*—or they are in adjacent cycles.

Historically, the "cyclic categories" were so-called in relation to the Transformational Cycle. One such cycle *C* is defined with respect to a sequence *S* of ordered rules, stipulating that any given rule R_i in *S* only applies within the scope of *C* if all other relevant rules ordered prior to R_i have already applied. After *C* is exhausted, *S* is computed again, so that the very same rules can reapply (in the next cycle), in the same fashion and until all applicable rules have exhausted their orderly application. Kayne (1969) is the first methodical application of the Transformational Cycle within syntax, where it is shown how the cyclic use of transformational rules provides a principled explanation of clitic placement and related phenomena in French verbal dependencies.[3] It is an empirical question which particular categories are cyclic (within which the Transformational Cycle must be exhausted). Chomsky's (1973) intuition was, in any case, that NP and sentences are cycles of the relevant kind.[4]

As it turns out, the Subjacency Condition as such did relatively little work in Chomsky (1973). It did capture the effects of Ross's Complex NP Constraint in (6), if both NP and S happen to be cyclic categories. There was actually much confusion about this and related matters in the literature, for a curious reason. At the time, the higher clause label (currently, CP) was taken to be S̄, and the lower one S, per Bresnan (1970). That is

(18) *S′ → Comp S*

But, mysteriously and without an explanation, Chomsky (1973) reversed this, assuming

(19) *S → Comp S′*

So when he asserted in that article that S is a cyclic node for the purposes of subjacency, Chomsky actually meant the higher clausal node! It is for this very reason that the Subjacency Condition could not cover Wh-Island effects in this formulation, which we leave as an exercise for readers to verify—until we come back to the matter as reformulated in Chomsky (1977). Returning to complex NPs, bear in mind that displacement may not skip a cyclic node, as that would render the movement nonsubjacent. For this reason, the condition led to a new observation: that extraction of something out of an NP that is inside another NP is degraded:

(20) **What did you receive* [*requests for* [*articles about* __]]?

In displacing to the outer (later called CP) cyclic node as in (20) *what* must skip over the NP headed by *articles* (that is one cyclic domain) *and* the NP headed by *requests* (the second cyclic domain)—so that is not a subjacent movement. But for that same general reasoning, the fact that subjects are islands did not fall under the Subjacency Condition:

(21) a. **Who did* [*stories about* __] *terrify John*?

b.

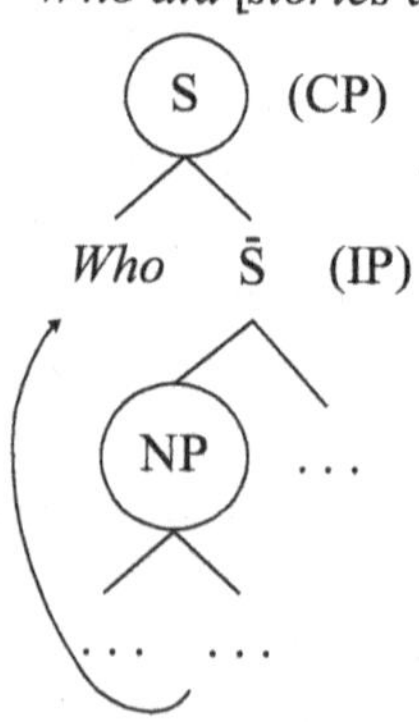

Again, for Chomsky (1973) the higher clause node (S, now CP) was the hypothesized cyclic node (circled in (21b)), not the lower one (S̄, now IP). If that is the case, displacement as in (21) only crosses the subject cyclic node—so it does involve subjacent cycles, in satisfaction of (17).

As for his scruples concerning the limitations of a broad Wh-rule as in (2), Chomsky (1973) decomposed the process. As one component of the account, he considered a ban on extraction from an embedded question, falling under one of two conditions:

(22) *Tensed Sentence Condition* (*TSC*)
No rule can involve *X*, *Y* in structure . . . X . . . $[_{\alpha}$ . . . Y . . .] . . . where α is a tensed S.

(23) *Specified Subject Condition* (*SSC*)
No rule can involve *X*, *Y* in structure . . . X . . . $[_{\alpha}$ . . . Z . . . $-WYN$ . . .] . . . where *Z* is the specified subject of *WYV* in α.

The good news about said conditions is that they are supposed to rule, more generally, over binding specifications, a matter we return to. The not so good news is that they require further definitions (e.g., "specified subject").[5] In Chomsky's (1973) view, all movement processes (not just passive or raising transformations) are subject to (22) and (23)—a view that was abandoned by Chomsky (1977) and is not part of the Principles and Parameters (P&P) approach in Chomsky (1981). As a second component of the account regarding a Wh-rule as in (2), Chomsky proposed the Superiority Condition:[6]

(24) *Superiority Condition*
No rule can involve *X*, *Y* in structure . . . X . . . $[_{\alpha}$ . . . Z . . . $-WYN$ . . .] . . . where the rule applies ambiguously to *Z* and *Y* and *Z* is superior to *Y*.

Like the A-over-A Condition in Chomsky's (1973) view, the Superiority Condition is taken to restrict the possible ambiguity of rule application:

> The condition requires that a rule must select the superior term where that rule is ambiguous in application, that is, where the structure given in [(24)] will satisfy the structural condition defining the rule in question with either *Z* or *Y* selected as the factor satisfying a given term of this condition. (246)

3.2 Toward Successive-Cyclic Wh-Movement

The ensuing theory had the consequence of predicting that what, until then, had been considered unbounded Wh-movement is instead constituted of a series of short movements—although this is harder to demonstrate than it may seem at first. Observe:

(25) a. $[_S$ *What did* [*you say* $[_S$ *that* [*Bill likes*__]]]]

b. $[_S$ *What did* [*you say* $[_S$ *that* [*you think* $[_S$ *that* [*Bill likes*__]]]]]]

Curiously, movement as in (25a) does not violate the Subjacency Condition, as two cyclic nodes are not crossed.[7] However, movement as in (25b) does violate the condition, as it is across two cyclic nodes. Chomsky thus hypothesized that movement has to be broken down into smaller steps, for theory-internal reasons. Concretely, he proposed that the "intermediate complementizer" positions, marked as *X* in (26), should be invoked:

(26) [$_S$ *What did* [*you say* [$_S$ *X that* [*you think* [$_S$ *X that* [*Bill likes*__]]]]]]

Remarkably, du Plessis (1977) found evidence from Afrikaans that such movements are empirically attested. Witness, for instance:

(27) *met wie het jy nou weer gesê met wie het Sarie gedog met wie*
with who did you now again said with who did Sarie thought with who
gaan Jan trou?
go Jan marry
"Whom did you say (again) Sarie thought Jan is going to marry?"

Observe how *met wie* 'with who' repeats after each intermediate verb. Du Plessis interpreted this as an indication that there is a movement residue on each "intermediate Comp." Since then, researchers have validated this point across multiple languages and conditions, a matter we will not go into now (see Boeckx 2008 for a summary).

Despite its notable empirical consequences, Chomsky's (1973) attempt at a unification raised several conceptual and empirical difficulties. We have already shown in (25a) how the theory as then stated does not predict an intermediate step of movement in the lowest S, but observe the clear presence of *met wie* 'with who' in the lowest cycle in (27) (after *gedog* 'thought'). Moreover, witness a Wh-island violation as in (28):

(28) ?*[$_S$ *What did* [*you wonder* [$_S$ *whether* [*Bill likes*__]]]]

The unacceptability in (28) could not be related to the Subjacency Condition in the terms stated, even if the intermediate Comp related to *whether* cannot be visited. That movement still only crosses from one cyclic node (boldfaced in (28)) to the next and is thus a subjacent process. If one were to invoke the TSC in (22) or SSC in (23) (the embedded clause is tensed or has a "specified subject"), it is then unclear how the application of said conditions would render grammatical the equivalent (26).[8]

Chomsky (1977:111) made an interesting adjustment to the theory where many relevant difficulties were addressed: he finally assumed the familiar (18) instead of the stranger formulation in (19), and, concomitantly, he crucially assumed that the cyclic nodes should be NP and S (not $\bar{S}$ or what we would now call CP). Although we should also point out that—even though Chomsky (1977) still uses the expression "cyclic"—such domains (for intermediate steps of movement or binding configurations as relevant to conditions like (22) or (23)) stopped being related to the cyclic application of ordered rules.[9] That being said, the domains themselves may still be playing a significant role within the system. This is just what was assumed by Chomsky (1981:305–308), when the name "bounding node" replaced the cyclic undertones attributed to NP and (in this formulation) S, while still keeping to the intuition that movement is bounded. The bottom-line idea thus remained that movement cannot be across two separate instances of NP or S in a subjacent configuration, with the "cyclic" intuition gaining a new meaning.

That had consequences for Ross's constraints. Chomsky (1977:112) observes how the Sentential Subject Constraint in (14) follows from the Subjacency Condition, if one assumes that movement via an intermediate complementizer site as in (29a) (see note 10) is ungrammatical, forcing movement across two bounding domains (as boldfaced):

(29) *The teacher . . .*

a. * . . . $[_{\bar{S}}$ *who* $[_{S}$ *that* $[_{\bar{S}}$ $[_{S}$ *the principal would fire*__]] *was expected*]] . . .

b. . . . $[_{\bar{S}}$ *who* $[_{S}$ *it was expected* $[_{\bar{S}}$ *that* $[_{S}$ *the principal would fire*__]]]] . . .

. . . *is an old fizzlebotch.*

It is interesting to ponder which particular complementizer domains allow movement "across," but we set that aside now.[10] Another topic that is not our focus here is how, among Ross's original constraints, several others can also be predicted in terms of the 1977 version of the Subjacency Condition. This should be obvious for the Complex NP Constraint as in (8), inasmuch as relevant movement involves displacement across S and NP. For similar reasons, the ungrammaticality of (18) (with movement across two NPs) is also predicted in the 1977 treatment (though recall that this was not one of Ross's constraints).[11] Finally, it is easy to show how the 1977 approach also predicts standard Wh-island violations (not one among Ross's [1967] constraints either), in contrast to what we saw for (24), now more appropriately labeled as in (30):

(30) *$[_{\bar{S}}$ *What did* $[_{S}$ *you wonder* $[_{\bar{S}}$ *whether* $[_{S}$ *Bill likes*__]]]]

Because the intermediate Comp where *whether* is generated does not allow a displacement through that domain, a nonsubjacent movement must be from the object of *likes* to the sentence periphery, across two S bounding nodes.

Thus, this version of the theory fully predicts successive cyclicity, contrary to what we saw for (25a), repeated now as (31):

(31) *[$_{\bar{S}}$ *What did* [$_S$ *you say* [$_{\bar{S}}$ *(that)* [$_S$ *Bill likes*__]]]]

In this instance, even Wh-movement to the first intermediate site is required because, skipping this site, the movement would have to be across two S bounding nodes (that being the difference vis-à-vis the 1973 account). This is then fully consistent with du Plessis's (1977) data as presented in (27).

All of that being said as favorable circumstances, a difficulty arises for grammatical examples as in (7), if the derivation is to proceed as in (32):

(32) [$_{\bar{S}}$ *Who did* [$_S$ *you say* [$_{NP}$ *a picture of*__]]]

The movement here is clearly across two bounding nodes. Chomsky (1977:112) says it was "for this reason that Subjacency was not extended to S in Chomksy [1973]." In 1977 he wants to reason things out in such a way that (32) is "the special case," and pursuing an analysis by Bach and Horn (1976), he argues that in such situations there is an intermediate step of movement bypassing the NP bounding node, via PP extraposition, an analysis that we will not review in the present context.

3.3 Expanding on Locality Effects

Throughout the development of the P&P model, considerations as discussed fueled theoretical progress and, concomitantly, the discovery of new phenomena. Another unification attempt, partly based on Lasnik and Saito (1984, 1992), was the *Barriers* framework (Chomsky 1986a), which sought a principled theory of bounding nodes. The core idea is that any XP is potentially a barrier, even though the XP that happens to be the complement of a lexical head (V, N, A, and maybe P) is actually not a barrier. This yields a "subject/object asymmetry" that was already pointed out by Chomsky (1973) and that Huang (1982) generalized as a "complement/non-complement asymmetry":

(33) a. [$_{\bar{S}}$ *Who did (you say)* [$_S$ *you like* [$_{NP}$ *friends of* _]]]?

b. *[$_{\bar{S}}$ *Who did (you say)* [$_S$ [$_{NP}$ *friends of* _] *like you*]]]?

If NP, as the XP that it is, can be a barrier—but only if not a complement to a lexical head like V, the subject subextraction in (33b) is predicted to be ungrammatical, while the comparable object subextraction in (33a) should be fine, across no barriers. This approach also accounts for Huang's observation that extraction out of adjuncts is barred:

(34) **Which player did the Red Sox remain winless* [*because they traded* __]?

Unfortunately, to handle a range of facts that we will not review, Chomsky's (1986a) theory became complicated. Coincidentally, the field then experimented with derivational economy and representational minimality considerations aimed at implementing what Chomsky (2005) was to call "third factors" of language design. In the context of Chomsky (2000, 2001), the notion "barrier" was replaced by "derivational phase," which at the time was assumed to be the categories CP and *v*P (a functional "shell" over VP, in the sense of Larson [1988]). The intuition in Chomsky (2001:12) for why these particular projections are phases is that they are "verbal phrases with full argument structure and CP with force indicators."[12] We have considered elsewhere whether that is empirically and theoretically sound, but what interests us now is *that* such special categories should arise within any version of the theory, for those constitute arguments for structure. In a nutshell, it is crucial for the various models that given designated elements be opaque or transparent to syntactic correlations across, precisely, such elaborate domains.

In the Minimalist proposals of recent years, the classical Subjacency Condition is replaced by a Phase-Impenetrability Condition (PIC):

(35) *Phase Impenetrability Condition*
For phase HP with head H, the domain of H is not accessible to operations outside HP; only H and its edge are accessible to such operations, the edge being the residue outside $\bar{H}$, either specifiers or elements adjoined to HP.

This new approach to "barrierhood" meshes with a new approach to derivations: Structure is built strictly bottom up.[13] In the classical P&P proposal there was an entire level of representation of D-structure as the locus of thematic relations, projected from structures equivalent to those arising in phrase structure rules (if enriched with headedness and selectional considerations). Only after such a level was formed did the transformational component begin its work, which led to a model posing empirical and conceptual difficulties that we will not review (but see Lasnik and Uriagereka [2005:chapters 1–3], as well as section 3.8). In contrast, the Minimalist idea is that movement processes dynamically intersperse with structure-building ones (and see note 13). Furthermore, phonological and semantic interpretation is performed cyclically, although now not so much in terms of a checklist of obligatory transformations, but rather as a consequence of systemic design. This creates phases in the derivational system that, once reached, entail the transfer of syntactic material from the preceding phase to interface components. "Islandhood" is then a consequence of this kind of multiple spell-out to the external components of the grammar. Once a structure is sent for phonological interpretation, its component elements are derivationally frozen.

A significant difference between the minimalist proposal and its predecessors can be witnessed when reflecting on an observation of Ross (1969): that island violations are dramatically ameliorated by deletion (S [IP] deletion in "Sluicing"):

(36) *I believe that he bit someone, but they don't know who (I believe that he bit __).*

(37) a. **I believe the claim that he bit someone, but they don't know who I believe the claim that he bit __.* (Complex NP Constraint)

b. (?)*I believe the claim that he bit someone, but they don't know who ~~I believe the claim that he bit __~~.*

(38) a. **Irv and someone were dancing together, but I don't know who Irv and__were dancing together.* (Coordinate Structure Constraint)

b. (?)*Irv and someone were dancing together, but I don't know who ~~Irv and__were dancing together~~.*

(39) a. **That he'll hire someone is possible, but I won't divulge who that he'll hire__ is possible.* (Sentential Subject Constraint)

b. (?)*That he'll hire someone is possible, but I won't divulge who ~~that he'll hire__ is possible~~.*

If "islandhood" results from material being frozen in place, per the PIC in (35), how is this kind of "island repair" possible, computationally speaking (see Merchant 2001; Lasnik 2001)? This problem could be posed for any of the broad proposals we have sketched, because, for example, a sluicing as in (37b)—if it is to follow from a transformation of the form implicit in (37a)—should be violating the Subjacency Condition of the P&P model. Interestingly, the highly dynamical minimalist approach does offer a possibility to deal with Ross's otherwise recalcitrant data.

Suppose that islands of the sort in (36)–(39) arise in the conditions explored in Uriagereka (1999, 2012), within a minimalist model of Bare Phrase Structure (BPS) that obeys Kayne's (1994) Linear Correspondence Axiom (LCA). The key derivational idea separating head-complement relations from any other is that one need not invoke a separate derivational space to assemble mere collections of head-complement relations (a simple formal fact that we leave as an exercise for readers).[14] However, the moment one tries to build (bottom-up) in a derivation any noncomplement—be it a specifier or an adjunct—if this noncomplement is phrasally complex, a fortiori it will have to be assembled in a separate derivational space:

(40) a. *A man met a woman.*

b. {*met*, {*a*, *woman*}}

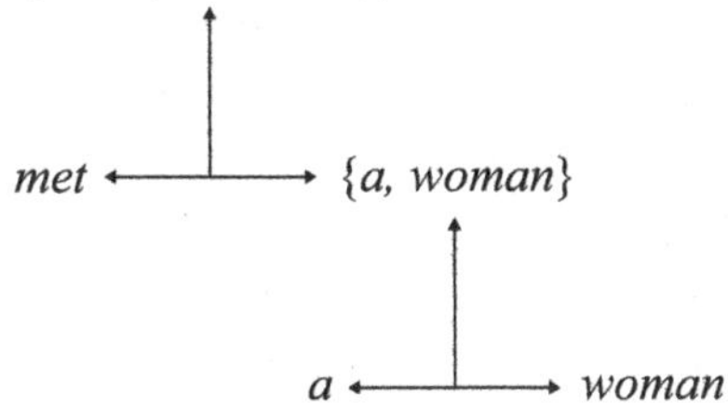

c. {*the*, *man*}

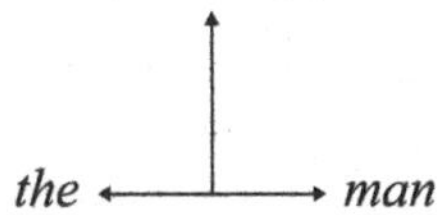

d. {{*the*, *man*}, {*met*, {*a*, *woman*}}}

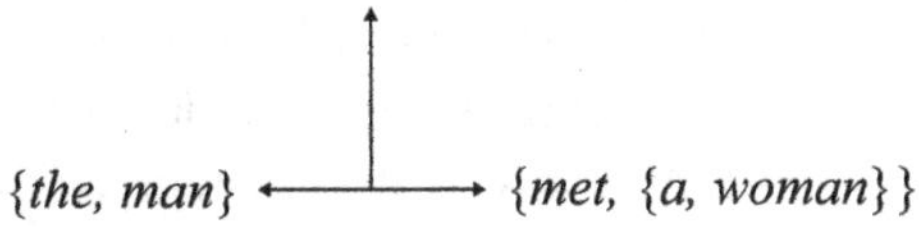

That said, the BPS derivation itself, by its very dynamics, separates collections of head-complement relations that can monotonically assemble (as in *met a woman*) from anything "derivationally off line" as implied by a complex specifier (like *the man*) or for that matter a complex adjunct (e.g., adding *in the park* in (40)). Under certain assumptions, one version of Kayne's LCA can then be made to force the system to go into dynamical spell-out if the linearization of phrases in the PF component is executed only through mapping c-command relations among terminals to precedence statements:

(41) *Linear Correspondence Axiom*
For *X*, *Y* terminals, if *X* c-commands *Y* in syntax, *X* precedes *Y* in phonology.

This is not Kayne's LCA, which was taken to apply to phrases in general. In contrast, Chomsky (1995:337) assumes that the LCA applies after the morphological component, as a matter of sensory-motor demands. This is important to our reasoning. The LCA works within simple head-complement sequences (c-command units), organizing complex phrasal dependencies dealing with dominance among phrases into ultimately sensory-motor instructions dealing, instead, with precedence among words. However, whenever the system hits complex materials outside a c-command unit (specifiers or adjuncts), the only way (41) can apply is if the process of Spell-out, presupposing the LCA, applies multiply—in such a way that the noncomplement is linearized independently of the c-command unit.[15] Importantly, material thus "flattened" for the purposes of the PF interface (where there are phonemes, syllables, or metrical feet, but not phrasal brackets or c-command dependencies) will be immune to internal manipulation. The effect of this Multiple Spell-out (MSO) is equivalent to that of the PIC in (35), except without any need to stipulate which portion of the derivation is transferred: whatever transfers does so to satisfy this (phonologically driven) LCA. As a consequence of this approach, something very much like the *Barriers* framework ensues, separating complements from the rest, for principled reasons if one assumes BPS and an LCA driven by sensory-motor demands.

As Hornstein et al. (2007) shows, this has consequences for Ross's puzzle. The key to Ross's ameliorations is the fact that the island violations *are not pronounced*. That is the beauty of the examples: they are generated by ellipsis, and although the implied structure (parallel to the one in the antecedent clause) clearly violates standard island constraints, it is enough not to pronounce the offending domain for the ungrammaticality to reduce or (for some speakers) disappear. But this is what we expect if the "islandhood" arises in PF terms invoked by the version of the LCA in (41) and we eliminate the relevant PF—and with it the need to invoke a linearization process, for there is nothing to linearize: all relevant materials are elided. That being said, the dynamical derivation proceeds as if there were no constraints for the long-distance movements across the islands. The reasoning holds only if the LCA demands are connected to phonology, for if they were derivation-internal, it should not matter whether relevant (unlinearizable) domains happen not to be pronounced. If this approach turns out to be correct, the argument for structure is even more sophisticated: the system is not just sensitive to whether it encounters a complement or a noncomplement. It is furthermore sensitive to whether the noncomplement in point is in need to obtain a phonological representation, or it depends, instead, on the parallel antecedent to embody its *syntax of silence*, to use Jason Merchant's (2001) apt expression. So, what we have is nothing short of the structure *of silence*, to which we return when considering the very globality of its survival in parallel conditions, as Ross (1969) observed.

It is worth bearing in mind that the MSO model is fully compatible with the PIC, as these related, but different, ideas make reference to different portions of a standard structure: the PIC concentrates on CP and *v*P complements within a derivational c-command unit, whereas the MSO model separates c-command units from the rest of the structure (complex specifiers and adjuncts). This is important when pondering how ideas relating to extraction and islandhood relate to other forms of grammatical dependency and in particular rules of construal among NPs (anaphoric dependencies and obviation conditions). We saw in the previous section how in Chomsky's (1973) model the TSC in (22) and SSC (23) were considered relevant to Wh-movement, although by Chomsky (1977) this idea was given up—though surely not the conditions as such.

3.4 Construal Relations

Anaphoric pronouns were derived in Chomsky (1955) from full NPs, while reflexives were derived from pronouns. That work (534) also hinted at the locality of reflexives with regard to their antecedent. Lees and Klima (1963) state this locality in terms of a "clause-mate" condition. Langacker (1969) remarked how in core circumstances reflexives stand in complementary distribution with pronouns, which he captures (163) by ordering the "reflexivization" before the "pronominalization" rule. In that piece, Langacker also deals with the conditions under which such processes obtain, noting (165) that it is nothing as simple as either linear ordering or depth of embedding. Then he zooms in on a better structural notion (167): a node *A* "commands" another node *B* if (i) neither *A* nor *B* dominates the other; and (ii) the S-node that most immediately dominates *A* also dominates *B*. The only difference between this "command" and the now standard c-command (i.e., constituent-command, as in Reinhart [1976]) is that the latter obtains within any constituent (as opposed to just S) that dominates the relevant categories. The latter notion is equivalent to—or possibly the converse of—Klima's (1964) "in-construction-with" as proposed in his investigations of the scope of negation. This transformational tradition also led to important work on the theory of what was later to be known as the control of null categories, which we touch on only in passing.

Such is the context in which Chomsky (1973) developed his conditions to handle movement; he then showed how these conditions can also deal with certain interpretive (in particular, obviation effects). Thereafter, in note 20 for reflexives and a series of considerations (too complex for us to rehash) for reciprocals, he suggested that such anaphoric processes also fall under the conditions in point, basically so as to handle clause-mate restrictions on said processes. The TSC in (22) and SCC in (23) prevent anaphoric dependencies of the relevant sort.[16] By 1972, and developing ideas of Jackendoff (1969) and Dougherty (1969), Jackendoff explored the alternative view that pronouns and reflexives are representationally present in the base component and have their antecedents entirely determined in the semantic component. As he put it:

> In this . . . interpretive theory, noun phrases are unmarked for coreference relations in deep structure. Rules of semantic interpretation establish relations between pairs of noun phrases, marking them coreferential or noncoreferential with each other. . . . Instead of being produced by transformations, pronouns and reflexives will be generated by the base component as lexical items, marked with the feature [+pro], but like other noun phrases, unmarked for reference. Reflexives, in addition, will be marked with the feature [+refl]. (108)

A reason to pursue an interpretive theory stems from the fact that anaphoricity as such need not be pronominal in any obvious sense. Witness the behavior of the elements that Jackendoff called epithets, as follows:

(42) a. *I wanted Charlie to help me, but the bastard wouldn't do it.*
b. *Irving was besieged by a horde of bills and the poor guy couldn't pay them.*

As Jackendoff noted, we would

> miss a generalization if we did not handle [these elements] by a rule of the same kind as pronominalization. . . . In a transformational framework, however, the generalization cannot be captured. The pronominalization transformation changes NPs into pronouns. In a consistent treatment, in certain contexts an NP could be turned into a pronominal epithet instead. But then which pronominal epithet should the NP be changed into? . . . In an interpretive framework, we can mark epithets as special lexical items which may function as pronouns in certain contexts of the pronominalization rule. . . . Thus no change need be made in the nature of the interpretive theory in order to include these cases. (111)

Though the plot thickened with regard to the epithets, as we will discuss.

By 1976, Lasnik had observed how, although a pronominalization transformation can rule out (43a) in favor of (43b), it could say nothing about (43c), given that *He* in (43d) is capable of referring to Oscar even when no pronominalization is relevant:

(43) a. **Oscar finally realized that Oscar is unpopular.*
b. *Oscar finally realized that he is unpopular.*
c. (*)*He finally realized that Oscar is unpopular.*
d. *He finally realized that Mary is unpopular.*

So whatever is problematic about the relevant reading in (43c) seems to be at right angles with a putative pronominalization process (if that process even exists).

"Split antecedents" in the sense of Anderson (1970) also pose a significant problem, as summarized in Lasnik (1976, 1981). Observe:

(44) *After John talked to Mary, they left the concert.*

It is unclear how *they* pronominalizes *John* or *Mary*. Anderson explored whether *they* is a substitute for a conjoined *he* and *she*, but the faulty parenthetical in (45) questions that:

(45) *After John talked to Paul, they* (**he and he/him*) *left the room.*

Interestingly, problems with split antecedents dissipate if, as such, a pronoun like *they* is free to refer to any plurality—as long as conditions on name obviation are satisfied.

Lasnik also observed how epithets as discussed by Jackendoff actually behave more like names than like pronouns, which is contrary to what Jackendoff expected:

(46) a. *John realized that he / *the idiot is going to lose.*
  b. *He realized that he / *the idiot is going to lose.*
  c. *The idiot realizes that he / *the idiot is going to lose.*

In (46) we see various circumstances in which a pronoun is possible, unlike an epithet. Like names more generally, epithets are obviative with regard to c-commanding antecedents. As it turns out, however, one broad aspect of Jackendoff's (1972) theory of coreference could be used to unify the new phenomenology: it was formalized as a binary relation holding between two NPs in a certain structural configuration, which is the focus of the present study. Jackendoff expressed his dependencies in terms of a *coreference table* tracking coreferentiality or lack thereof, a matter that we return to in chapter 4.[17]

Chomsky (1976) considers anaphoric relations of the sort Jackendoff studied as rules of grammar in their own right. The TSC and SSC were then taken to constrain said anaphoric relations in themselves. Chomsky took from Fiengo (1974) the idea that the relation between an NP that has undergone NP Movement (as in a passive or raising) and the position from which it moved is one of bound anaphora too, abstractly.[18] The thought was that anaphoric dependencies (as in reflexives) and what began to be known as A-movement fall under the same construal conditions. Chomsky thus concludes that "we can regard SSC [or TSC], in such cases, as a condition on surface structures applying quite generally to anaphora (hence to the NP-trace relation), rather than a condition on transformations" (179). This is actually why the 1973 piece was called *Conditions on Transformations* while the 1976 one was called, instead, (surface) *Conditions on Rules of Grammar*.

That machinery became the basis for the definition of binding domains (originally, "governing categories") in the P&P model. This was done through the proposals in Chomsky (1980a), where the notions "bound" and "free" are first introduced:

(47) a. An anaphor α is bound in β if:
There is a category c-commanding and co-indexed with α in β.
b. Otherwise, α is free in β.

In this work, Chomsky argued that just as NP-traces behave like anaphors, so too do Wh-traces behave like names, in the process beginning to characterize A-dependencies (as seen in passive and raising transformations) as distinct from Ā (A-bar) dependencies like Wh-movement, a matter that we return to in chapter 4. Descriptively, one could say that A-dependencies are subject to local anaphoric licensing (in some form), whereas Ā-dependencies are subject, instead, to obviation and Subjacency (or barrier, PIC, MSO, etc.) considerations.[19] A priori such a unification could come from one of three possibilities: (i) perhaps all A-movement relations share with anaphoric dependencies some representational stricture that gets satisfied within a local domain *D* (defined by the TSC and SSC, or relevant updates); (ii) perhaps anaphoric dependencies actually involve more or less hidden derivational processes of the A-movement sort (again, restricted by the TSC and SSC or updates); (iii) perhaps for some underlying reason domain *D* is relevant both to A-movement and construal (binding) considerations. At our level of abstraction, it is immaterial which of these possibilities, which researchers continue to pursue in various guises, turns out to be correct. What is relevant to our argument for structure is the need, in all instantiations, of a domain *D* somehow related to very specific structural conditions like the TSC and SSC, or updated variants as the case may be.

Within the current Minimalist Program—and through an interesting history that we will not rehash—there appears to be a tacit assumption that local anaphoric and obviation relations are to be satisfied in terms of the PIC. While that may be true for a class of anaphoric dependencies and pronominal obviation, it is far from obvious for all such anaphoric and obviative situations. The complexity of the problem is compounded by the fact that Minimalism does not assume levels of representation (like D-structure or S-structure) other than the ones deemed necessary for linguistic interfaces (PF and LF). It was customary within the P&P model to ask at which level of representation binding conditions apply or even whether in particular the licensing conditions could take place as the derivation unfolds. Within Minimalism, matters are drastically restricted: representationally, binding conditions can only be imposed at LF, while it is still possible that some licensing phenomena may occur within the derivation. That entire project could not even be stated were it not for an assumption that dates back to Ross (1967) (and in some form, also to Chomsky [1955]): movement can be decomposed into more elementary components, including copying. To see the significance of this process, let's take a step back.

Consider a grammatical example like (48):

(48) [[*Which pictures of himself*$_{i/j}$] *did John*$_i$ *think* [*Fred*$_j$ *liked*__]]

As Barss (1986) notes, the antecedent for *himself* can be either *John* or *Fred*, neither of which actually c-commands the anaphor. Having *Fred* as an antecedent is surprising in that obviously *himself* is far away from this subject. At the same time, there is by hypothesis a stage in the derivation in which the Wh-phrase is in its thematic position:

(49) [*John thinks* [*Fred liked* [*which pictures of himself*]]]

Perhaps *himself* gets A-bound at that stage, sufficing for its anaphoric licensing. But as (48) shows, *John* can also be the antecedent. Note that this, in itself, is a remarkable argument for the "successive cyclic" Wh-movement that Chomsky hypothesized as a result of his approach to the Subjacency Condition in 1973. In particular, if the following intermediate configuration obtains, the anaphor could be locally licensed there, as proposed in comparable examples in Belletti and Rizzi (1988):

(50) [*John thinks* [[*which pictures of himself*] [*Fred liked* __]]]

Finally, note that if movement operations are a result of leaving copies behind, which get "chopped" in Ross's terminology, we would find ourselves with representations along the following lines (with the superscripts conventionally representing the copied material):

(51) [[*Which pictures of himself*] [*John thinks* [$^{[which\ pictures\ of\ himsef]}$ [*Fred liked* $^{[which\ pictures\ of\ himself]}$]]]]

To be sure, a theory of the sort implied in (51) will have to elicit which particular copy gets interpreted (presumably as a result of not being chopped), but having the copies in the domains that (51) makes explicit opens up the possibility that the anaphor *himself* can take whichever antecedent is in its local domain, its appropriate binding then becoming relatively straightforward at that level of representation. This, in turn, ups the ante on what counts as linguistic structure: entire sets of copies-to-be-chopped distributed throughout the derivation, no less.

There is more to say about the relations and redundancies among constraints and components, from A-over-A to the MSO assumption or other such minimalistic considerations. One wants to know how to treat binding dependencies (whether as movement or otherwise) or how A- and Ā-dependencies differ and how that may relate to the sorts of constraints that limit their scope. None of these are settled matters, although differences in approaching them reduce to in-house disputes. Syntacticians passionately argue whether it is best to treat construal relations as movement transformations or to analyze them as equivalent representational dependencies. However, no syntactician denies the reality of these phenomena, which is the bedrock for our argument on structure. At this level of abstraction, it is immaterial whether domain *D* for local binding and obviation follows from the PIC or is to be understood in some other terms, for example, comparing domains of ideal binding (as in Chomsky 1986b). Important proposals exist in all regards, some of which we return to. But the key now is that, irrespective of the explanatory choice, it would be irrational to deny the existence of domain *D*. Therein our essential argument: domain *D*, details of execution aside, is a structural entity, which has the sophistication of phrases as in chapter 1, the relational reality of subjects as in chapter 2, and then some: for example, incorporating the effects of the TSC and SSC, the phasal nature of derivations if the PIC is relevant, or even something else entirely. The Devil will certainly be in such details, but we are only ascertaining the existence of some such structural Devil.

3.5 Beyond Locality Effects

The issue of globality in syntactic computations, which is behind derivations by phase, is addressed in many recent works (e.g., Chomsky 2007). But the concerns go as far back as Chomsky (1973), where it was proposed that all construal rules obey locality—except pronominal coreference. Chomsky (1976) qualified that exception as an error, attributing to Lasnik (1976) the idea that no rule of grammar at all is needed for an example like (52a):

(52) a. *John thinks Mary likes him.*
b. (*)*He thinks Mary likes John.*
c. *No actor thinks reviewers like him* (*and no actress does either*).

That claim, however, is somewhat misleading. It is correct that no construal rule was invoked for that particular example in Lasnik (1976), "accidental coreference" sufficing to express the semantic fact that *him* in (52a) can refer to *John*, just as it can refer to any other male in discourse.[20] That said, the same piece explicitly argued for a rule of grammar to characterize the ungrammaticality of (52b) when *he* is taken to be coreferential with *John* (the standard obviation effect). Lasnik also argued that bound-variable pronouns as in (52c) invoke a rule, as shown by the fact that, in the relevant reading, *him* covaries with the values of the variable instantiation associated to *no actor*. This is so much so that, in the elliptical continuation in parenthesis, the bound variable can no longer be *him* and must instead be *her*, as it covaries with the instantiations of *no actress*. To get that machinery to work one needs more than a pragmatic-based accidental coreference, as there is no referent in the domain of discourse that a negative quantifier picks out, in a sentence like (52c) asserting an existential absence. The entire (intricate) referential dependencies there ought to be the consequence of some rule of grammar.

Computational phases—or any process leading to transferring derivational chunks to interpretation—aim at cutting computational complexity. But many syntactic situations do not seem reducible in this fashion, which we would like to discuss now without attempting to be particularly exhaustive. Consider, first, quantifier scope interactions:

(53) a. *Some man likes every woman.*
b. *Some man believes* [*every woman to be remarkable*].
c. *Some man believes* [*that every woman is remarkable*].
d. *Some woman is liked by every man.*
e. [*Some woman is said* (*to be believed* . . .) [*to be liked by every man*]].

In the reading that interests us in (53a), *every woman* has scope over *some man* (though not for all speakers). Such a reading cannot be contemplated other than by correlating both quantifiers, so that the syntactically lower one inverts its scope over the other. Depending on what constitutes a derivational phase *X* and where the lower quantifier sits within *X*, this operation may be problematic. We can complicate matters by separating the two quantifiers. The bad news is that they can be separated at least as much as in (53b), with quantifier interaction surviving. The good news, that if the separation crosses a finite clausal boundary, as in (53c), in general the quantifier interaction fails (May 1977). That being said, how the lower quantifier interacts *over* the higher one in (53b), crucially respecting phase boundaries, is not straightforward. Moreover, in passive situations as in (53d) nothing prevents each quantifier from arbitrarily separating from the other, as more passive embeddings are added (53e). These conditions might be accommodated if quantifier interaction is calculated *as the derivation unfolds.* In any case, a situation like (53e) highlights how a dependency can lead to successful grammatical interactions that—at least in parsing terms—are effectively unbounded.

Consider next Wh- in situ conditions.

(54) a. *What does John think* (*he said* . . .) [*Mary bought*]?
b. [*What* [*does John think* [^{what} (*he said* . . . [^{what} . . .) [*Mary bought* ^{what}]]]]]?
c. *Who thinks* [*Mary bought what*]?
d. *Zhangsan yiwei* *Lisi mai-le* *shenme?*
Zhangsan thinks Lisi bought-asp what
"What does Zhangsan think Lisa bought?"

Example (54a) is a standard Wh-question, relating *what* to a gap arbitrarily far down a series of complement sentences. These are the conditions giving raise to "successive cyclicity": in the relevant movement, the operator is copied at the edge of relevant bounding nodes, or phases in the computation. In (54b) we are representing intermediate copies with superscripts. Things get more complicated as in (54c), where *what* has not displaced overtly, and yet its scope can be understood as equivalent to that of the other operator in the sentence, *who*.[21] We return to these kinds of examples in section 3.7, because Kuno and Robinson (1972) claimed that not everyone obtains such a reading unless the two Wh-phrases are clause-mates (and see section 3.7 for further nuances pointed out in Grano and Lasnik [2018]). Less obviously, in this instance one could still argue that some successive cyclicity is preserved for *what* in terms of a parasitic relation with *who*. But in a language like Chinese, the normal way of asking a question like (54a) is as in (54d), where the single operator in the expression, *shenme* 'what', is clearly left in situ—yet it takes scope over the entire sentence, as shown by Huang (1982).[22] This process is as global as it gets, particularly if, as Huang argued, it is not sensitive to island effects. That alone suggests that derivational phases are at right angles with the scope-taking abilities of *shenme*.

We have seen English anaphors obeying clause-mate conditions. However, in many languages anaphors take long-distance antecedents. Consider for instance the following Chinese examples:[23]

(55) [*Zhangsani renwei* [*Lisi*$_j$ *zhidao* [*Wangwu*$_k$ *xihuan ziji*$_{i/j/k}$]]]
Zhangsan think Lisi know Wangwu like self
"Zhangsan thinks that Lisi knows that Wangwu likes him/himself."

An anaphor like *ziji* can pick out its antecedent in *any* higher clause—unboundedly so. Data of this abstract sort (although involving anaphors within NPs and more limited in distribution) was discussed in Chomsky (1980a).[24] Such examples pose a challenge for clause-mateness restrictions for anaphors and, in addition, clearly do not exhibit complementary distribution with regard to pronouns. Witness:

(56) a. *Peter thought that* [*pictures of himself were on sale*].
b. *Peter thought that* [*pictures of him were on sale*].

Here reflexive and pronoun are not in complementary distribution in (56), and their antecedent is not a clause-mate. This lack of complementarity led Chomsky (1986b) to a representational proposal for binding domains in terms of the ideal context in which Binding Theory can be satisfied for the element whose licensing or filtering is being evaluated. We will not explore this now, beyond pointing out that such a characterization is rather different from the one sketched in section 3.4 (e.g., in terms of TSC and SSC). In particular, there cannot be a single unique structural domain in which an anaphor must be bound *and* a corresponding pronoun must be not bound. In any case, whatever definition we attempt here, it will push us beyond a phasal domain. In Lasnik and Uriagereka (2005:chapter 7) an idea is sketched for these "domain extensions" that we will return to, but the bottom line is that they are, well, extensions of standard local domains.

Consider, also, the obviation effects summarized in (57), where all examples except (57c) are bad on the coreferential reading:[25]

(57) a. (*)*He/the bastard killed John.*
b. (*)[*He/the bastard said* [(*I thought . . .*) [*John was dead*]]].
c. [[*His/the bastard's assistant*] *said* [(*I thought . . .*) [*John was dead*]]].
d. (*)[*He/the bastard wonders* [*whether* [*John was dead*]]].

To repeat, pronominal *he* (or for that matter epithets like *the bastard*) cannot be coreferent with *John* in instances in which the latter is c-commanded by the former—no matter how distant the relation is between the two, as seen in (57b). There have been many attempts since Chomsky (1976, 1982) to have facts along these lines dismissed or follow from something outside the syntactic considerations of a binding theory. We confess not to understand how any of them avoids the conclusion that there is nothing semantically or informationally ill-formed in (57b) any more than there is in the comparable (57c). The difference between (57b) and (57c) is only that in the nonobviative example the would-be antecedent does not c-command the name, whereas in (57b) c-command does obtain between the pronoun/epithet and the name. Note that introducing a Wh-island between the would-be antecedent and the name/epithet (as in (57d)) has no bearing on the data: the relation between these nominal elements is as obviative when an island mediates among them as when it does not. That suggests cyclicity, islandhood, barrierhood, phasehood (or whatever we want to call the bounding phenomenon) is at right angles with the conditions arising for name obviation. That, to us, is a purely structural relation if there is one—and a long-distance one at that.

It is worth bearing in mind, in that regard, that obviation for pronouns (Condition B of the Binding Theory in Chomsky [1981]) differs drastically from obviation for names (Condition C of that theory). An interesting possibility, pace facts along the lines in (56), is that Condition B effects arise in complementarity with anaphoric licensing (Condition A effects). That is, Condition A of the Binding Theory demands the local binding of anaphors (say, within a derivational phase) and when such a binding does not obtain, a pronoun is licensed instead (see Hornstein [2001] or Kayne [2002] for a minimalist version of this idea).[26] Note, first, that such a reasoning is global in itself. In principle, the grammar has to allow for the possibility of a pronoun like *him/her* associated to the predicate *self*, so as to seek an antecedent, which yields a grammatical result if said antecedent is local (within the relevant binding domain) and c-commanding the anaphoric element. If, however, such an antecedent is *not* found, the grammar has to have the possibility of either erasing the *self* bit or considering an alternative derivation without the *self*. Either situation is global in that, at the time of introducing the pronoun with *self*, the system cannot tell whether there will be an antecedent. Once the derivation unfolds, the antecedent will or will not exist. If it does not, the grammar should be able to license a derivation *without the self*. Finally, when the grammar selects a name for insertion, it has no way of telling whether further up in the derivation there will be an element bearing possible antecedence (agreeing in morphological shape) with regard to that element.

3.6 Reconstruction Effects

A stronger type of argument for computational globality comes from the precise understanding of "reconstruction effects" as in (51), which motivate the Copy Theory of movement. Such processes are interesting in that, as already observed in Kayne (1969:8), while they allow (in fact, force) the pronunciation of any one of the occurrences, at most one such item can be pronounced. Kayne uses the impossibility of (58d) and (58e) as an argument that *tous* 'all' is moving, as opposed to being base-generated in multiple positions (which ought to allow precisely for combinations as in (58d) or (58e)).

(58) a. ***Tous*** *les garçons sont partis à la guerre.*
all the boys are departed to the war
"All the boys have gone to war."

b. *Les garçons sont* ***tous*** *partis à la guerre.*
the boys are all departed to the war
"The boys have all gone to war."

c. *Les garçons sont partis* ***tous*** *à la guerre.*
the boys are departed all to the war
"The boys have gone all to war."

d. ****Tous*** *les garçons sont partis* ***tous*** *à la guerre.*
all the boys are departed all to the war

e. **Les garçons sont* ***tous*** *partis* ***tous*** *à la guerre.*
the boys are all departed all to the war.

While that is taken for granted in standard treatments, the matter is far from trivial if movement is copying and chopping, as in Ross (1967). The copying is unproblematic, but the chopping (deletion) may be tricky in that it cannot take place before the copying—and if it does thereafter, the process is "too late" for a strictly phase-bound system.

Next recall our treatment of the reading for (51), in which *Fred* is the antecedent for *himself*, and suppose these two are in the same binding domain early on in the derivation. That anaphoric licensing seems unproblematic. But now consider the reading in which *John* is the intended antecedent. The derivation unfolds up to that point without licensing *himself* anaphorically on *Fred*. But what does that mean for the phrase *pictures of himself*? Does it get interpreted at that site? If it did, it would force the anaphoricity on Fred or an ungrammaticality, if the anaphor finds no antecedent. So suppose *pictures* (and only that) is interpreted in the thematic position (satisfying a theme dependency for *liked*) and the rest of the copied phrase is chopped/deleted after having been copied in the intermediate Comp domain. Now we are in that site and the derivation continues, introducing *John*, which could then be an antecedent for *himself* as desired. Or not: if the sentence is leading to a derivation as follows:

(59) [*Peter says* [$^{[\textit{which pictures of himself}]}$ [*John thinks* [$^{[\textit{which pictures of himself}]}$ [*Fred liked* $^{[\textit{which pictures of himself}]}$]]]]]

The point is that until the Wh-phrase ends in some final landing site, there is no obvious way of guaranteeing how *that* is going to be the place to sanction an interpretation. It could be (if there is a local antecedent), but there may be other licensing sites further up. Importantly, there seems to be a way to bound this computational matter: we just need to look at the entire Wh-chain (the set of its occurrences) and establish whether the various anaphoric licensings that occur do or do not achieve their binding goal.

Consider also a situation, as in (60), where no anaphoricity is at issue (so we do not limit our discussion to construal and referential strictures):

(60) a. [*I don't think* [*Mary likes you*]]
b. [*I not think* [*Mary* ^{not} *likes you*]]
c. [*I don't think* [*Mary doesn't like you*]]

In these situations of "Negative Raising," the negative associated to the matrix verb is actually denying the embedded verb. Example (60a) is not expressing your absence of a thought regarding Mary's preferences; rather, it expresses a concrete thought of yours: that Mary does not like you. In short, the scope of *not* is *likes*, not *think*. One way of representing that is as reconstructed in Horn (1989), with a copy+chopping of the negative as in (60b). But now we must be careful: we want to prevent (60b) from allowing for a representation as in (60c), or we should obtain the meaning that a sentence with two negatives allows: your not having a thought about Mary not liking you (so she kind of likes you). A way of achieving that is to force the chopping of the lower *not*, in a way similar to what Kayne noted for *tous* as in (58d) or (58e). It is not clear, as the derivation unfolds,[27] how the system "decides" not to interpret *not* then and there. At that stage, that proposition could end up embedded under a verb like *think*, associated to which a displaced *not* is interpreted effectively as a clitic that has "climbed" or as any other verb. However, most embedding verbs disallow the Negative Raising interpretation:

(61) a. *I didn't say* [*Mary likes you*]
 b. *I don't wish* [*Mary liked you*]

It is interesting to combine the "reconstruction" issues with this matter of a copy only being interpreted at a single site, even if it has been displaced over several phrasal contexts. Right away we must clarify that observation. Witness:

(62) *Offensive pictures may seem to each other's authors to be taken maliciously.*

In (62) the anaphor *each other* can only be licensed after *offensive pictures* has been raised to subject position. But to give *offensive pictures* its thematic role as the object of *taken*, and come up with a standard idiomatic interpretation for *take a picture*, it is often assumed that the displaced phrase is actually interpreted in its "base" position.[28] Does this not, then, count as one copy of *offensive pictures* being interpreted UP and another interpreted DOWN? It depends on how syntax interfaces the semantics. Here we have been arguing that various levels of the formal hierarchy in chapter 1 are grammatically real, leading to differing interpretations. We have not yet discussed how interpretation achieves such a result—a matter we return to in chapter 5. A straightforward way for this to happen is if the semantics is opportunistic, interfacing the syntax as the derivation unfolds, much in the spirit of Chomsky (1955). If so, it is possible that in (62) the semantics interprets the phrase *take offensive pictures* before any movement has taken place, as an idiomatic expression with whatever thematic roles are configurationally relevant, in the sense of Hale and Keyser (2002). Thereafter, a chain is formed via copying. It is only then that we worry about how to interpret said chain, for example, with the copy at the top as needed to license the anaphor in (60). No more than one copy need then be interpreted.

Lasnik and Funakoshi (2011) consider other recalcitrant examples for the idea of a single occurrence per chain being interpreted, in the spirit of Lebeaux (1990, 2009):

(63) *No criticisms of each other$_{1/2}$'s theory seem to any two linguists$_1$ to appear to their advisors$_2$ to be without merit.*

This is ambiguous, depending on whether the antecedent for *each other* is *any two linguists* or *their advisors*. Note, also, that the polarity item *any* has to be in the scope of the *no* heading the phrase in subject position, which "pins down" *no criticisms of each other's theory* to that position. But in the reading that matters now, *each other* has to be in the immediate scope of any two linguists, so that it is locally bound by *any two linguists*. That seems to demand "scattered deletion":[29]

(64) *No criticisms* $^{\textit{of each other's theory}}$ *seem to any two linguists*$_1$ $^{\textit{no criticisms}}$ *of each other*$_1$*'s theory to appear to their advisors*$_2$ $^{\textit{no criticisms of each other's theory}}$ *to be without merit.*

The point of our raising such examples now is that they involve a global analysis of the derivational situation: the only way the grammar "can be certain" that a given chain occurrence is to remain, and in which configuration it is, is entirely dependent on contextual elements in said configuration (which "pin down" the occurrence in terms needed for binding, polarity licensing, and the like).

It is interesting to evaluate the spirit of Lebeaux's (1990, 2009) chain uniqueness requirement (which he called "the single tree" condition) in light of examples like (61). As Lasnik and Funakoshi (2011) argue, this kind of case is a prima facie violation of that condition, requiring "scattered chain deletion." Then again, a further issue is exactly how many chains the displacement of *no criticism of each other's theory* creates, and whether the obvious A-movement across subject positions contains a further DP-internal chain within. If there are multiple chains in hiding, one could conceive ways of salvaging the uniqueness of each, in terms of relevant licensing conditions for each such chain, separately. That would not take away the globality of the case that concerns us now, but it is an important matter to elucidate in itself.[30] Perhaps (65), a less complex example built on analogy with (62), but with a negative quantifier, could help us in this regard:

(65) *No one seemed/appeared* [*to care*]
  a. *No one SEEMED/APPEARED* [*to care*]*—but they did, so something was done.*
     Rough LF: *No one seemed/appeared* [$^{\textit{no one}}$ *to care*]
  b. *It seemed/appeared that* [*no one cared*]*—so nothing was done.*
     Rough LF: $^{\textit{No one}}$ *seemed/appeared* [*no one to care*]
  c. **No one/someone SEEMED/APPEARED* [*not to care*]
     BAD LFs: *No one seemed/appeared* [*no one to care*]
     $^{\textit{no}}$ *one seemed/appeared* [*no* $^{\textit{one}}$ *to care*]

Clearly (65) is ambiguous, with a wide scope for *no one* as in (65a) or, instead, a narrow scope for this element as in (65b). What is impossible is a reading for the negative element in both the matrix and the embedded clause, as in (65c)—which would arguably obtain if a single A-chain could be interpreted UP and DOWN simultaneously, if not presuming chain uniqueness. Iatridou and Sichel (2011:600) argue that verbs that allow for Negative Raising (like *seem* or *appear* and unlike *be certain*) correlate with these structural ambiguities. The important point is that both A-chain occurrences cannot be interpreted simultaneously, or we would arguably license an LF as in (65c), contrary to fact. Once again, this seems like a consideration spanning the A-chain.

Although somewhat technically, (66) also allows us to reach the same conclusion:

(66) a. **Ourselves*$_1$ *seem to each other*$_1$ *to appear tired at the end of the day.*
(cf. *We ourselves*$_1$ *seem to each other*$_1$ *to appear tired at the end of the day.*)
b. [$^{Ourselves}{}_1$ *seem* [*to each other*]$_1$ [*ourselves*$_1$ *to appear* [*ourselves*$_1$ *tired*]]]
c. [*Ourselves*$_1$ *seem* [***to each other***]$_1$ [*ourselves*$_1$ *to appear*[$^{ourselves}{}_1$ *tired*]]]
d. [***Ourselves***$_1$ *seem* [*to each other*]$_1$ [*ourselves*$_1$ *to appear* [$^{ourselves}{}_1$ *tired*]]]

This is ungrammatical, which cannot be easily explained away—as is simply seen by adding *we* at the beginning of the sentence, which renders it grammatical. A condition on chain uniqueness would again take care of this bad example, simply by preventing (66b) (licensing anaphor *ourselves* by way of the boldfaced antecedent ***to each other***) and (66c) (licensing anaphor *each other*) by way of the boldfaced antecedent ***ourselves***) from co-occurring, resulting in occurrences as in (66d). That is only possible if the chain of *ourselves* collapses DOWN and, nonuniquely, also UP.

Recall, also, Ross's (1969) "repair by ellipsis" examples, which we discussed in section 3.3 ((36)–(39)). Just to make the further point about long-range correlations, let's now repeat (39):

(67) a. **That he'll hire someone is possible, but I won't divulge who that he'll hire is possible.* (Sentential Subject Constraint)
b. (?)*That he'll hire someone is possible, but I won't divulge who.*

As Ross observed in 1969, this phenomenon seems to demand "globality" in the repair of the island violation in the context of an antecedent it is parallel to. It may seem as if the Hornstein et al. (2007) treatment we sketched—which piggy-backs on the fact that the elided material lacks a PF, thus posing no spell-out problems giving rise to islands—bypasses globality: for that approach all that matters is that, with no PF, the relevant material is sheer "syntax of silence."

But the silent structure requires its being elliptical on (an unboundedly large) parallel representation. Worse, one can build an ellipsis on the basis of a sentence someone else said, as in this famous *Casablanca* dialogue:

(68) Ugarte: *You despise me . . .*
Rick: *If I gave you any thought I probably would.*

To complete a VP after *would*, Rick must have a mental representation of Ugarte's LF and turn it around in such a way that *me* becomes *you* in the exchange.

It is bad enough that one has to keep representational track of "what others say"; in addition, that information has to be structured in particular ways that allow access to it. To see this, compare the following examples, which is a dialogue about the Kennedy clan:

(69) A: *JFK's mother liked his children.*
B: *Pat did too* [*like his* (*JFK's*) *children/like her* (*Pat's*) *children*].

(70) A: *JFK's mother liked his children.*
B: *Pat's husband did too* [*like his* (*JFK's*) *children/*like her* (*Pat's*) *children*].

Once ellipsis "across discourse" is accepted, (69) is expected, with a strict and a sloppy reading (Pat, JFK's sister, can thus be said to have liked JFK's two kids or her own four kids with Peter Lawford). But now consider (70), in which case we are adding Lawford (Pat's husband) to the mix. Note, first, that in the real world it is just as (if not more) likely for him to like his own children as it is to like JFK's. Still, very curiously the sloppy reading is bad in these elided contexts, even if the strict one is good: B in (70) is only committed to Pat's husband liking JFK's children, not his! Ross (1967) already hinted at, and Lasnik (1976) and Reinhart (1983) fully demonstrated how, for a sloppy reading to be licensed in elliptical contexts, the antecedent for the silent variable must c-command this variable. Remarkable in itself, this is even more so in cross-discourse contexts, because it entails that hearers must be storing *a full syntactic representation* of earlier information heard in at least the immediate discourse. So ellipsis is a highly constrained process that cannot target just any old verbal element. Things would have been easier if the process were so unrestrained that any imaginable antecedent does the trick. But that seems far from the reality we are encountering, with c-command strictures (into missing material, no less!) clearly arising, so as to structure the syntax of silence.

Matters elliptical are so subtle that parallel conditions extend to scopal nuances of the sort we discussed in (53), as Fox (2000) showed:

(71) a. *Some boy read books by every author; some girl did too.*
b. *Johnny read books by every author; some girl did too.*

If *every* takes wide scope in the antecedent clause, it must also in the elided one. Note that *every* cannot take wide scope in (71b) even when this would determine, in parallel conditions, a universal wide-scope reading for the elided material, yielding a distributed interpretation. Fox reasons that this is the case because the raising of *every author* over *Johnny* has no scopal effect on the antecedent clause in (71b), as names are scope rigid. In other words, the grammar has to "know" that this step, which has no interpretational consequences, is not justified. This is a very global reasoning indeed, presupposing a computation spanning over scores of steps. And to make things even more intriguing for the purposes of our general argument, as Lasnik (1972) showed, the relevant facts extend beyond ellipsis proper, to "copy-intonation" as in (72) (and see also Tancredi 1992):

(72) a. *Some boy read books by every author; some girl did* ^{too} *read books by every author.*
b. *Johnny read books by every author; some girl did* ^{too} *read books by every author.*

For us what matters now is not so much ellipsis proper or lack thereof, but whatever the parallelism condition is that presupposes that phenomenon or, as it turns out, also the (in that parallelism regard) clearly equivalent process of copy intonation.

3.7 Gate Effects

Next we want to discuss connectivity effects that again argue for sophisticated structures. Let us start with Ross's (1967:29) observation that Wh-extraction from infinitival embedded sentences is better than from clauses with a finite verb (recall Chomsky's Wh-island):

(73) a. ?**Which books did he tell you why/whether we read?*
b. ?*Which books did he tell you why/whether to read?*

The question is why the Wh-island is weakened. Does this have anything to do with the silent subject (PRO) in the infinitival instance, vis-à-vis a regular subject like *we*? This is a matter that Lasnik (2018) reflects on, based on ideas going back to Uriagereka (1988).

Another well-known phenomenon where null subjects of infinitival clauses make a radical difference are "clitic-climbing" conditions of the sort first raised in Kayne (1969). Rivero (1970), for instance, points out how clitics in a language like Spanish are moved to a preverbal position, often over intervening (nonthematically related) verbs, but never across a sentence boundary—except in nonfinite embedded sentences:

(74) a. ***Lo** hice.*
it did.I
"I did it."
b. *Quiero que tú **lo** hagas.*
want.I that you it do.II
"I want you to do it."
c. ****Lo** quiero que tú hagas.*
it want.I that you do.II
d. *Quiero hacer**lo**.*
want.I do.INF.it
"I want to do it."
e. ***Lo** quiero hacer.*
it want.I do.INF
"I want to do it."

Postal (1974) argues that, under certain circumstances, a full clause becomes a quasi-clause in some sense. Is it possible to relate these clitic-climbing observations to the Wh-movement situations discussed in (73), in terms of some unified account?

Next, let's consider reciprocal interpretation, as in (75):

(75) a. *John and Mary kissed each other.*
b. *John and Mary want [to kiss each other].*
c. **John and Mary want [Bill to kiss each other].*
d. *John and Mary thought [they had kissed each other].*

Example (75a) is the standard instance, but (75b) is already more subtle, in that the interpretation may distribute in the embedded *kiss* or in the matrix *want*, as in the paraphrases in (76):

(76) a. *John and Mary want [to each kiss the other]*
b. *John and Mary each want [to kiss the other]*

For the interpretation paraphrased as in (76a), both John and Mary, who perhaps have declared their love for one another, have the same desire of each kissing the other. In contrast, for the reading that (76b) paraphrases, the wish is separate, and perhaps John doesn't know about Mary's desire and vice versa. Example (75c) is ungrammatical (the anaphor not being local to its antecedent). The interesting case is then (75d), which in some regard is like (75c)—although there is a local antecedent for the reciprocal in this instance.[31] That should sanction the sort of reading that (77a) paraphrases. Surprisingly, however, a reading paraphrased as in (77b) also seems possible for many speakers:

(77) a. *John and Mary thought [they each had kissed the other]*
b. *John and Mary each thought [they had kissed the other]*

That is, (75d) can describe an independent thought of John of recalling having kissed Mary and, vice versa, Mary's own thought of having kissed John. Indeed, for that particular reading it could even be the case that John and Mary were actually never in a relationship, but they each could think of an occasion in which they had happened to kiss the other. It is very intriguing how the reciprocal manages to "hook up" not with the local *they* (for that would yield the wrong interpretation), but actually with the long-distance *John and Mary*, one entire clause up. Actually, it is most noteworthy that this kind of interpretation for (75d) goes away if *they* does not refer back to John and Mary, and instead it refers to some entirely different plural entity, like Romeo and Juliet. Needless to say, (75d) can describe John and Mary thinking of the famous Shakespearean affair, but not John thinking of Romeo and Juliet kissing him and Mary thinking of Romeo and Juliet kissing her, entertaining as such thoughts may be.

Consider next other normally local relations $R(x, y)$ that somehow happen across an infinitival *or* a finite clause—*if* that clause's subject is a bound pronoun. Let's start with gapping, a subcase of ellipsis as in (78a). Readers can see how pronouncing only an object, with everything else elided under parallel conditions, deteriorates with distance:

(78) a. *John read articles and Harry ~~read~~ monographs.*
b. *John wanted to read articles and Harry ~~wanted to read~~ monographs.*
c. **John wanted Bill to read articles and Harry ~~wanted Bill to read~~ monographs.*
d. **John thinks Bill will read articles and Harry ~~thinks Bill will read~~ monographs.*
e. ?*John thinks he will read articles and Harry ~~thinks he will read~~ monographs.*

The crucial example is (78e), to be compared to (78d). A helpful anonymous reviewer of Nishigauchi (1998) pointed out the remarkable circumstance. The way Nishigauchi puts it is "the clausemate restriction on Gapping is alleviated by an intervening pronoun" (150). However, consider the contrast in (79), built on analogy with the cases just discussed:

(79) a. *John*$_i$ *thinks that he*$_i$ *will see Susan and Harry*$_j$ *thinks that he*$_{j/*i}$ *will see Mary.*
b. **John thinks that I will see Susan and Harry thinks that I will see Mary.*

In (79a) we see the long-distance gapping succeed if the elided *he* is coreferential with *Harry*, but not otherwise. For the same reasons (79b) is ungrammatical, because the elided *I* cannot be coreferential with Harry. So the alleviation in point requires a bound pronoun.

Grano and Lasnik (2018) (henceforth G&L) show other paradigms involving a relation with difficulties across a tensed clause, which improves with a bound pronoun in the intervening subject position. We do not want to go off on a tangent, but here are some exemplars to give readers a sense of the phenomenon and its scope. We use mostly English, but contrasts extend to other languages that researchers have tested to various degrees of thoroughness. We will not unpack these paradigms for readers, so as to leave the matter as a fun exercise to test. That said, two caveats should be kept in mind. First, the data is in some instances relevant to speakers' dialects or even idiolects; second, often the bound variable signals a significant amelioration, but not total acceptability:

(80) Multiple Interrogation in some dialects (Kuno and Robinson 1972; Postal 1974)
   a. *Who kissed who?*
   b. **Who thought* [*Joan kissed who*]?
   c. *Who convinced who that it was time to leave?*
   d. **Who convinced Mary* [(*that*) *John kissed who*]?
   e. **Which man claims that Kevin lent Jill which magazine?*
   f. ?*Which man claims that he lent Jill which magazine*?

(81) Multiple Sluicing (Lasnik 2013)
   a. *Someone talked about syntax, but I don't know who talked about syntax.* (Sluicing)
   b. *Mary talked about something, but I don't know about what Mary talked.*
   c. *Someone talked about something, but I don't know who about what.* (Multiple)
   d. *Someone wanted* [__ *to talk about something*], *but I don't know who about what.*
   e. *Someone wanted* [*me to talk about something*] **but I don't know who about what.*
   f. *A certain boy decided* [__ *to talk to a certain girl*] *I forget which boy to which girl.* (Barrie 2005)
   g. ?*Each professor$_i$ said* [*he$_i$ was working on a different one of these topics*], *but I can't remember which on which one.* (Lasnik [2013], based on an observation in Merchant [2001])
   h. **Each professor said* [*I was working on a different one of these topics*], *but I can't remember which on which one.* (Jason Merchant, personal communication, April 10, 2006)
   i. *A certain boy$_i$ said* [*he$_i$ would talk to a certain girl*] *I forget which boy to which girl.* (Barrie 2005)

(82) Extraposition ("Complex NP Shift")
(Usually clause-bound, Ross [1967]; Grosu [1973]: Right Roof Constraint)
a. *I will discover [exactly what happened to Rosa Luxemburg] tomorrow.*
a′. *I will discover tomorrow [exactly what happened to Rosa Luxemburg].*
b. *I have wanted to know [exactly what happened to Rosa Luxemburg] for years.*
b′. *I have wanted to know for years [exactly what happened to Rosa Luxemburg].*
b″. **I have wanted you to know for years [exactly what happened to Rosa Luxemburg].* (Postal 1974)
c. *The absent-minded professor$_i$ will say [that {he$_i$/*Lucy} is working, if you press him, on a new molecular compound for flubber].*
(Jason Merchant, personal communication, April 10, 2006)

So the question that G&L sought to technically implement is how a bound subject keeps a clausal domain "open" for relations across (be they clitic climbing, reciprocal licensing, overt movement, gapping, or other such relations of grammar), even when the clause is finite. If we assume, in standard Minimalist terms, that derivations proceed strictly bottom-up) and that "clause-mate phenomena" are constrained by derivational phases, then the PIC in (35) should be relevant. This is particularly so if C is a phase head, so that its TP complement is sealed off on transfer, as we have already discussed in section 3.3. The issue then is how to find a way to halt that transfer, an idea first discussed in Lasnik and Uriagereka (2005:chapter 7). We may suppose that a characteristic of bound pronouns is that they are introduced into a structure with unvalued agreement features, whose value is to be specified when the antecedent is introduced into the structure.[32] An interesting, if technical, question that we will not go into now is exactly what effects the crucial postponement of the application of Transfer, thus keeping the phase open for further relations to, as a result, become available.[33] Two aspects of this general approach are central to our concerns here, as was the case already in Lasnik and Uriagereka (2005:chapter 7): obviously this makes derivations extremely more dynamical than would be the case if phase transfer were always dependent on hitting designated elements (like *v* or C), and importantly for the overall argument, as a result of these processes, phase transfer could be halted indefinitely, as the derivation is forced to wait for a relevant antecedent to bind the crucial bound pronoun. These are, then, true "gate" effects—the gate being able to remain open for indefinite amounts of derivational time, at least for some speakers. It is even conceivable that said differences among speakers in licensing these phenomena might relate to individual memory specificities.[34]

3.8 Parasitic Gaps, Tough Movement, and Beyond

We do not want to give readers the impression that we have shown already "all there is to globality" in derivations. There is so much more that we could write an entire monograph just on those extensions. But we cannot resist at least providing a sampler.

Another one of Ross's wonderful discoveries are so-called parasitic gaps. We will not go into a detailed presentation, for which we refer readers to Lasnik and Uriagereka (1988). Here we would like to simply point out that, prima facie, these phenomena go well beyond standard chains, in that two (or arbitrarily many) chains connect into a sort of super-chain including multiple variable instantiations. For instance:

(83) a. *Which book did you shelve after reading* (*without having purchased*)?
b. Which book x is such that you shelved x after reading x without having purchased x?

Obviously, there is a chain associated to each of the verbs in (83a) and, somehow, these dependencies end up being part of a unified (rough) logical form as in (83b). There are scores of properties of these creatures that we cannot review now, which we will illustrate with examples for readers to play with. If speakers disagree with our judgments, welcome to the club: this is a domain in which individual variation is rampant:

(84) a. *Which book did you shelve __ after you/?? Mary read e?*
b. ???*Which book did you shelve __ after you said e costs a lot too?*
c. ?**Which book __ impressed everyone after you said e costs a lot too?*
d. ?*Which book did you say __ impressed everyone after saying e costs a lot too?*
e. *Whose house did you paint __ after building/*after consulting?*
f. *Who did you show a picture of __ to __?*

In each example, the "real gap" of Wh-movement is marked with a dash and the parasitic one with the symbol ***e***. In (84a), we see the standard instance pointed out by Ross, and we see right away a gate effect: somehow having *Mary* "in between" as the subject of the embedded clause makes the example worse than having the bound *you*. Example (84b) presents a certain "parallelism" in the abstract form of the two gaps, real and parasitic: speakers tend to prefer them for some reason if the two coincide in general case/agreement specifications (in (84a), for instance, both gaps are direct objects). Example (84c) illustrates the structural fact that the real gap must not c-command the parasitic gap—otherwise the result degrades. Actually, this might well be related to the fact that if the real gap is in subject position and we intend for this element to bind the G&L-style "gate" pronoun, then the parasitic gap will end up being (indirectly) A-bound by this element, in violation of obviation conditions; if, to avoid that fate, we do not invoke a "gate" pronoun bound from the outside, the G&L effects discussed in section 3.7 may emerge. Example (84d) shows an instance that, although it would seem to satisfy all the requirements implicit in the discussion thus far, is still far from perfect. In a sense, it appears to be the case that the real and parasitic gap have to be subjacent or some such (and perhaps they are too far apart in this instance).[35] Example (84e) is constructed so as to show that apparently what is at stake in constructing these superchain dependencies is not just a variable; rather, what matters is a syntactic gap. That is, semantically the variable in (84e) ranges over people: we are asking about the individual whose house was painted. Still, that does not suffice to license a parasitic gap, because the operator *whose* in a language like English is obligatorily "pied-piped" with the fronted nominal expression; indeed, that nominal ranging over houses in this example can license a parasitic gap. Finally (84f) is one of our favorite examples, because it was amply discussed in Chomsky (1982), although we do not share the grammaticality judgment. We reported in Lasnik and Uriagereka (1988:84) how for many speakers this means something "entirely crazy": which is the pair of individuals (x, y) such that you show a picture of x to y. We know of no direct way of achieving that representation; Chomsky and others apparently get a meaning along the lines of $x = y$ for our pair. If that were grammatical, it could be a parasitic gap.

Our showing such intricacies is not capricious: as Chomsky (1982) insightfully argued, these marginal cases often reveal more about the grammar than very common structures do. None of the examples in (82) are abundant (or even present!) in data corpuses, and yet speakers have robust (often passionate) intuitions about them. It should be clear, in any case, that whatever superchains are being formed in these instances and not in others go well beyond anything we have explored thus far or will explore in the remainder of the book. We finish with another such wonderful monstrosity, which has an amount of significance for the Minimalist Program like no other.

(85) a. *John is easy [for anyone) to please* __].
b. *A man who is easy to convince is easy* [(*for anyone*) *to please* __].
c. *This book is difficult* [*to convince people* [*to read* __]].
d. *This book is difficult* [*to convince people* [*that they/*I ought to read* __]].
(Chomksy 1981)

Examples like (85a) appear at the end of Chomsky (1981:309). The problem for that system is that, while *John* feels like it ought to have A-moved from the object of *please* (as in subject-to-subject raising, mutatis mutandis), it is impossible to license the trace of A-movement in such a domain.[36] Thus, *John* must be directly inserted in its surface position; but if this happens at D-structure, the Theta Criterion is violated because *John* is an argument but lacks a theta role at that level. Following the power of his convictions, Chomsky makes the reasonable move of liberalizing lexical insertion in such a way that *John* can be inserted in surface syntax, not in D-structure. The idea is that a complex predicate *(for anyone) to please x* can be formed by moving some empty operator *Op* to the periphery of that chunk of structure, thereby predicating that material from the newly inserted *John*. As it turns out, Kevin Kearney entirely destroyed that possibility in Howard Lasnik's 1980 seminar, by noting how the subject of these constructions can be of arbitrary complexity, including structures involving all sorts of transformations, hence most assuredly not in the lexicon. One could liberalize lexical insertion all one wants and still not obtain *a man who is easy to convince*—a structure in which the very transformation under scrutiny has applied. D-structure is, thus, doomed as a level of representation and a return to the generalized transformations of Chomsky (1955) is required. One has to assemble that entire chunk of structure in some separate derivational space Δ, then to associate the output of that derivational subroutine to whatever is assembled elsewhere (e.g., *is easy [for anyone] to please*). These are precisely the sorts of highly dynamical representations that we are after here.

Things get even better. The gap in these predicative constructions can be arbitrarily far down, as the collection of infinitivals in (85c) shows. In Chomsky's (1981) terms, these domains ought to present an abstract PRO subject, to satisfy the relevant thematic role. Curiously, when we make this subject explicit, the construction is sensitive to whether the (then) overt subject is a bound pronoun (like *they* in (85d)) or not (like *I*). This looks like another G&L gate effect to add to the class we have been presenting. But it ought to be clear that the phenomenon somehow arises in the construction of what we are dubbing a super-chain. In short, there is no single chain, in any traditional sense of the term, from the gapped instances in (85) and whatever is in subject position. The dependency goes beyond chains, into some sort of entanglement that illustrates perfectly just how intricate structural dependencies can get to be.

3.9 Conclusions

As this chapter has advanced, we have presented more and more elaborate arguments for structure. To pick examples at random, parasitic gaps or *tough* movements as seen in the section 3.8 are intuitively "more complex" than, say, whatever is going on in Lear's "No, no, no, no! (Come, let's away to prison.)" Aside from that being intuitive, we have provided already (see chapter 1) a formal apparatus to make such a claim precise. In our view, all of that is language structure—in some instances pretty flat structure, in others highly entangled dependencies. In between, simpler structures abound. Structuralists were fond of constituent analysis, but the best among them already realized that such "boxing procedures" are not enough. Following insights that date back at least to Zellig Harris's manipulations beyond constituents, Chomsky boldly postulated his now-famous transformations. Soon after, the field started studying how possibly to constrain such a powerful tool, which without limitations would end up manipulating structures with only computability as a boundary. The seminal work of the giants in the 1960s, very especially Ross, led to an entire industry that has lived multiple incarnations and is still in progress. We do not want to claim that any of that is a finalized project. But we do want to emphasize that it is a project that has continued to thrive based on prior results, finessing it as needed, thus leading to the sorts of entanglements we discussed in section 3.8. It would be a mistake to ignore these results from hundreds of colleagues working for dozens of years . . . on the basis of the field still lacking a totally crisp formulation to describe them beyond the sorts of generalizations we have been introducing. We may not understand what c-command stems from in a derivation, for example, but it surely is a pretty robust and, as such, precise generalization. To help focus this discussion, we will present our own tools in chapter 4, so as to let readers glimpse a possible future, at least from our perspective. But even if we are exactly wrong in our attempt, what remains is hard to dismiss. That, in a nutshell, is what we had in mind in chapter 2 when we said that empirical arguments for structure abound.

4 Reducing Reduced Phrase Markers

We have been presenting an argument for structure based on the empirical analysis of language phenomena and the proposal of a formal, computational apparatus that can model such data. We have done this by tracking various levels of syntactic complexity, in the sense of the Formal Language Hierarchy (FLH). At the simplest such level, matters are formally safe and mostly boring. We do not mean that disparagingly: there are "flat" components of language and describing them in finite-state terms seems appropriate. As we see in section 5.1, also, such phenomena may play a role in "internal" language change, so there is no reason to be dismissive about them. At the same time, our careers have been spent looking at higher levels of the hierarchy in point, where things get more interesting and formally less predictable. While no linguist denies the existence of phrases, many debate whether they should be characterized from the top or the bottom, or even in some parsing-dependent way. These are hard matters to elucidate. As one delves into such structural considerations, mathematical theorems become virtually intractable, perhaps because formal theorists have not been studying them for very long.

That all comes with the territory; for centuries physics was done with half-baked numerical theories—and much of what came to be central in the twentieth century would not have been even conceivable to the likes of Copernicus. Chomsky has often remarked that we are still at a pre-Copernican age in linguistics. Regardless, the only way forward is to forge ahead, pushing metaphors when nothing else is available and, in the process, attempting the best formalization possible to try to be predictive and explanatory. Our ideas in the present chapter ought to be seen in that light. Given the overwhelming evidence for structure that we have reviewed up to this point, the question arises as to how that is to be formalized. Importantly, our conclusions have gone beyond phrase structure, so phrase structure formalisms will only give us part of what we need. A related question, from a Minimalist perspective, is why structure has the properties it does. All that follows is what we take to be a tentative conjecture about a direction toward addressing such questions, given certain empirical facts that we take to be established. Even a speculation at the (broadly) context-sensitive level of the FLH presupposes all that formally exists below that level; this is why we will be formulating our transformational proposal starting from a phrase structure base. But what has been profitable in well over half a century of theorizing at that level is all *beyond* phrase structure: transformations to start with, but also relevant constraints for variables within those transformations, the operations themselves, other rules of grammar presupposing such transformations (e.g., construal limitations), and perhaps even the derivations carrying said processes. From our perspective, all of this is "fair game," although which particular game one may be playing depends on nuanced matters.

Note that we will not be focusing now on locality considerations. This is not because they have no interest to us. But there are thought-provoking ideas that could reasonably account for that part of the puzzle, some of which we ourselves have contributed to developing. For example, although one may debate whether phases should be described in this or that way, have this or that scope, entail this or that amount of freezing, we believe they exist, regardless of whether we call them that or any other name. Similarly, especially in a bottom-up (bare) phrase structure system of deriving phrasal structures, it is a formal fact that some derivations only invoke a single derivational space Δ, while fully recursive ones invoke that and placing structural material "off line" (with respect to Δ) too. That much is a boundary condition on the sorts of systems we are assuming; the question is whether to make substantive use of such conditions. The MSO idea that we will assume for the remainder of the book answers that question positively. Which means we need not go there again, as we search for more problematic forms of structures to provide an account of. We are thinking of long-range correlations, which we have argued for in chapter 3—particularly those, like long-distance obviation, that seem irreducible to local treatments.

We will not have much to say, even speculatively, about some phenomena we consider very real. One such example are chain occurrences and the perplexing property of their "distributed" existence possibly reducing to a single configuration in the interpretive components. There are very few attempts to deal with this. In the case of PF, Nunes (2004) discusses the matter in a way that relates to MSO and Kayne's (1984) LCA under certain interpretations. In the case of LF, Orús et al. (2017) present an explicit discussion, by way of a formalism that we will not go into. There is also a long history of "multidominance" proposals that relate to the matter, but which pose issues too numerous to mention in this context—and in any case, in our view do not address this "occurrence problem."[1] Which is all to say that we will also not be addressing it here, as the formalism we will be exploring (while compatible with treatments of the difficulty) has nothing deep to say about it. There are even more complex problems that we will also not be accounting for, especially of the sort discussed at the end of chapter 3. These are very dear to our hearts, but once again our formalism is not clever enough to resolve them, even if it seems compatible with a resolution that will have to await future work.

4.1 Reduced Phrase Markers

Chomsky (1981) assumes the formal system in Lasnik and Kupin (1977) (henceforth L&K). As seen in chapter 1, Chomsky's (1955) context-free PS grammars consist of:[2]

(1) a. A designated initial symbol (or set thereof);
 b. Rules consisting of a single symbol to be rewritten by at least one symbol.

For instance, given grammar (2), the phrase structure representation (P-marker) of *John laughs* is (3), the set of all lines in any of the equivalent derivations of the terminal string. By convention, in Chomsky-grammar rules apply strictly one at a time. Equivalent derivations provide the same constituent structure information, as they involve the same rewrite rules the same number of times, though applied in a different sequence. That crucial piece of linguistic information is as in (4).

(2) a. Designated initial symbol: S
 b. Rewrite rules: $S \rightarrow NP\ VP$
 $NP \rightarrow N$
 $VP \rightarrow V$
 $N \rightarrow John$
 $V \rightarrow laughs$

(3) {*S, NP VP, NP V, N V, N VP, John VP, John V, NP laughs, N laughs, John laughs*}

(4) a. *John left* is an S.
 b. *John* is an N.
 c. *John* is an NP.
 d. *left* is a V.
 e. *left* is a VP.

According to Chomsky (1955), linguistic theory need not express more than, for each portion ψ of the terminal string, whether ψ is a constituent, and if so what the name of this constituent is. If a notation encodes more than this information—and the extraneous notation is not linguistically relevant—it is a formalism that makes spurious generalizations. Following this thinking, L&K noted how P-markers as in (3) encode more than is needed to determine "is a" relations.

Some members of the set in (3) present exactly one nonterminal symbol. These are called "monostrings" in L&K, and are boldfaced in the version of (3) in (5):

(5) {*S, NP VP, NP V, N V, N VP, John* ***VP****, John* ***V****,* ***NP*** *laughs,* ***N*** *laughs, John laughs*}

Importantly, comparing the monostrings with the terminal string one by one, one can compute all and only the "is a" relations in the following fashion. From comparing *John laughs* with *John* VP, one can deduce that *laughs* is a VP. From comparing *John laughs* with *John* V, one deduces that *laughs* is a V. From comparing *John laughs* with NP *laughs*, one deduces that *John* is an NP. And so on. So as it turns out, the object in (3) and (5), a PM as in chapter 1 that obviously contains more than the terminal string and the monostrings, provides too much information that appears to be irrelevant. L&K thus proposed a construct they called "reduced phrase marker" (RPM), which only includes the terminal string and the monostrings. Their argument is, in a sense, squarely minimalistic.[3]

An RPM considers the relation between the monostrings and the element within the set that is not a monostring: the terminal string, as highlighted in L&K (176): "in addition to the terminal string, there is one and only one element in the reduced phrase marker for each distinct non-terminal in the phrase marker." Syntactic relations in L&K ("is a," "dominates," and "precedes") "are defined on monostrings on a set of strings, each monostring representing a particular occurrence of a non-terminal" (176). Central to the "completeness"/"consistency" conditions is the fact that "every pair of elements of an RPM satisfies *dominates* or *precedes* [and] every RPM has at least two elements: a single non-terminal and a string of terminals" (177). So the RPMS are hybrid, introducing information about contextualized nonterminals (i.e., nonterminals plus portions of the terminal string that locate them) and about the terminal string, in a way that we return to.

It is convenient to look at the admissibility conditions that the L&K system deploys, in order to meet completeness/consistency requirements:

(6) a. The RPM provides a consistent analysis of the terminal string.
b. The terminal string and the terminal portions of each monostring "agree."
c. An RPM can only be the counterpart of a rooted tree and never of a forest.
d. Every RPM element (except string of terminals) is a monostring.

The central result within RPMs is a deductive consequence of the way in which *monostrings relate to the terminal*, given these conditions on the RPMs.

Transformations work by affecting sub-RPMs (proper parts of RPMs), assuming:[4]

(7) There are implicit variables in between any two consecutive sub-RPMs, entailing that at this level of abstraction adjacency conditions cannot be stated.

(8) Transformations hold of the system's ontology (strings), disallowing any second-order operations over Boolean combinations thereof.

(9) Transformations index only nonterminals, which entails that transformations only hold of constituents (given the shape of monostrings) and prevents terminal manipulation in the transformational component.

Presented as less central are also the following:

(10) There can be at most two constituents affected in any transformation.

(11) Per transformation, there can only be one "catalyst" (or sub-RMP required as context for a transformation to apply, but not a part thereof).

Uriagereka (2012:chapter 7) notes how, although L&K could not have foreseen this, (10) and (11) can be made central to the RPM architecture by bringing into the system Chomsky's (1994, 2005) intuition about Move as Internal Merge, as in (12):

(12) Where sub-RPM K is a proper part of sub-RPM L, T only relates L to K if:
a. K contains one monostring ψ.
b. In addition to ψ, L contains a different token ψ of the identical monostring.
c. T targets ψ in K and ψ' in L.

If (12) holds, inasmuch as implicit variables are assumed (7), its net effect is that the source and target of the transformation involve a nonterminal *of the same type*. This, coupled with the fact that nonterminals are embedded within monostrings, entails that (10) and (11) are a natural part of (12). This is all to show how the RPM is amenable to familiar considerations, making some of its general conditions more natural.

In what follows, we study how to come up with an RPM when assuming BPS objects as in (13). In our view this is related to the issue of linearizing (13) as (14):

(13) {*will*, {*will*, {*v*, {{*one*, {*one*, {*man*}}}, {*v*, {*v*, {*meet*, {*meet*, {*a*, {*a*, {*woman*}}}}}}}}}}}

(14) ⟨*will*, *one*, *man*, *v*, *meet*, *a*, *woman*⟩

For clarity, in (13) labels are conventionally underlined in the formal object.[5] Let's assume (13) is prior to any movement, so *will* sits in Infl and there has not been any displacement. Let's also assume Chomsky's (1995) definition of term and label:

(15) *Term*
Members-of-members of *K* are terms.

(16) *Label*
A lexical item that is not a term is a label.

4.2 Reducing Reduced Phrase Markers

Following Guimarães (2000), suppose that "at the bottom of each merge path" there is a self-merge. This is to avoid linearization problems with Kayne's (1994) LCA, mapping the c-command among terminals to precedence relations.[6] But two words that merge as any derivational space becomes active (in situations in which such words come out straight from a lexical array selected from the lexicon, without any mediation of a Merge process) ipso facto c-command one another, so one cannot asymmetrically c-command the other. Guimarães's idea to remedy this problem is to have any one of those two objects, say β, self-merge, yielding the set-theoretic object $\{\beta\}$. Then α can be said to asymmetrically c-command {β}, and therefore α can precede β. As a consequence, at the bottom of each merge path there is a labeled lexical item *K* (per (16)), seen as a term in the sense of (15) after self-merge {*K*}. This distinguishes "first-merge complements" from anything else in the PM, in that (i) their binary merge reduces to a single term instead of two, (ii) the term immediately and exhaustively dominates a terminal label, and (iii) such elements, unlike all other lexical items in the PM (in different structural conditions), are such that, while being terminal, are not also terms.

Now, let's limit this bottom of a merge path situation as in the following:

(17) *Anchoring Condition*
Only nouns self-merge.

In general, adpositions take nouns as their complement and verbal transitive structures bottom out in a noun. There are intransitive verbs, but these have been argued by Hale and Keyser (2002) to be hidden transitives. Many nouns do not take complements at all (thus they bottom out as nouns), and when they take a complement, this complement is typically adpositional (thus presenting a noun complement). Finally, there are adjectives, which arguably also bottom out as presenting a noun complement if their various classifications are implicitly sorted out as in (18), with complements that can be made explicit; inasmuch as said complements are adpositional, assumption (17) follows:

(18) a. Opinion: *good/cheap* (in value), *delicious/peculiar* (in taste)
 b. Measure: *large/round* (in shape), *fast/slow* (in speed)
 c. Age: *young/old/new* (in age)
 d. Color: *red/black/pale* (in color)
 e. Origin: *Dutch/Iowan/classy* (in origin)

With that said, suppose the way to obtain an RPM from the BPS object is through a *tensor product* of (i) the list of labels (generated bottom-up in standard ways) as in the underlined elements in (13) times (ii) the terminal string.[7] That is:

(19) $\langle \textit{label list} \rangle \otimes \langle \textit{terminal list} \rangle$

The list of terminals we have in mind for (19) (here *the, man, meet,* etc.) is the one corresponding to the particular PM we are seeking to linearize (as opposed to just any random word collection), therefore meeting the LCA. The tensor product is

(20)
$$\begin{bmatrix} will \\ v \\ one \\ man \\ v \\ meet \\ a \\ woman \end{bmatrix} \otimes \begin{bmatrix} will \\ one \\ man \\ v \\ meet \\ a \\ woman \end{bmatrix} = \begin{bmatrix} will, & [will, one, man, v, meet, a, woman] \\ v, & [will, one, man, v, meet, a, woman] \\ one, & [will, one, man, v, meet, a, woman] \\ man, & [will, one, man, v, meet, a, woman] \\ v, & [will, one, man, v, meet, a, woman] \\ meet, & [will, one, man, v, meet, a, woman] \\ a, & [will, one, man, v, meet, a, woman] \\ woman, & [will, one, man, v, meet, a, woman] \end{bmatrix}$$

The result can be naturally mapped into a set of monostrings constituting an RPM for (13) by working *bottom up* the resulting matrix in (20), subscripting an element in the second column by way, in succession, of an element in the first column. The subscripting is by matching: first an identical element, next a list containing an identical element and what has already been subscripted, if compatible with the BPS rules. And so on:

(21)
$$\begin{bmatrix} will, & [will, one, man, v, meet, a, woman] \\ v, & [will, one, man, v, meet, a, woman] \\ one, & [will, one, man, v, meet, a, woman] \\ man, & [will, one, man, v, meet, a, woman] \\ v, & [will, one, man, v, meet, a, woman] \\ meet, & [will, one, man, v, meet, a, woman] \\ a, & [will, one, man, v, meet, a, woman] \\ woman, & [will, one, man, v, meet, a, woman] \end{bmatrix} = \begin{bmatrix} [_{will}\, will, & one, & man, & v, & meet, & a, & woman] \\ will, & [_{v}\, one, & man, & v, & meet, & a, & woman] \\ will, & [_{one}\, one, & man], & v, & meet, & a, & woman \\ will, & one, & [_{man}\, man], & v, & meet, & a, & woman \\ will, & one, & man, & [_{v}\, v, & meet, & a, & woman] \\ will, & one, & man, & v, & [_{meet}\, meet, & a, & woman] \\ will, & one, & man, & v, & meet, & [_{meet}\, a, & woman] \\ will, & one, & man, & v, & meet, & a, & [_{woman}\, woman] \end{bmatrix}$$

Note that a discontinuity arises when a given element in the left column does not associate to anything that has already been subscripted or contained within any such list (in satisfaction of BPS rules). For instance, when we are trying to deploy *man* as a subscript, there is no way for it to associate to $[_v\, v,$ *meet*, *a*, *woman*] or any part thereof, according to the BPS rules. So a new subscripting has to arise, and the process has to be repeated. These points of, effectively, derivational discontinuity will be crucial.

It can seem as if the subscripting process in (21), which generates monostrings, in a sense recapitulates the BPS process. This, however, is only a residue of a Deep Structure approach to these matters. Suppose lexical insertion, following Otero (1976) and also in the spirit of current Distributed Morphology proposals, is a "surface structure" phenomenon. Then what BPS yields are category lists, as in the first column in (22), to match (via the tensor product) a given list of words:

(22)
$$\begin{bmatrix} Aux \\ v \\ Num \\ N \\ v \\ V \\ Num \\ N \end{bmatrix} \otimes \begin{bmatrix} will \\ one \\ man \\ v \\ meet \\ a \\ woman \end{bmatrix} = \begin{bmatrix} Aux, & [will, one, man, v, meet, a, woman] \\ v, & [will, one, man, v, meet, a, woman] \\ Num, & [will, one, man, v, meet, a, woman] \\ N, & [will, one, man, v, meet, a, woman] \\ v, & [will, one, man, v, meet, a, woman] \\ V, & [will, one, man, v, meet, a, woman] \\ Num, & [will, one, man, v, meet, a, woman] \\ N, & [will, one, man, v, meet, a, woman] \end{bmatrix}$$

Then the subscripting in (21) is effectively lexical insertion, appropriately matching a syntactic label to the relevant nonterminal in the monostring:

(23)
$$\begin{bmatrix} Aux, & [will, one, man, v, meet, a, woman] \\ v, & [will, one, man, v, meet, a, woman] \\ Num, & [will, one, man, v, meet, a, woman] \\ N, & [will, one, man, v, meet, a, woman] \\ v, & [will, one, man, v, meet, a, woman] \\ V, & [will, one, man, v, meet, a, woman] \\ Num, & [will, one, man, v, meet, a, woman] \\ N, & [will, one, man, v, meet, a, woman] \end{bmatrix} = \begin{bmatrix} [_{N}\, will, & one, & man, & v, & meet, & a, & woman] \\ will, & [_{v}\, one, & man, & v, & meet, & a, & woman] \\ will, & [_{Num}\, one, & man], & v, & meet, & a, & woman \\ will, & one, & [_{N}\, man], & v, & meet, & a, & woman \\ will, & one, & man, & [_{v}\, v, & meet, & a, & woman] \\ will, & one, & man, & v, & [_{V}\, meet, & a, & woman] \\ will, & one, & man, & v, & meet, & [_{Num}\, a, & woman] \\ will, & one, & man, & v, & meet, & a, & [_{N}\, woman] \end{bmatrix}$$

To approximate monostrings in the L&K sense more accurately, we can ignore the terminal elements within the labeled brackets, as in (24). The ensuing matrix covers all of the information an RPM does. The classical RPM had monostrings (strings of terminals, including the empty string, with a nonterminal in between) and, somewhat oddly, the terminal string too. That was required so as to keep all the monostrings related. Here the monostrings are related because they are part of the same matrix.[8]

$$(24)\quad \begin{bmatrix} Aux, & [will, one, man, v, meet, a, woman] \\ v, & [will, one, man, v, meet, a, woman] \\ Num, & [will, one, man, v, meet, a, woman] \\ N, & [will, one, man, v, meet, a, woman] \\ v, & [will, one, man, v, meet, a, woman] \\ V, & [will, one, man, v, meet, a, woman] \\ Num, & [will, one, man, v, meet, a, woman] \\ N, & [will, one, man, v, meet, a, woman] \end{bmatrix} = \begin{bmatrix} [_N0, & 0, & 0, & v, & 0, & 0, & 0] \\ will, & [_v0, & 0, & 0, & 0, & 0, & 0] \\ will, & [_{Num}0, & 0], & v, & meet, & a, & woman \\ will, & one, & [_N0], & v, & meet, & a, & woman \\ will, & one, & man, & [_v0, & 0, & 0, & 0] \\ will, & one, & man, & v, & [_V0, & 0, & 0] \\ will, & one, & man, & v, & meet, & [_{Num}0, & 0] \\ will, & one, & man, & v, & meet, & a, & [_N0] \end{bmatrix}$$

This "reduced" RPM, or R^2PM can be reduced even further, as we see shortly, and it is a set of monostrings only (without the terminal string). The terminal string did go into its construction, in the tensor product in (22), which "clashes" against the organized set of labels a BPS object yields. But after that product ensues, the effects of the terminal string are implicit in the resulting array, without it being an object in its own right thereafter.

A curious property of the theoretical move in (24) is shared with RPMs: the monostring for a labeled category has no lexical information about the contents of what that particular category is taken to dominate. One may wonder whether this spells trouble for semantic representation, or whether one, then, needs to recapitulate the phrasal representation as it is shipped to interpretation. That is a highly theoretical question: It is not the same to do compositional semantics in Montogovian terms as in Neo-Davidsonian terms, for instance. If the way in which semantics works is akin to categorial grammar, having gone to an object along the lines in (24) is not practical, because we would then need to restructure relevant, merge-like, dependencies. But in a Neo-Davidsonian approach what we seek are predicates, the variables they hold of, roles, and quantificational elements taking scope (aside from implicit conjunctions). In that kind of semantics, it makes sense to know whether there is a label *v* at stake (introducing transitive relations involving appropriate theta roles), how many N labels the system needs to interact with—each an argument to play a specific role in articulating relevant events—or for that matter which Ds constitute the quantificational elements in whatever scope is relevant.

That is more important, at that "first pass" semantic level, than "encyclopedic" knowledge on whether the arguments are men or women (as opposed to, say, aardvarks) or the verb denotes an event of meeting, hating, or what. That ends up being important—but it is tricky to establish derivationally when such nuances get cashed out. Take for instance examples that show an obviation effect as seen in chapter 3:

(25) a. *He likes Santa Claus.*
b. *He likes Banksy.*
c. *He likes Noam Chomsky.*
d. *It squares to 1.*
e. *It squares into a stack of cards.*

It does not matter whether the referent of the object is imaginary, unknown, famous, or abstract. It is true that the only real numbers that square to 1 are −1 and 1. Still, (25d) does not seem like a felicitous way to express the thought that in fact 1 squares to 1. Whatever is going on is at right angles to the abstract nature of the truth claim being made: it looks like an automatic grammatical reflex that kicks in before we worry about the actual meaning of these terms. A bunch of cards can square into a stack if appropriately arranged, a sense of squaring that has relatively little to do with the arithmetic one, beyond the obvious metaphor; no matter, (25e) is still obviative, presumably on the basis of the mere fact that the two arguments of the verb *square* stand in a particular relation.

In the spirit of that discussion, from a Neo-Davidsonian point of view, it is apparently important to construct an active set of semantic files (reminiscent of Jackendoff's [1972] referential tables discussed in chapter 3), so that certain event descriptions, participants, and mutual dependencies are recorded. Computational phase transfers as such may be essential in keeping track of the event descriptions, whose effect in a sentence is cumulative, adding to relevant presuppositions. But in addition, one needs information argument files, which the phases do not fully determine (as in any given phase there can be up to three major arguments, and possibly several more oblique dependents). It seems telling that grammatical studies, well before generative grammar and back to antiquity, have mostly been about the interplays among NPs. All the major phenomena from traditional grammar (case, concord, anaphora, actant vs. circumstance specifications, etc.) revolve around such elements. In generative grammar too, the major subtheories of the P&P model specified Case, Movement, Construal (of binding and control dependencies), and so on. The same is true in the Minimalist Program: Agree is about such long-range correlations. There are conditions of grammar that hold of all categories (e.g., Merge) and of just nominals (e.g., Case). We don't know of any such condition that holds only of a category X (not all categories) if $X \neq N$ (or some variant, like DP, QP, etc.). These elements seem special, and part of their being so is the need the grammar has to keep track of them in files of some sort—whatever the reason.

Returning to the information that an object like (23) presents, note that in going from it to (24) we ignored the terminal elements in between the brackets. But it is equally possible to ignore those outside the brackets. For comparison to the R^2PM, let's call that a "reduced" RRPM, or R^3PM. This version of our core matrix in (23) does not involve monostrings—but it seems as legitimate a reduction of (23) as (24) was, giving an identity interpretation to elements that, from a certain perspective, are deemed irrelevant.

(26)
$$\begin{bmatrix} Aux, & [will, one, man, v, meet, a, woman] \\ v, & [will, one, man, v, meet, a, woman] \\ Num, & [will, one, man, v, meet, a, woman] \\ N, & [will, one, man, v, meet, a, woman] \\ v, & [will, one, man, v, meet, a, woman] \\ V, & [will, one, man, v, meet, a, woman] \\ Num, & [will, one, man, v, meet, a, woman] \\ N, & [will, one, man, v, meet, a, woman] \end{bmatrix} = \begin{bmatrix} [_N will, & one, & man, & v, & meet, & a, & woman] \\ 0, & [_v one, & man, & v, & meet, & a, & woman] \\ 0, & [_{Num} one, & man], & 0, & 0, & 0, & 0 \\ 0, & 0, & [_N man], & 0, & 0, & 0, & 0 \\ 0, & 0, & 0, & [_v v, & meet, & a, & woman] \\ 0, & 0, & 0, & 0, & [_V meet, & a, & woman] \\ 0, & 0, & 0, & 0, & 0, & [_{Num} a, & woman] \\ 0, & 0, & 0, & 0, & 0, & 0, & [_N woman] \end{bmatrix}$$

This manipulation in (26) allows us to create a formal extension of the monostring with significance to the formation of files. To see that, note, first, that a matrix can be seen as equivalent to a concatenation of vectors, as follows:

(27)
$$\begin{bmatrix} [_N will, & one, & man, & v, & meet, & a, & woman] \\ 0, & [_v one, & man, & v, & meet, & a, & woman] \\ 0, & [_{Num} one, & man], & 0, & 0, & 0, & 0 \\ 0, & 0, & [_N man], & 0, & 0, & 0, & 0 \\ 0, & 0, & 0, & [_v v, & meet, & a, & woman] \\ 0, & 0, & 0, & 0, & [_V meet, & a, & woman] \\ 0, & 0, & 0, & 0, & 0, & [_{Num} a, & woman] \\ 0, & 0, & 0, & 0, & 0, & 0, & [_N woman] \end{bmatrix} = |[_N will, \ldots woman]\rangle + |0, \ldots 0\rangle + \ldots + |0, \ldots [_N woman]\rangle$$

That said, we can then ask about the "component vectors" concatenated to the right of the equation in (27), where the plus sign simply means concatenation. But we can also ask how the vectors relate to one another numerically in terms of their vector sum or superposition. Note that these match-up differently via addition/superposition depending on where the zeroes in the vector happen to fall. To properly sum two vectors, we need to make their component elements correspond. While adding something-or-other (including the bracketed expressions that we have created in step (24)) to zero is a straightforward operation, yielding the exact same object, literally adding a bracketed expression to another is meaningless. The idea is that a sum as in (28a) results in an object as in (28b):

(28) a. $|0, [_{Num}\ one, man], 0, 0, 0, 0\rangle + |0, 0, 0, 0, 0, [_{Num}\ a, woman]\rangle =$

b. $= |0, [_{Num}\ one, man], 0, 0, 0, [_{Num}\ a, woman]\rangle$

Let's call such an object a "bistring," because it contains two nonterminal labeled portions.[9]

4.3 Bistrings

In the context of matrix (26), an object like (28b) is equivalent to one of those in (29):

(29) a. |*will*, [$_{Num}$ 0, 0], *v*, *meet*, [$_{Num}$ 0,0]⟩
  b. |*will*, [$_{Num}$ *one, man*], *v*, *meet*, [$_{Num}$ *a, woman*]⟩

The idea is to use bistrings to construct referential files for the purposes of establishing construal relations among the nonterminals within. Note that, as things have unfolded formally, bistrings (or for that matter monostrings) can be seen as vectors, with all the operational implications for such objects. It is by vectorially adding monostrings within the same R^3PM that we obtain bistrings. Recall that the main difference between the classical RPM and our reduced R^2PM is that the latter object (obtained via the cross product of a Chomsky-style BPS PM and a compatible terminal string) does not contain the terminal string—it is just an ordered collection of monostrings. In other words, while the terminal string is used in mapping the R^2PM itself, giving terminal contexts to its internal labels, once that is achieved the terminal string plays no further role in the formal object. In turn, we reduce the R^2PM even further by ignoring those terminal contexts, presumably at the point of transfer to the interfaces. This is when said contexts are effectively zero structures, which allows us to sum relevant monostrings, creating something comparable to Jackendoff's (1972) referential tables. We also need substantive restrictions on the bistrings, so that only some matter for construal; intuitively, bistrings in which one of the nonterminals is not a nominal projection ought to be irrelevant, or for that matter bistrings in which neither nonterminal c-commands the other—for which we need to build in structural nuances. As such, the bistring is literally anything in the RPM that has resulted from adding two monostrings.

Note that bistrings from an object like (26) may come in four varieties, considering the logic of c-command conditions:

(30) a. Neither nonterminal c-commanding the other:
⟨*will, one*, [$_N$ *man*], *v*, *meet, a*, [$_N$ *woman*]⟩.
  b. The left nonterminal c-commanding the other:
⟨*will*, [$_{Num}$ *one, man*], *v*, *meet*, [$_{Num}$ *a, woman*]⟩
  c. The right nonterminal c-commanding the other:
⟨*will, one*, [$_N$ *man*], [$_v$ *v*, *meet, a, woman*]⟩
  d. Mutual c-command of the nonterminals:
⟨*will*, [$_{Num}$ *one, man*], [$_v$*v*, *meet, a, woman*]⟩.

Typically, grammatical conditions hold from a c-commanding "antecedent." It is curious why that should be (eliminating grammatical conditions for situations as in (30a)) and why c-command conditions, in these bistring terms, should care about precedence (eliminating situations as in (30c) in favor of (30b)). Bear in mind that BPS objects as in (13) do not code precedence and are assumed to obtain under binary Merge. In contrast, the string in (14) is meant to code only precedence. Kayne (1994) argued that only binary merge is possible because (14) is obtained from something like (13) by mapping c-command relations among terminals onto precedence relations: an *n*-ary merge yields unlinearizable objects in such terms.[10] But why should c-command itself obtain?

Berwick and Wexler (1987) (henceforth B&W) blame c-command on the effective parsing of variable binding of pronouns by quantifiers. The parsing problem involves the (nonlocal) relation between the relevant pronoun and whatever quantifier serves as its antecedent. They specify their proposal within the two-pushdown (last in, first out, or LIFO) stack, left-to-right, parser in Marcus (1980). In such a parser, one stack is called the "input buffer," in that it holds a finite number of words from whatever sentence is being parsed; the other is the "active phrase stack," where words in storage are partially analyzed into relevant structures. Structures in the active phrase stack may be only partly constructed, awaiting some information at the input buffer. Such partially constructed phrases are accessible to the parser depending on how recently they have been assembled, given the stack's LIFO memory regime. The binding task involves connecting information in the input buffer and the active phrase stack. A c-command restriction limits access *to the very last layer of structure* within the active phrase stack. B&W shows how complexity grows explosively without such a restriction. So the idea boils down to justifying why, under assumptions about learnability,[11] a grammaticalized c-command restriction has the effect of making grammars containing it easier to learn.

In the formulation implicit in (30), and for the purposes of understanding a subclass of construal relations, we may assume that each nonterminal in the bistring corresponds to one of the terms in the antecedent-variable dependency. Only bistrings of the form in (30b) both allow long-distance relations altogether (unlike (30d), where the nonterminals are local) and in efficient parsing terms (unlike (30a) or (30c)). The latter is obvious for (30c): any parsing treatment would be irrelevant if c-command matters and the buffered element is "to the right." The entire rationale of parsing is that buffered elements emerge "to the left"—or to be precise, are encountered before they need to be recalled, so as to provide some key information that resolves an unspecified matter. In turn, for (30a) the issue has to be with the importance of c-command, which is more directly relevant to the specific B&W approach: in this instance neither nonterminal in the bistring c-commands the other, which renders the bistring irrelevant.

Then again, c-command restrictions certainly exist beyond bound-variable binding. Consider the list in (31), which is not meant to be exhaustive:

(31) a. Predication and theta relations hold under mutual c-command.
b. The internal domain of a Probe is its c-command scope.
c. Case dependencies hold under c-command from the assigner.
d. Displacement is to a position c-commanding its origin.
e. Theta, Case, and Agreement hierarchies are described in c-command terms.
f. Binding of anaphoric dependencies is under c-command from the antecedent.
g. Licensing of polarity items is under c-command from the licensor.
h. Switch-reference holds under c-command from the anchor.
i. Obligatory control holds only under c-command.
j. Obviation holds only under c-command.
k. A quantifier restriction is normally its c-command domain at surface syntax.
l. The scope of a quantifier is its c-command domain at LF.
m. Some quantificational elements raise to LF-commanding restriction sites.

Some of these may reduce to one another; for example, the licensing conditions may be under Probe-Goal dependencies of the sort in (31b)—though at the expense of expanding one's understanding of what agreement boils down to (cf. the phenomena of polarity licensing or switch reference). But it is not obvious how a justification for c-command in all of these sorts of dependencies could amount to parsing considerations as in B&W. Uriagereka (2012) suggests that Probe-Goal relations share elements of such a treatment, assuming that what needs to be parsed under agreement conditions is a given valuation of the Probe in terms of information in the Goal. In other words, encountering a Probe is in some regard the converse of encountering an antecedent, and in each instance one needs to resolve the relevant relation in terms of locating the goal. An antecedent can have full information to provide to what it antecedes; in contrast, a Probe needs to get some information (a value) from the Goal. Then again, one could have the Probe like the antecedent (and in fact for arguably better parsing reasons, because it "wears its needs for information" on its very shape) go into a memory stack that, as in the binding task, involves connecting information with the input buffer.

Things get much trickier for obviation. While it is easy to come up with licensing approaches as sketched (in terms of Probe-Goal dependencies, with the issues just alluded to), we know of no treatment of filtering conditions in any such terms. One can argue that, with squinting, a Probe is like an antecedent, in that both "miss something" to be found through the parse—information "traveling down" for the antecedent and "up" for the Probe. As noted, for anaphora even this is far from obvious, for most relevant antecedents licensing anaphors are as grammatical with as without the anaphoric resolution. But one can again speculate in the direction of Wh-phrases, which, in languages where they displace, "wear" their construal needs on their "faces," and the grammatical contexts of Probes. It is conceivable that the grammar generalizes to this worst-case scenario for all forms of construal. That is, instead of having a type of relation *R* under c-command for Probe-Goal dependencies and Wh-information questions that move, and a more permissive relation *R′* elsewhere (where the parsing issue is not signaled), the grammar may have evolved to stick to the efficient solution that may entail better learnability. That said, it is not even obvious that in filtering conditions involving the *inability* to permit a name under given (obviative) conditions—when in the c-command domain of a coreferential pronoun—there is any construal proper. If anything, there is *lack* of construal. One can always claim that, for some reason, in (counterfactual) situations in which the grammar *would* sanction relation *R* for licensing of some construal dependency, a relation *R′* that has nothing to do with construal, but simply prevents it, is activated. But that seems like describing the problem, not solving it.[12]

After we have stated the issue in terms of bistrings as in (30), given the anchoring statement about nouns in (17), we could take a different approach. Consider again the two stacks in the Marcus (1980) parser or, in terms related to the formalization of BPS in Collins and Stabler (2016), simply a derivational spine (in the shape of a buffer or any other, but not to be manipulated internally) and a derivational space Δ. In those terms, for a derivational construction, the issue is less a LIFO regime than the assumption that derivations are monotonically built bottom-up, starting with some merge as in (17) and proceeding in continued merge steps until the derivation of the spine as such is halted and a separate derivational flow is invoked in Δ, so as to assemble a specifier (or adjunct, though let's set those aside), Δ by hypothesis adds information only at the top (following the so-called Extension Condition) and is not to "tamper with" information that was already assembled—even in terms of Agree, only unvalued features become valued. Interestingly for us, it is meaningful to ask whether a given derivational flow that must start on a noun (per assumption (17)) also ends on a noun or instead ends on a non-noun. Could this make any difference for construal dependencies?

In our view, the first important fact ever found by linguists was the distinction between consonants and vowels that ancient alphabetic writing systems presuppose. Only second to that, at least historically, must be Pāṇini's famous statement in his Sūtra 1.4.14: "A word [in Sanskrit] is something that ends with either a *sup* (nominal affix) or a *tiṅ* (verbal affix)," from where he then proceeded to cover the functions of these word types in the rest of his grammar (see Kiparsky 2008). While these discoveries date back to at least the second and first millennia BCE, respectively, the treatment of this basic distinction in terms of features is a postulate of twentieth-century grammarians. The notion "distinctive feature" stems from an insight by Roman Jakobson in trying to pursue Ferdinand de Saussure's views (inspired by Pāṇini's) within a phonological plane of linguistic analysis (see Jakobson et al. [1952] and Jakobson and Halle [1956]). While the idea was first applied to the consonant/vowel and comparable distinctions, Chomsky (1974) extended it also to the traditional distinction between nouns and verbs. Both formalizations share an abstract point in common: consonants are taken to be as maximally distinct from vowels as a phoneme can be, just as verbs are taken to be as maximally distinct from nouns as a word can be. Such notions can be made precise, for example, within vector spaces; thus, we say that a unit vector [1, 0] is orthogonal (at right angles with) a unit vector [0, 1]. Mutatis mutandis, we can say that a vowel is [+*V*, −*C*], while a consonant is [−*V*, +*C*];[13] in similar terms Chomsky argued that a noun is [+*N*, −*V*] and a verb is [−*N*, +*V*]. The distinctive features allow us to "orthogonalize" the categories these features hold of, be they phonemes (per Jakobson) or words (per Chomsky). In a grammar of this sort, it makes no sense to consider the phonemes or the word classes other than in relation to one another, in a system where "all hangs together."

With all of that said, whether a syntactic derivational space should be anchored on a noun ought to be every bit as momentous as whether a phonological derivational space is anchored on a vowel. The latter is the basis of syllable structure, built around vowels (at any rate, phonemes presenting a feature +*V*—as a syllable can also be quasi-vocalic). A syllable is not one if it is not built around a phonological space that is continuant; in fact, the syllabic nucleus is in a definable sense maximally "sonorous" vis-à-vis corresponding non-nucleic (consonantal) boundaries to such a space. In an (arguably) formally analogous way, per statement (17) syntactic derivational spaces are anchored on nouns, if only those self-merge. What are the consequences of such an anchoring? Semantically (cognitively), they seem basic, although this is not our focus. Surely only noun spaces are felicitously named, deictically signaled, flexibly pronominalized for anaphoric purposes, and more. It may have been no accident for Sanskrit grammarians to think how central nouns are to the system or that philosophers of all ages have discussed relevant puzzles that arise around nominal denotations, from reference to quantification. More importantly for our purposes, children bootstrap their lexicon, starting with a handful of nouns, to anchor verbal and other dependencies.[14] Syntactically, it seems as if nouns are equally central, as noted, in establishing case and agreement systems, binding and obviation construals, nuanced displacements, and long-range correlations. To what extent is any of that related to the fact that a syntactic derivational space Δ is anchored on a noun? For the phonological example, aside from the vocalic nature relating to the stress salience of a syllabic nucleus (see note 13), its sheer perceptual clarity plays a role in phonological bootstrapping.[15] Should things be any different for syntactic features?

Descriptively, a transitive clause has the general, schematized, form in (32), where the pairs of Ns at the bottom of the trees are meant to represent self-merge. Bear in mind that each of these arises in a separate derivational flow, so that, if we have been operating on the construction of (32a) in derivational space Δ, (32b) must have been placed "off line," in some (memory) portion that the derivation is not working on.[16] Conversely, we can associate the object in (32a) to (32b) by activating the latter, placing it into Δ and continuing the operation, in a way we discuss in chapter 5:

(32) a. Subject: b. Predicate:

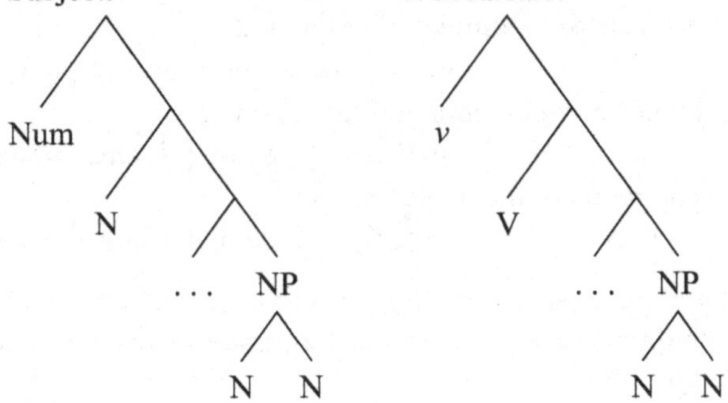

The dots in (32) signal the fact that structures of this sort can iterate indefinitely, with the verb in predicate position, or the noun in subject position, taking a complement that is more complex than an NP. Complexity notwithstanding, at the end (bottom) of such iterations, by hypothesis there still is an NP where self-merge has taken place, per (17). The issue, then, is whether the two "extended projection paths" in (32) correspond to anything with structural significance, simply because of their uniformity contrasts. Given the assumptions discussed, while a subject begins its "projection life" as an N and ends it also as an (extended) N projection, a predicate that begins as an N ends the projection life as an (extended) V projection. (Let's set aside prepositional, adjectival, or other "noncore" elements.) In that regard, (32a) is obviously uniform in a way that (32b) is not. But could that affect the shape of relevant bistrings, for file-formation purposes?

4.4 Orthogonal Labels and the Construction of Files

Pursuing the idea that nouns and verbs are orthogonal, Orús et al. (2017) postulate a system of features relevant to that distinction. While nominal projections present a label whose attribute is the real expression 1 (in its negative guise), verbal projections present a label with the complex i ($\sqrt{-1}$, in its positive guise) as attribute. V and N are then orthogonal in a formal sense, as follows (within the complex plane):

(33) a. $V = \sqrt{-1} = -1^{\frac{1}{2}} = i$ b. $N = i^2 = -1$

Per this system, relevant bistrings involving extended subject and predicate projections have numerical labels as in (34) (the labels expressed as subscripts). In (34) we have signaled in bold the nonterminals in uniform bistrings only:

(34) a. Neither nonterminal c-commanding the other:

⟨*will*, *one*, [$_{-1}$ *man*], *v*, *meet*, *a*, [$_{-1}$ *woman*]⟩

b. The left nonterminal c-commanding the other:

⟨*will*, [$_{-1}$ *one*, *man*], *v*, *meet*, [$_{-1}$ *a*, *woman*]⟩

c. The right nonterminal c-commanding the other:

⟨*will*, *one*, [$_{-1}$ *man*], [$_{i}$ *v*, *meet*, *a*, *woman*]⟩

d. Mutual c-command of the nonterminals:

⟨*will*, [$_{-1}$ *one*, *man*], [$_{i}$ *v*, *meet*, *a*, *woman*]⟩

Suppose we demand, perhaps for interpretive purposes, that only bistrings *of a uniform kind* should be acceptable to the formation of relevant construal dependencies as files:

(35) File bistrings are conceptually nonorthogonal in label terms.

The intuition for relevant oblique elements is that they occupy a space in which each is visible to the other. An old magician's trick to make a flat object like a card or coin "disappear" is to present its edge to the audience: a disk looks like a disk if presented in full view, but it starts looking like an ellipse at some tilting angle, until at a 0° angle from the viewer it presents just an edge, which may not be perceived at all (has an ideal zero dimensionality at that angle). In a similar sense, within the vector space in which they can be seen to formally exist in the terms being considered, the N-labeled (again, formally −1 labeled) and V-labeled (formally *i* labeled) elements are literally at right angles to one another. So it would be fair to say that, depending on which "interpretive perspective" one takes (nominal/real or verbal/imaginary), certain representations are effectively invisible from that angle, which we signal with a strikethrough notation:

(36) *From the* ***nominal*** **(*real*)** *perspective:*
 a. Neither nonterminal c-commanding the other:
  <*will*, *one*, [$_{-1}$ *man*], *v*, *meet*, *a*, [$_{-1}$ *woman*]>.
 b. The left nonterminal c-commanding the other:
  <*will*, [$_{-1}$ *one*, *man*], *v*, *meet*, [$_{-1}$ *a*, *woman*]>.
 c. The right nonterminal c-commanding the other:
  <*will*, *one*, [$_{-1}$ *man*], ~~[$_i$ *v*, *meet*, *a*, *woman*]~~>.
 d. Mutual c-command of the nonterminals:
  <*will*, [$_{-1}$ *the*, *man*], ~~[$_i$ *v*, *meet*, *a*, *woman*]~~>.

(37) *From the* **verbal (complex)** *perspective:*
 a. Neither nonterminal c-commanding the other:
  <*will*, *one*, ~~[$_{-1}$ *man*]~~, *v*, *meet*, *a*, ~~[$_{-1}$ *woman*]~~>.
 b. The left nonterminal c-commanding the other:
  <*will*, ~~[$_{-1}$ *one*, *man*]~~, *v*, *meet*, ~~[$_{-1}$ *a*, *woman*]~~>.
 c. The right nonterminal c-commanding the other:
  <*will*, *one*, ~~[$_{-1}$ *man*]~~, [$_i$ *v*, *meet*, *a*, *woman*]>.
 d. Mutual c-command of the nonterminals:
  <*will*, ~~[$_{-1}$ *the*, *man*]~~, [$_i$ *v*, *meet*, *a*, *woman*]>.

Again, it is not as if the orthogonal expressions cease to exist, any more than the magician's disk would when being presented orthogonally to the viewer—but they have a zero measure in one another's domain of existence. To put things more traditionally: if we consider the representations from a nominal perspective, we get some *neutralized* verbal information; vice versa, from a verbal perspective we get some neutralized nominal information. Several asymmetries arise in these terms in (36) and (37) once we factor in labeling considerations and their putative orthogonalities. Indeed, the only bistrings that are entirely visible in the particular sense we are considering are (36a) and (36b). There is nothing mystical to why there is less "visible stuff" in bistrings from a verbal perspective: this is a consequence of the fact that we stipulated (17), which has merge projections start at a noun self-merge. Had we stipulated the opposite, the equation would tilt into the complex realm, for the same formal reason. But the important point for us now is only that asymmetries emerge, which we hope we can utilize to distinguish bistrings that can harbor successful construals from those that cannot.

The broad intuition we are pursuing is as formalistic as the one behind the idea that only certain (vowel-centered) syllables exist, or category projections preserve headedness, and so on. Each is an empirical claim about language structure.[17] Just as (17) was rationalized as an ultimately lexico-conceptual anchoring, we could also rationalize (35) in information terms seeking referential files that keep track of construal relations among nouns. In particular, we can think of the system as seeking to axiomatize a syntax/semantic mapping in terms of uniform bistrings only, which come in two guises:[18]

(38) Uniform (nonorthogonal) bistrings:

a. Parallel Condition (PC): Neither nonterminal c-commanding the other:
⟨*will*, *one*, [$_{-1}$ *man*], *v*, *meet*, *a*, [$_{-1}$ *woman*]⟩

b. Oblique Condition (OC): The left nonterminal c-commanding the other:
⟨*will*, [$_{-1}$ *one*, *man*], *v*, *meet*, [$_{-1}$ *a*, *woman*]⟩

To begin with, bistrings as in (38) are interesting in that, of the four logically possible bistring situations as in (34) that arise for a matrix as in (26), only the two in (38) are uniform. That is, an R^{3}PM as in (26) contains many logical combinations among nonterminals that may end up in a bistring, including non-NPs and elements that do not c-command one another, all of which we seek to eliminate as relevant construal dependencies for our referential files. Uniform bistrings in the sense in (38) drastically limit possibilities to what we are calling the PC and OC conditions. It remains to be seen whether all relevant dependencies can be thus described.

It is useful to "dress up" the schematized objects in (38) with words to facilitate our intuitions about them in understanding their structural behavior.[19] Observe for the PC and OC and concentrating on coreferential or covariant readings only how judgment patterns differ significantly, as follows:

(39) Parallel Condition (PC):

a. *Will* [*John's friend*] *recognize* [*his mother*]?

a′. ??*Will* [*no one's friend*] *recognize* [*his mother*]?

b. ?*Will* [*his friend*] *recognize* [*John's mother*]?

b′. ?**Will* [*his friend*] *recognize* [*no one's mother*]? (weak crossover)

(40) Oblique Condition (OC):

a. *Will John *(say people) recognize him?* (coreference ok if nonlocal)

a′. *Will no one *(say people) recognize him?* (covariance ok if nonlocal)

b. **Will he say people recognize John?* (obviation)

b′. **Will he say people recognize no one?* (strong crossover)

For the PC, the main difficulty arises when attempting covariance between a pronoun and a non-c-commanding quantifier (as in (39a′) and (39b′))—with worse results if the quantifier comes after (39b′).[20] The PC yields perfect results for any kind of coreference as in (39a) and, at worst, may induce strangeness if the coreference involves the pronoun preceding the name, as in (39b). Matters are different for the OC, where covariance may arise naturally (if nonlocal for a pronoun)[21] as in (40a′) and is entirely impossible in the converse situation, as in (40b′). In the same structural circumstance, a strong obviation effect arises for coreferent elements (40b), which leads to no ungrammaticality in the converse, so long as locality does not obtain for the pronoun vis-à-vis its antecedent.[22] For those familiar with Binding Conditions in the sense of Chomsky (1981), none of these results are surprising. The issue is whether we can capture these effects in ways that are not stipulative for the formalism we have been exploring. In particular, can something equivalent to Binding Conditions be postulated within the confines of uniform bistrings, which we are attempting to construct referential files from?

A possible factor in some of the unacceptabilities in (39) and (40) may relate to the Familiarity/Novelty Condition (F/NC) in Karttunen (1968), Kamp (1981), or Heim (1982), building on earlier work by Jespersen (1949) and others in traditional grammar.[23] As Lasnik and Stowell (1991) note for comparable cases, (39b′) improves as follows:[24]

(41) ?*No mother* (*in the costume party*), *do I expect* [*her friend*] *to recognize.*

Whether (41) still violates the F/NC depends, first of all, on exactly how this condition is ultimately specified. For our purposes, it would be natural to try a statement as in (42):

(42) *Familiarity/Novelty Condition* (*F/NC*)
Within a construal file, referential anchors precede their anaphoric recollection.

Recall that we are taking construal files to be limited to uniform bistrings, by grammatical design. Right away that suggests that (42) is too weak, for this pragmatic condition surely obtains, also, across texts. Thus, for instance, if a narrative starts by stating that "the man arrived at the house," then to continue in a different sentence by affirming that "then a man screamed," we take the men to refer to different entities—in a way that is unnecessary (possibly even pragmatically odd) for the converse order of descriptions: "a man arrived at the house; then the man screamed." That being said, we are mostly concerned here with sentence grammar, not discourse analysis. Apparently, the F/NC holds in some version also within sentences, though the statement in (43) suggests that this is the case only within uniform bistrings that we use to specify a construal file. All that may be odd about (39b) for some speakers, as compared to (39a), could reduce to their permissibility with the F/NC as in (42).[25]

In that regard, displacement as in (41) may be enough for the F/NC to be satisfied, if this information-driven condition, in itself, cares mainly about precedence (though see note 25). None of that has a bearing on the less acceptable examples in (39), which involve quantificational expressions. Apparently, a further issue arises with relations of grammar, like the one that must obtain between a quantifier and the element covarying with the variable said quantifier ranges over. We return to this momentarily.

Note that the sharply ungrammatical (40b) does not ameliorate as in (43), where we are trying to use a displacement gambit as in Lasnik and Stowell (1991):

(43) **John, he will say people recognized.* (Bad under coreference)

The topicalization having no amelioration effect already suggests that whatever problem arises for the coreferent expressions in (40), for the oblique condition, goes well beyond (relatively weak) F/NC matters. As we saw in chapter 3, the description of the problem with (40) and the like goes back to Lasnik (1976),[26] a construal rule that gave raise to what later became Condition C of the Binding Theory in Chomsky (1981). The dependency arises in situations involving c-command, which in our terms reduce to what we are calling oblique bistrings. Certainly, other construal dependencies happen under c-command too, like the relation between a quantifier and the element covarying with its variable. This is what sanctions (40a′) as grammatical. By the same reasoning, (40b′) is entirely ungrammatical. In turn, this time not involving quantificational expressions, while (40a) is perfectly fine, in the converse situation we get an obviation effect. Thus paradigm (40) contrasts sharply with paradigm (39), in that only for the OC can a relation of grammar obtain within a bistring, while in the PC coreference, if it takes place, is merely accidental from a syntactic point of view—no construal process ensures it or prevents it.

Several attempts, since at least Chomsky (1982) and Reinhart (1983), exist in the literature to have whatever underlies these effects follow from something else. It is not our intention here to contribute to a further understanding of this problem: we simply want to attest that it arises in what we have called the oblique circumstance within a bistring—and it does not reduce to F/NC effects. It may ultimately be that the obviation effect in some sense correlates, as a counterpart of sorts, with the kinds of conditions that B&W argued as reasonably involving c-command. For example, it could be that, in the LF component, the assumption of rigidity for names entails "scoping them out" to the point-of-view domain of whichever judge (the speaker or some reported perspective) assumes such designations—as suggested in Uriagereka (1988:chapter 5). If so, (40b) may perhaps become akin to (43) at LF, involving actual (covert) phrasal displacement, thus in some very abstract sense reducing to the B&W rationale. That being said, verifying the consequences of an analysis along those lines is beyond our scope. The important point now is simply that our way of encoding orthogonal labels allows us to reduce bistrings from four possible scenarios to only two, both of which are attested as useful for referential conditions, although in our terms only one of them (the OC) leads to the establishment of construal relations.

We should emphasize that our (35) does not entail that the grammar cannot identify, for example, conditions of mutual c-command as in (36d) or (37d). Rather, what we take the grammar not to be able to do is to create bistrings for such conceptually orthogonal labels and therefore open a construal file in such terms.

Conditions beyond (32) also surely arise, for example, in relational terms:

(44) a. Possessor: b. Relational noun:

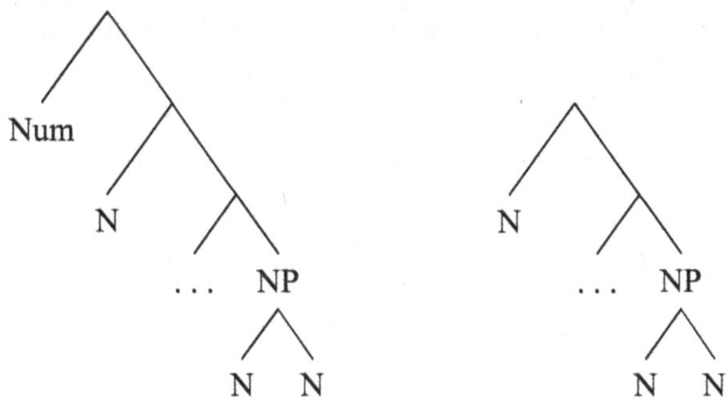

Interestingly, the way such dependencies typically materialize is as in (45):

(45) a. *The jaguar is a relative of the lion.*
  b. *The jaguar is the lion's relative.*
  c. *The jaguar is a lion relative.*

Examples (45a) and (45b) may not pose much of a problem, because *of the lion* is a PP (a category with a $-i$ label in the Orús et al. [2017] system) and *'s relative* is a $\bar{\mathrm{D}}$ (a category with a i label in that system)—in both instances, these are labels orthogonal to the nominal one (again, -1). Example (45c) is more interesting, in that *a lion* seems to be a nominal predicate of the relational noun, and they both ought to have parallel labels in our terms (-1 for the head nominal and either another -1 for the modificational nominal or 1 if it is seen as adjectival in some sense, again in the terms of Orús et al. [2017]). If the nominal projections each "see" the other, we should be able to form a construal file in terms of bistrings as discussed in section 4.3. This, in turn, predicts curious referential properties for expressions as in (46):

(46) a. *Every critic is a critic critic* (*a critic of* (*their*) *critics*).
  b. *Every lover is a lover lover* (*a lover of* (*their*) *lovers*).
  c. *Every relative is a relative relative* (*a relative of* (*their*) *relatives*).

Such sentences may perhaps be possible.[27] But it is worth thinking about truth conditions obtaining for such self-critics, self-relatives, and so on. Imagine a universe with a single lover who loves himself only, as there is no one else to love. Does (46b) come out true there? Or is there a disjoint-reference effect and *a lover lover* means something like "a lover of lovers not including themselves"? We will not impose our judgments on readers, but the prediction of our approach is clear: we cannot rule out bistrings of the form in (46), as they clearly involve parallel (extended) projections. Therefore, binding and obviation effects may well kick in for these residual situations.

Before abandoning this discussion, it is worth asking whether, just as we formed bistrings, via addition/superposition of simple monostrings, we couldn't have equally formed tristrings, tetrastrings, and more generally *n*-ary-strings if relevant "match up" conditions obtain. Obviously one can do that, formally. However, it is worth noting that, no matter what the condition of the *n*-ary-string may be (how many nonterminals it may involve), these will or will not be orthogonal to one another. To be sure, that too is theory-dependent. Classically, phonemes start on the consonant/vowel opposition of orthogonal elements, just as words start on the verb/noun comparable opposition. But there is no reason why there couldn't have been more such orthogonalities.[28] We have no reason to suspect that, in the case of language, the system is more complex, and thus one routinely assumes in syntax that attributes $\pm N$ and $\pm V$ (or, equivalently, $\pm 1/\pm i$) describe the entire inventory of the substantive parts of speech. If so, with a base along those lines, the conditions for bistrings may reduce to the four logical possibilities in (14), at least in a system that only allows for the four basic labels i (verbs), -1 (nouns), $-i$ (adpositions), and 1 (adjectives). Each such label is or is not orthogonal to the others, then yielding the "visibility" conditions sketched and no others.

Given derivational dynamics, bistrings in our terms pose a crucial divide in the derivation between what a part of the interpretive system "sees" (while in a certain perspective)—being able to put it in a referential file buffer—and what remains within the hidden computation interactions. This creates something like a computational stack if information in construal files is to be parsed. That amounts to a bifurcation in the system, separating what is computed in general from what is actually, in some narrower sense, interpreted. While that is somewhat hard to square with a Montogovian semantics, it fits with the Neo-Davidsonian project, with its emphasis on separating event descriptions (events typically being instantiated via verbs and adpositions) from event participants (encoded via arguments that can, in turn, be quantificationally expressed)—with modifiers conjunctively added. There could be other ways of making sense of the bifurcation we are emphasizing, for example in Discourse Representation terms. But the syntax we are sketching emphasizes some sort of divide, so that not all interpretive components are equal. This follows from two substantive axioms: the fundamental assumption of the (classical) orthogonality between verbs and nouns and the conceptual anchoring of derivations on the self-merger of nouns. Clearly, a recursive system like this needs to bottom out somewhere, and self-merge at the bottom is a legitimate way to do so. But nothing in the formal system would require it to be nouns that anchor everything; it could have been any of the other parts of speech, and perhaps, in some other logically possible language, that does happen. The ensuing system would still have the broad formal bifurcation we are emphasizing now in the formation of uniform bistrings. However, instead of highlighting uniform paths that start in noun-labeled elements and end in like categories, it would start in, say, verb-labeled elements, ending up the same way. For such a system, one would expect the mirror syntax of what one witnesses in human language: case/agreement specifications for verbs, those same elements acting as "arguments" of nouns, "binding conditions," and "control" for verbal projections, and so on. This is easy to imagine, but describes a world that is not ours and that seems relatively chaotic if one is into using language to describe dynamical events by way of (relatively) static arguments. That perceived limitation may just be lack of imagination on our part. More to the point of our considerations here, Jackendoff (1972) already limited construal relations to binary dependencies, even if more putative construals in principle emerge within a text. That reasonable stipulation, adapted to our machinery in terms of bistrings, follows for us from our above-mentioned specifications.

4.5 In Search of Dependencies within and across Chains

In chapter 3 we discussed transformational conditions that, at some level of abstraction, are best understood as "chain formation," but we did not provide a formalism for chains. Chomsky (1995:252) takes a chain to be a pair $CH = \langle\langle\alpha, K\rangle, \langle\alpha, \beta\rangle\rangle$ within the derivation of a syntactic object, where (simplifying to the general case) a specifier α moves from context β to context K. Certainly all standard (argument) Wh-movement is from a Case-checking site (in Minimalist terms, either a specifier or a position agreeing with a specifier that must invoke said specifier in further movement) and into some clausal periphery also involving a specifier. That is, from an A-position into an Ā-position, which we need to characterize too. As for A-chains themselves, the majority also involve specifier-to-specifier movement, for example, from an external argument position in a *v*P specifier to an IP (TP) Case checking site, or a Case-less site in an intermediate such movement toward a Case-checking position, if such displacements exist for A-movement. The only situations that apparently differ from this pattern, involving a complement in the first chain step, are passive constructions or possibly corresponding displacements from an underlying (transitive) object position to the specifier of a corresponding *v*P. Even in such situations, under the interpretation in Lasnik (1995) matters are more nuanced and such (ultimately "unaccusative") contexts involve a base-generated specifier too. Another way of thinking of the matter is in terms of defining a specifier as the last dependent in a projection XP (immediately dominated by XP). Evidently, in an "unaccusative" situation, with XP presenting a single dependent, that one dependent will be both a complement and a specifier. It thus seems sound to conceive of (argument) chains as being specifier-to-specifier.

Chomsky (1995:252) goes so far as to suggest that a chain *CH* "is actually (K, β) if we adopt the more austere version" of the notation he introduces; that is, some sort of concatenation of contexts associated by way of the displaced item α. This is a very interesting way of thinking of the entire transformational process, particularly from the perspective of a BPS theory and the MSO proposal. As we noted in chapter 3, in a BPS model one requires a separate derivational space Δ to articulate full recursion, in the sense of arbitrary complexity on two derivational branches: some sort of "spine" and whatever associates "off-the-spine" if this element is phrasally complex. We also noted how an interpretation of Kayne's (1994) LCA entails the separate spell-out of complex specifiers (and possibly adjuncts, but we are setting them aside) so as to treat said elements as, effectively, compounds or frozen idioms of sorts, capable of c-commanding as a terminal α (and thus, preceding) the structure that associates to this critical site.[29] That is the essence of the MSO proposal. Now while literally sending a specifier α to Spell-out in association to some structure K does have the desired effect of "terminalizing" α, it should also result in this "terminalized" α being anchored to K's context in the PF component. While that may be just what we want for α, it may also be useful to retain α accessible to computations with a PF reflex as related to the satisfaction of whatever featural requirements are still live in a given derivation, beyond K's associated PF. We could see a chain CH as allowing just that, as follows.

Recall from our treatment of Ross's (1969) "repair by ellipsis" in chapter 3.2 that LCA problems arise in Minimalist terms only if the relevant phrasal material has a PF to start with. We call this "Minimalist" because, in Kayne's original treatment, the LCA was axiomatic for phrases regardless of their phonological interpretation. But Chomsky (1995:337) correlates linearization matters to the interface domain where linearity is an issue: the perceptual/articulatory component. From this point of view, if a structure has no phonology, how to linearize it is a nonissue: there is nothing to linearize. This is what happens to some chain links: they have no PF. So the timing matter we need for MSO is straightforward, if subtle: the chain link that we want to linearize is precisely the one with a PF component, however that is determined. The reason we are being coy about that, and not just saying "the highest link of the chain," is because we saw plenty of situations in chapter 3 in which, for example, a Wh-dependency is not linearized UP within a chain. An even simpler version of that arises in pro-drop languages in which, very typically, a *v*P internal subject agreeing with T as a subject nevertheless materializes in some structurally lower position, which Rizzi (1986) correlates with many other interesting properties of languages that allow such structures. In those circumstances the chain specifier that goes to PF is not UP (in TP), but DOWN (say, in *v*P)—and see Pesetsky (2000) for much related discussion.

So in an ideal world, apparently a chain CH links relevant contexts (K, β), per Chomsky's (1995) definition, with the α that serves as the link between (K, β) materializing in one of those sites in the PF component—the other site(s) being irrelevant for PF purposes as no pronunciation is involved. We may think of that as the "PF collapse" of CH at either K or β. Importantly, CH has to remain a unit during the derivation or we would lose the main empirical payoff of the MSO model: to predict the sort of island effects we discussed in chapter 3. Recall that those followed for us only inasmuch as the "collapsed" material is no longer phrasal, so one cannot state a context-dependent transformation within. Indeed, the way we permitted Ross-style island violations (i.e., in a certain sense, "repairs") within the ellipsis sites is by having no reason to spell-out the elided material, so syntactic contexts within them remain live. But we know empirically that chain links are not accessible to extraction. Witness:[30]

(47) *[$_{CP}$ *Which car*$_i$ *was* [$_{TP}$ [*the driver of* t_i]$_j$ [$_{vP}$ *awarded* t_j *a prize*]]]?

We want to prevent a subextraction from the lower link of the chain formed by the displacement of *the driver of which car*, more specifically in the site that has not been spelled-out because it has no PF content. Takahashi (1994) and Ormazabal et al. (1994) accounted for such impossibilities in terms of a presumed "chain uniformity condition," which essentially assumes that all chain links must be identical. A condition along those lines was first proposed in Browning (1987), harking back to ideas first systematically explored in Emonds (1976) in broader terms; the condition was also used by Chomsky and Lasnik (1993) to predict important differences between argument and adjunct chains, which we cannot go into here (but see Lasnik and Uriagereka 2005:chapter 4).

In that regard, movement chains differ from ellipsis dependencies as discussed in chapter 3; for example, in a situation as follows, where the dependents are boldfaced:

(48) a. **That he'll hire someone is possible, but I won't divulge who that he'll hire is possible.* (Sentential Subject Constraint)

b. (?)***That he'll hire someone is possible***, *but I won't divulge who* ***that he'll hire is possible***.

In instances of this sort, what is expressed in the antecedent to anchor the ellipsis and what is recalled in the correlate are in no sense "uniform." That happens to be true even if we are not invoking a repair by ellipsis as simply seen in (49):

(49) ***John is hiring someone***, *but I won't divulge* ***who John is hiring***.

In the antecedent we have *John is hiring someone*, whereas the consequent presents either *John is hiring who* or even *he is hiring who*. These are related structures, but they are not obviously identical, a topic that has had much discussion over the decades. Chomsky (1995:252–253) suggests that in some sense ellipsis invokes "chains," mainly because there is a robust parallelism between antecedent and correlate. We are skeptical, however, for the reason alluded to:

we fail to see the strong uniformity one encounters across chain occurrences. We prefer to think of elliptical structures as in some sense "entangled," which we return to (because we think there are other such "entanglements"). For starters, Lasnik (1972) already noted how parallelism also arises in situations of "copy" intonation of examples with the structure in (50) (see Tancredi 1992):

(50) a. *Old McDonald kicked the bucket, and so did his cow kick the bucket.*
b. *Old McDonald kicked the bucket, and so did his cow* *kick the bucket*.
c. *Old McDonald kicked the bucket, and so did* ***HIS COW kick the bucket.***

The classic argument for parallelism is that such nuances as idiom interpretation (as opposed to a literal meaning) are preserved in the correlate if invoked in the antecedent, as in (50b). But clearly that condition holds with the copy intonation too—and with no ellipsis. In our terms, this should be yet another entanglement, but not a chain proper.

It is one thing to assume that *CH* is a chain, and even that *CH* obeys a strong form of uniformity (stronger than whatever parallelism may be invoked in entanglements), and a very different thing to understand what that really means. This is particularly so when we want a displaced α connecting context β to context K to "collapse" at either configuration at the point of interpretation, not both instances or in neither. We may think of that chain situation as a "superposition" of contexts and the interpretation of a chain copy in one and only one configuration, as its collapse, which we know not to be necessarily the same in PF and in LF: indeed, in "reconstruction" situations, a chain occurrence collapses in different occurrences in PF and in LF. To be candid, we are introducing these terms with scare quotes because nothing in Chomsky's formalism predicts this surprising phenomenology. We would take a real account to be able to appropriately concatenate the phrasal contexts K and β that α links in its displacement and—the most perplexing bit—for α to collapse in either of those contexts, but not both or neither, in any of the interpretive components. In an ideal world, the "superposition" (K, β) (whatever that means) should entail the collapse of α as a sister of either K or β (also whatever that means, particularly when it differs for the interpretive components). This is surely a computable process, as shown in the detailed analysis in Collins and Stabler (2016). But the issue is why it makes sense, as opposed to alternative algorithms: for example, "linking K and β has no bearing whatsoever on α." Or "linking K and β by copying α as a sister of K and a sister of β ends up with α interpreted both at K and at β." Or "if α collapses as a sister of K at PF, then α must collapse as a sister of β at LF." All of those seem equally reasonable, but they do not describe the facts. We simply need to understand why the grammar goes with one option over the others.

If that weren't daunting enough, the system presupposes a well-established distinction between A- and Ā-chains. This entirely fundamental divide has always been a definitional embarrassment. Chomsky (1981:47) characterized an A-position as "a potential θ-position."[31] Chomsky (1995:196) invoked the notion "L(exical)-relatedness": thematic dependents (complements or specifiers) of an argument-taker V were assumed to be L-related to V. Movement within L-related domains is A-movement—otherwise, Ā-movement. If V moves to some X via head-movement as in Emonds (1976) and Pollock (1989), assuming V *substitutes* into X, the L-related categories continue to be so within the newly formed head-chain, thus extending the domain of L-relatedness. The problem with this definition postulated in chapter 3 of Chomsky (1995) is that by chapter 4 Chomsky had given up on verb movement by substitution, under the assumption that such a process cannot be "last-resort."[32] As a result, the domain of L-relatedness at best extends one head up, to whatever is the first X that V adjoins to; subsequent adjunctions could not be V adjunctions, but could be X adjunctions, which are no longer L-related to V's dependents. While a verb V head-moves to Infl (and thus the IP specifier would be L-related to V, creating an A-movement site), by chapter 4 Chomsky had also extended functional categories beyond Infl, into at least *v*, the domain of external arguments and accusative Case checking. At that point, definitions fall apart: V is L-related to *v* only, not beyond, assuming V head-moves (overtly or covertly) to *v* via adjunction. So there is no direct way of making the IP specifier an A-position in terms of L-relatedness. In current works, Chomsky and others assume that agreement processes define A-positions, but to us that just tracks the facts. We know since Chung and Georgopoulos (1988) that Ā-chains involve agreement in a language like Chamorro, so it could not simply be the case that A-movement correlates with agreement while Ā-movement does not. One could relativize agreement to the relevant types, but that is equivalent to saying that we have A-agreement and we have Ā-agreement, and we have no idea what it is to be of the A or Ā type.

Now regardless of how A- and Ā-chains are defined, their behavior is drastically different. We have spoken of the collapse of an α displaced from β to K at either K or β. Puzzling though that may be for A-movement, complexity compounds if the α displacing is a Wh-operator and the operation is Ā-movement. In an (argumental, setting aside adjuncts) Ā-dependency we first need to get the Wh-phrase out of its thematic context, a kind of uninterpretability if the Wh-operator is "the wrong type" (see Lasnik and Uriagereka 2005:chapter 7). But we also need a variable in argument position or the thematic roles of the relevant projection would not be satisfied. The way to have our cake and eat it too is apparently by creating a dual object, where a part of the DP (the NumP) stays in the theta position and a different part (the D) ends up elsewhere in the structure but in a correlated position that still relates to the NumP in theta position. This would appear to presuppose some form of antecedence, in that the displaced operator hooks up to the variable that survives the thematic dependencies in situ. The grammar as such does not give us operators or variables, only syntactic categories—so, somehow, we must find a reasonable syntax-semantic mapping to do the job. Such antecedence, in turn, presupposes that the displaced element gains scope over the context it originally occupied. "Displacing downward" into the structure would not work for an operator if semantics is compositional. In turn, the (semantic) variable element within the NumP for some reason related to thematic considerations must be interpreted in its base position, or at the very least the position in which Case is realized, somewhat mysteriously. In its turn, the part of the NumP corresponding to the quantificational restriction is what appears to be able to collapse at a higher or lower context, which "reconstruction" tracks.

Moreover, as we discussed in chapter 3, Ā-dependencies are surely not as local as A-dependencies are, so the former may take place across clauses. In original treatments of these matters in the 1960s, "local" versus "nonlocal" was definitional for each type of dependency. In the P&P system, the relevant differences stemmed from the fact that the traces of A-movement were taken to be anaphors amenable to Condition A of the Binding Theory, while those of Ā-movement were taken to be the equivalent of names and subject to Condition C. The locality versus lack thereof was thus understood in terms of Condition A needing to be satisfied within a binding domain, as opposed to Condition C entailing a form of global obviation.[33] Within the present system, there exist speculations in the direction of phase impenetrability and minimality constraints of a relativized sort, though it is unclear what in the system predicts these empirical differences, particularly when the A and Ā distinction is imprecise (thus making it difficult to decide what to even relativize). Just as we need to understand what it substantively means for a chain to be uniform, we also need to understand what it means for its occurrences to obey minimality conditions or to exist across phases. Researchers have relativized matters to the point of proposing "criterial" conditions for different specifiers, within the Cartographic Project of Cinque and Rizzi (2008). In our view, at the limit that would mean relativizing matters well beyond the A versus Ā distinction, into specifiers for each and every category one may be finding. One often finds metaphors to sort out the ensuing category collection, for example, with mention of "fields" (as in *the CP field*) or "domains" (as in *prolific domains*), although without any characterization of why categories in a certain configuration should constitute a field and in what sense it is field-like. Moreover, beyond interesting factual discussions, so far as we know there is no attempt yet to relate the (non)locality and reconstruction phenomenology, making one wonder whether all logical combinations apply, possibly across languages.

It is worth recalling, also, that the antecedence relation (apparently relevant in Ā-dependencies) is *a*symmetrical (the antecedent *antecedes* its consequent), whereas A-dependencies seem symmetrical in that, across languages, collapses UP and DOWN a relevant displacement domain seem possible. Chomsky (1995, 2005) also argued that A-dependencies within a phase are "equidistant" from a target outside the phase, also suggesting a kind of A-symmetry internal to phases.) This symmetry of A-dependencies was used by Hornstein (1995) and Kitahara (1996) to predict core quantification interaction facts as discussed in section 3.3—distributing quantificational readings in terms of whether A-chains collapse UP at the Case position or DOWN at the thematic configuration instead. We also know that while all Ā-dependencies (of the argumental sort) presuppose an A-dependency at the first chain occurrence, the converse is not true. If one way to distinguish A- from Ā-dependencies is in terms of a symmetrical syntax-semantics correlation vis-à-vis an asymmetrical such dependency, it would be nice to relate that intuitive fact to the locality and the reconstruction phenomenology.

This is the bread and butter of generative linguistics, as are morphological dependencies (structural Case, agreement, and more) often surfacing in tandem with the long-range correlations. For most of it, though, we honestly believe we do not, yet, have a solid understanding, beyond the fact that it all seems to exist. It is our hope that the sorts of tensorizations we have exercised with in this chapter, which allow us to capture dependencies within what we have called bistrings and establish types thereof, may be used to come up with a framework to at least state these various (a)symmetries. To start with, Lasnik and Kupin's (1977) objects were compatible with the global dependencies in Chomsky (1981), like Binding Condition C. Any solution to global dependencies will require objects of the right size to even state them. Our R^3PMs present both size and the possibility of capturing type distinctions. This, in itself, does not tell us why there are, say, obviation conditions in the grammar—only *how* they can be stated. There may be other global systems that could work, including traditional PMs as originally defined in Chomsky ([1955] 1975) and more powerful graphs, as in many proposals in the literature. But here we were aiming at the most reduced such object that still preserves globality, and at the same time, one that can be trivially constructed from BPS objects (in our instance, literally multiplying such standard phrasal objects in terms of tensor products involving a terminal string or phonological representation). We also think that the vectorial system that ensues from our proposal is amenable to chain considerations that, to date, are merely tracked.

It seems interesting that a vectorization of the sort entertained here allows the addition of component elements. Perhaps what we have called "superposition" chain conditions reduce to a class of such additions, which may be defined also for inverse situations within systems of orthogonal features. A key difference between addition and subtraction is the fact that only the first is symmetrical. This might be used to model the A versus Ā distinction in a more principled and formal way. All other things being equal, one would want the grammatical system to choose symmetrical specifications like those of addition for the A-dependencies and asymmetrical ones like those of subtraction for the Ā-dependencies. More generally, it is our hope that chains could be understood as computational procedures to link phrasal contexts in domains of full recursion, when more than one "derivational spine" is invoked across that process and a separate Δ. This is, in any case, the spirit of the Orús et al. (2017) proposal, which we cannot go into here.

Again, that is all happening within the confines of mere chains, as arising in garden-variety expressions like *who seems to like puzzles*? But in the process of characterizing the simplicity of such sentences, generative grammar has also unearthed concomitant extensions that have given us as much pause as entertainment:

(51) a. *John has tried to solve the puzzle.*
  b. *To solve the puzzle tends to be fun* (*for anyone*).
  c. *This puzzle is tough* (*for John*) *to solve.*
  d. *Which puzzle did you solve after proposing?*
  e. *I like my puzzles stated my way and you probably do too.*

It is through such instances of obligatory (47a) and arbitrary (47b) control, "tough" movement (47c), parasitic gaps (47d), or ellipsis as reviewed above (47e) that we get into the glory of such "entanglements" as "gate" effects, "vehicle changes," and more of the sort touched on at the end of chapter 3. To us, these are situations where multiple chains manage to entangle, in some sense or another, so that denotational decisions made in one chain carry over to the others. We do not think these are situations arising in chain "superpositions;" we find them less uniform, which opens up a whole new can of worms, posing interesting long-range construals. Needless to say, we will not be able to understand chain entanglement if we do not know how even simple chain occurrences superpose in "reconstruction" situations. We are open to the possibility, for instance, that some instances of "successive cyclicity" may well be of this entangled sort, or for that matter the very connection between an Ā-chain and the A-chain that starts the derivational life of any Ā-chain. In any event, we propose R^3PMs as a move toward formulating these matters, but we are the first to admit that this is only a small step and not the leap that may be needed.

4.6 Tentative Conclusions

Having considered correlations taking place beyond phases/cycles in chapter 3, in the present one we have explored a formal apparatus that could allow us to express such correlations. One could assume that phenomena taking place beyond phases are not syntactic. We think, however, that such an approach is not useful because the pattern we witness exhibits syntactic strictures. In particular, standard obviation or anaphoric conditions do not arise across independent sentences or ignore c-command conditions that would appear to make little sense beyond syntax. One could also assume that the conditions in point arise within some formal object like the PMs in Chomsky (1955). However, L&K have shown how such objects (let alone graph-theoretic versions) present too much information that has no bearing on syntactic operations or representations. So the problem seems real.

Building on the L&K RPM, we first considered how to translate said objects to a current Minimalist system based on BPS. We showed how a basic tensorization simplifies the classic RPMs into a reduced version, which we called R^2PM: a tensor product of the bottom-up label list in an underlying phrasal object *times* (i.e., $\otimes$) the terminal string. That product is a matrix that can be directly mapped into a set of monostrings constituting an RPM. The procedure is most natural if lexical insertion is à la DM, with BPS yielding mere category lists (with no encyclopedic information) to match (via the tensor product) a given list of words. Then one can think of a subscripting mechanism yielding the appropriate ordering of rows and columns in the matrix as lexical insertion, or the matching of a syntactic label to the relevant nonterminal in a monostring. While the L&K formal object was a set (including arbitrarily many monostrings and the terminal string), the current object is a matrix including effectively monostrings only, with the role of the contextual terminal string now being organizing these monostrings into their matrix.

Our matrix R^2PM covers all of the information an RPM does, after having mapped a terminal string (a linear context) against the labels arising in a standard Minimalist PM as in Chomsky (1995). This added context is crucial in allowing for the long-range correlations we sought to describe. A further reduction of the matrix R^2PM into what we called a R^3PM allows a treatment of the monostrings as vectors, which we called a reduced R^2PM, or R^3PM. This manipulation of the monostrings into vectors allows us to construct an extension of the monostring with significance to the formation of discourse files. The idea is to decompose the R^{3}PM into component vectors, which concatenate into the R^{3}PM matrix. As vectors, these objects can be summed, resulting in what we called bistrings (or more generally *n*-ary-strings), as summed vectors composed of, in effect, contexts with two (or *n*) labels. It is these bistrings that allow us to state anaphoric or obviation dependencies without invoking any other structure. The implicit idea is that, although basic sensorimotor and conceptual information is transferred by phase/cycle to PF and LF, respectively, there is an intentional skeleton that remains active as the derivation unfolds until it ends.

Bistrings allow us to connect any two labels within a PM. While this is part of what we want (so as to determine long-range correlations between those syntactically connected elements), it is also too much in that it has no bearing on c-command strictures. The rest of the chapter sought a way to pursue c-command dependencies without having a PM to define the notion. One could do it in the R^{2}PM or R^{3}PM matrices, which are equivalent to RPMs in terms of dominance/precedence relations. But a more interesting and less global way to do this is to seek a characterization of c-command within the bistring itself. It can be done if the grammar (i) can define certain labels as orthogonal to others and (ii) the mechanism is insensitive to relations across nonuniform labels. The rest are substantive conditions on when (in particular, information) strictures arise, for example, in the formation of referential files. These seem more natural in the case of anaphoric dependencies subject to Novelty/Familiarity limitations than in the case of obviation, but it is not our intention to clarify this matter any further in this context, beyond having provided a way to state the long-range correlation itself, whatever its nature.

We ended the chapter by reflecting on the important difference between long-range correlations within phases/cycles (chains) and long-range correlations across such domains (super-chains), which we think are quite distinct. Although we have not resolved the matter, we have hinted at the possibility that tensorizations of the sort we have explored could allow us to separate each type of dependency in terms of superpositions versus entanglements, a matter we will not elucidate here. The important point for us is substantive: just because a long-range correlation exists, even if in similar substantive terms (anaphoricity, covariance, obviation, etc.), one need not conclude that we are dealing with the exact same dependency. While to someone with a hammer, everything may seem like a nail, it may be important to discover other tools and other forms of correlating the pieces in our workshop.

To conclude, we find it somewhat perplexing how, although much effort has gone into understanding the building of structure through intricate derivations, little is known about structural *disposal.* In a naturalistic system like, let's say, metabolism, while part of the physiological conundrum is how an organism processes energy from the environment so as to build its own proteins, another part is how to eliminate unwanted elements, which takes significant effort. Similarly for standard calculators, we cannot run our next computation if we haven't hit the clear key first. We have seen interesting theories of how to build structures, though little is ever specifically said about the relevant scaffoldings (brackets, indices, links, etc.) once they have served their purpose of articulating some meaning in terms of some form. Intuitively, we may want the arguments and predicates arranged in intricate ways, but whichever parentheses help us achieve that arrangement ought to be as irrelevant as such elements are in arithmetic as we proceed with solving our problems. In the case of accounting, we hit the clear key or simply erase the board, so that we can continue introducing new symbols. Does anything of the sort ever happen in language, as we go from one sentence to the next in mental processing? If so, does that not take an effort, perhaps akin to that involved in building structure, whatever that means in each instance? Does linguistically arranged information relevant to our understanding a situation perhaps end up recycled into the lexicon in the form of stored presuppositions? If so, what kind of a space is the lexicon, so that it can rapidly gain such information as we speak and listen, allowing us to update long-term thoughts with each new thought process? We have no answers to such questions, but we mention them because we see nothing structurally trivial about them.

In the last chapter, we return to some of these considerations, somewhat programmatically. The concerns get us closer to some architectural issues of the sort arising in neo-connectionist systems, for example, of the sort in Harmony Grammar (Smolensky and Legendre 2006). At the same time, we see no reason to get into the relevant architecture of competence/performance or the syntax/lexicon divide by way of ignoring the foundational results of generative grammar. We see our entire project as a way of being sensitive to these architectural concerns while, at the same time, building answers to generally familiar structural questions in terms of derivational systems that appear to present elaborate computational priors. This was obvious for context-free phrasal dependencies (presupposing phrases and more, like headedness or selectional restrictions) and perhaps less formally clear for context-sensitive correlations. But in the latter instance, too, constraints on locality, uniformity, or the morphological triggers of transformations, appear to be significant priors for the system. A workable theory of these matters cannot ignore such central presuppositions.

5 Structural Variation, Language Acquisition, and Machine Learning

Throughout this book, we have been arguing for the existence of structure, as perceived at various levels of complexity, in human language. One of our motivations for delving into this topic is that we perceive a tendency that would have us expect state-of-the-art machines to be able to pick up said structure "from the environment." Although we find that optimistic, we want to make it clear that we have nothing against machines, computational analysis, formal tools, or math, including the statistics that we use in our own work. In the present chapter we want to share some of our views on these matters, up to whatever scientific skepticism we also have in some important regards.

We come at these issues from the perspective of language variation, which is the key to language acquisition. We find that variation puzzling. There is no obvious variation in the visual or motor systems, let's say, and to the extent that there may be some (in color perception or gaits), these have a significant genetic component. There may be such variations in language too, correlating with handedness—but that is not what one normally means by "language variation." The difference between Chinese and Swahili has nothing to do with handedness, gaits, or color perception. Those who do not believe in innate structure in language seem delighted with the prospect of "endless forms," to use Darwin's famous phrase and intuition about the topic, which he extended from languages to species. Although we are not biologists, we align with Chomsky in his reservations (e.g., in 2009:part 1), presuming that what he calls third factors for language design also constrain natural selection (and see the controversial Berwick and Chomsky [2015] and Fodor and Piattelli-Palmarini [2010]). But if one takes this approach, one does owe an explanation regarding the sorts of variation that become possible within such confines.

All of that affects language acquisition (concomitantly, language change). Chomsky established his mentalist credentials in a debate with B. F. Skinner, which got more interesting when extended, in front of the Royaumont audience, (Piattelli-Palmarini 1980; see section 2.3) to Jean Piaget. Chomsky's argument in those contexts boils down to the impossibility of any associationist approach—based on general intelligence, whether of the sort Skinner defended in behaviorist terms or more broadly in the emergentist terms of Piaget—to account for the structure of language. As reviewed in chapters 1 and 2, the argument is simple. Take phenomenon *P* in language and find an explicit formal device *f* that can have *P* be inferred from an explicit data collection *D* without direct instruction. Some $f(D) = P$. This presupposes that first-language learners cannot be effectively instructed in the very language they are learning, and other forms of instruction are hard to specify. The Skinnerian or Piagetian accounts have been unable to address such processes as Auxiliary Fronting, so those are domains in which a miracle would seem to be invoked. For skeptics, postulating that some linguistic processes—the *f* in $f(D) = P$—must pre-exist the learning task also seems miraculous, this is even though by now it is pretty clear that many (all?) animal species present innate behaviors. The waggle dance that honey bees exhibit is highly surprising and remarkable the more we understand it, but it is far from obvious that it is, in any serious sense, learned by the bees.[1] Which, to us, puts the phenomenon of language on the same philosophical grounding: bees dance, we talk.

Have new artificial intelligence devices, which Skinner or Piaget would not have dreamed of, changed the situation? This is the question we want to pose in this chapter. In a sense, researchers probably ought to test the grounding of such a question in a relatively simpler instance, in which the neurophysiology is easier to grasp and ethical limitations are less patent. We seriously suggest that machine learning models ought to look into the acquisition of waggle dances. Robotic models, initially proposed by Landgraf et al. (2011), already exist and continue to be worked on, but what we are discussing now is not so much the computational modeling of the dance, but, instead, its acquisition and evolution.[2] The research program is easy to describe. It is possible to create an artificial life situation in which interacting agents mimic the life of a bee (with a hive, social individuals that protect it and are related to the same mother-queen, the need to feed in the surrounding areas, and so on).[3] The question is: Under what conditions do such a group of insects successfully evolve bee-dancing? Needless to say, one cannot presuppose either that the insects already communicate this way or that a programmer designs them to achieve this particular result. Bee-dancing is clearly computable. The issue is whether it can spontaneously emerge from artificial interactions in a computational environment and if so under what initial conditions. That would be useful as a first step, which could then be tested against an actual population of nondancing bees (see note 1), tweaking their environment as relevant on the basis of whatever was learned from the experiment, simply to see whether an organism acquires a systematic behavior that crucially was not part of its innate repertoire.

This is our first friendly challenge to the community and is meant in the spirit of cooperating in solving it. We are happy to offer our own expertise as linguists in a project of these characteristics, in the belief that succeeding, or even failing, could be worthy of our efforts. As we understand the literature, many of our colleagues already presuppose that what we are calling our first challenge is somewhat trivial, which may be why they can go and model, say, the emergence of subjects (or other such structural notions) from an apparently unstructured corpus of words.[4] We may be naïve, but if so it should be easy to prove us wrong. The reason we stick to our guns is that we have not seen, so far, even a real understanding of the challenge. In the case of honey bees we would not be surprised if the behavior can be modeled in finite-state terms and that it is universal to the relevant species in any part of the planet.[5] By contrast, in the case of human language, the structure, as we have shown throughout, goes fairly high up within a computational hierarchy as discussed in chapter 1. And to make life more interesting, said structure is stable only in its essentials, also presenting significant variation, which learners must acquire, from one community of users to the next.

In what follows we take a stab at bounding the nature of this puzzle in terms of the tools we have been presenting. We could be wrong-headed in our efforts, for boundary conditions are often empirical. If we knew already exactly what third factors constrain the nature of language, or what first factors contribute to its (epi)genetics and general neurophysiology, our problem would be simpler, effectively reduced to the second factors that chance has left open for history to set. But the fun here is that, at least in the case of language, we have little understanding of the first and practically none of the third factors, which some even doubt exist.[6] So we are speculating, we think in informed ways. Some guesses are more educated than others, so we hope ours help us guide research in a direction that is clear enough to test.

5.1 Three Kinds of Variation

While linguistic variation is obvious, it is harder to decide how a learner can acquire some structural nuances in the absence of explicit training. This is the POS argument reviewed in chapter 2. In part because of the Royaumont Debate (Piattelli-Palmarini 1980), where Monod and Jacob's Operon model was discussed, and certainly as a consequence of careful descriptive work at the time and a deeper understanding of generative grammars,[7] the P&P model came to fruition in the 1979 Pisa Lectures by Chomsky, later published as

Chomsky (1981). This effort led to the notion "I-language," understood by Chomsky (1986b) as an abstract, mentally encoded, generative procedure, where underlying principles (akin to genotypic specifications) get regulated by external (effectively epigenetic) information to result in observable language productions. Key here is the idea that primary linguistic data (PLD) is itself abstract: the sort of information that can activate whatever the underlying principles turn out to be into actual structures that constitute the syntactic backbone. Just as epigenetic proteins, light, temperature, and similar factors are not the same as the organs/behaviors they result in after interacting with genes in regulatory ways, so too PLD sets are not the same as the linguistic observables in the form of actual expressions after setting underlying conditions.[8] This is what we think of as a Language Acquisition Device, which Universal Grammar is a theory of. That raises many questions. What is the nature of the PLD? Is it unified, or can Language Acquisition Devices receive different types of PLD? Is any of this maturational? Is any of it affected by the microbiome? Does this model actually account for language variation? Does it account for language change? And above all, can the model provide an account for language acquisition?[9]

During the decade or so preceding this volume, the P&P theory has been criticized on two grounds. First, theoretically, as P&P morphed into the Minimalist Program, some have argued that there is no role for open parameters within the emerging program. Second, empirically, it is claimed that none of the parameters in the literature work—they all manifest counterexamples.

This is not the place to discuss why we disagree with taking Minimalism to entail a fixed grammar. Suffice it to say that biological systems, as they are coming to light from the perspective of molecular biology, appear to be the result of somewhat open programs, for which epigenetic regulation is every bit as central as genetic endowment. While Minimalist ideas are still too much of a hypothesis for anyone to decide on what is *kosher*,[10] at the relevant level of abstraction biology seems to have found relative stability beyond sheer genomes: in the proteome, the microbiome, possibly the connectome in the case of brains, and so on. All that is strictly *past genetic endowment*—what is endowed goes beyond the genome as such (as a particular set of genetic specifications). Which is all to say that, in our view, there is little one can conclude about putative linguistic parameters from general reflections on the biological substrate.

We will also not revisit the particular problems raised for parameters proposed in the literature. The general form of such counterexamples is as follows: "Your theory proposes parameter *P* regulating ±*property*. However, here is a language *L* that, in fact, presents +*property* in domain *D and* also –*property* in domain D'. Therefore L disproves P as a real parameter." That reasoning, as such, is straightforward. However, it is also limited to disproving the relevance of P. To disprove the general theory of parameters, one would have to come up with an alternative explanation to how children acquire language. (Or how languages effectively change.) This is not to say that we consider parameters proposed in the literature (the Pro-drop, Directionality, Polysynthesis parameters, and so on) the last word on the relevant topic or even proof that parameters are real. We are agnostic about that matter as such and have some practical thoughts to offer in that regard later in this chapter. Our point is more modest: we do not know, and cannot even think, of an alternative to a theory along the lines presupposing parametric differences that learners set and whose consequences reverberate throughout a grammar.[11]

We also want to mention how so-called microvariation may well be at right angles with the tough problem of language acquisition. Languages differ in small ways, which need not all be as trivial as Fred Astaire pronouncing *potato* or *tomato* in ways different enough from Ginger Rogers to inspire the Gershwins into an unforgettable tune. Again, it is far from trivial why this may be, and we are even prepared to argue that such minute differences can, in some instances, lead to serious language changes. However, for a learner to figure out such variances may be relatively easy if they are not hard to consciously spot even for adult song writers. We will go as far as to saying that this seems to us just the sort of information that a machine learning algorithm *can* (or should) abstract from a regular enough data corpus. All of that said, while the phenomenon is real and relevant to the whole picture—with possibly sociological consequences that actual human groups may be willing to go to war for—it is mostly orthogonal to the logical problem of language acquisition. Nobody denies that there are parts of language that differ from one community to another, are fairly easy to identify and, well, learn in strictly learning terms. If all of language were that way, there would not have been much of an argument between Chomsky and the likes of Skinner or Piaget. The problem is that some of language, to anyone's present understanding, is not easy to abstract in such a way from the raw data. We think it is impossible.

Just to be clear about this, when a learner "fixes a parameter"—on the basis of easily available information as opposed to explicit instruction from a tutor—the learner's decision is supposed to have consequences beyond the particular data set being acquired, crucially including structural aspects that are hard to systematically spot. If one is into the biopsychological reality of the language faculty, while there is obvious *microvariation*, it is simply not as relevant as what may be thought of as *dark macrovariation*. We use the adjective "dark" on purpose, to liken the situation to that of "dark data," in the sense of structures that underlie a surface information phenomenon. Internet moguls are interested in convincing us that much is going on behind our backs that we ought to pay attention to—and pay for. We are skeptical that computer scientists at this point understand what dark data amounts to, beyond existing, among other things because the workings of machine learning are, as such, effectively a black-box mystery.[12] So we mean the comment metaphorically, but also as an admission that we too do not understand yet what our "dark parameters" are beyond expecting them to be there.

With all those caveats out of our way, in a model along the lines we have sketched in this book, there are three places where we expect structural variation, each deeper than the next and tracking the FLH in chapter 1. To put the matter intuitively, consider ways in which your bicycle can differ, bearing in mind that it needs two wheels attached to a frame; a pedaling mechanism with something to steer; and incidentals like weight, height, color, and the like. The wheels and frame seem essential, the pedaling and steering mechanisms less so, and the rest is a necessary by-product. Where is the variation? Surely in the incidentals as this is what bicycle shops market. Historically, the pedaling and steering have changed considerably and may continue to change in the future. When it comes to the core structural matter of the two wheels attached to the frame, less than that gives you a unicycle and more, a tricycle. So too in the case of language we expect less variation, and with more drastic consequences, as one delves deeper into its basic structural nuances. This is our, we think testable, hypothesis.

We may tentatively pursue in that regard the specific proposal in Uriagereka (2018:chapter 4), which tracks the FLH discussed in chapter 1. That work distinguishes, at the core of the system (where transformations are stated), variation in terms of macroparameters. We want to resist the temptation of giving actual examples of this in language because part of what we are attempting to argue for is that the empirical task of discovering such dark parameters is difficult, requiring the type of efforts that finding dark matter poses for teams of physicists. At a less central component of the language faculty, in turn, we expect variation in which phrasal components are realized. Tentatively, it may be that the traditional Head parameter is of that sort, although it is unclear whether what varies from language to language is the position of complements vis-à-vis their heads or, instead, some morphosyntactic mechanism that in some language forces overt displacement, unlike in others (as argued in Kayne [1994]—and see also Fukui and Takano [1998] for a different view). We have no axe to grind in that regard, beyond noting that phrases, in principle, may linearize differently, simply because speech is linear and phrasal hierarchies are not. Finally, we expect microvariation. In our terms it is natural to think of that as superficial, tracking such obvious linguistic features as forms of pronunciation, putative iterations, perhaps some fixed (even "iconic")[13] linear orders and little else. In a sense, microvariation is as obvious as it is structurally feeble.

We do not intend the latter comment as patronizing. We are aware of the careful work of philologists showing how minute phonological changes (e.g., in vowel quality, stress retraction, syllabic structure) may have dramatic consequences that could affect entire morphophonemic paradigms. Those, in turn, may lead a generation of learners in a direction different from that of the previous generation, which in some instances can have consequences that may be systemic. Such changes can happen when, sadly often in history, a community conquers or enslaves another. But more importantly to the linguist, in principle they can also happen without such dire circumstances, more in line with the sociological scenarios studied by William Labov (e.g., in 2001), which may be important to group identity. We are willing to go as far as saying that such dynamics could have been central to the stabilization of dialects as language was evolving, particularly if early human groups sought a numerical optimum closer to the hamlet than the village.[14]

What matters to us here is simple: in principle there are (at least) three types of structural variation, with each type deeper than the previous one. If we are correct in this speculation, we expect drastic language changes (setting aside invasions and the like) that start in minute microvariations. This is because we can easily see, following Labovian pressures, how adolescents can change the way they talk and, with some probability (no matter how small), how their children may (though need not) reanalyze primary linguistic data in a way that results in a Lightfoot-style change.[15] But the only way we can see for changes to be equally drastic and proceed in the opposite direction (from core parameters to microvariations) is if communities live a multilingual reality, as first explored by Tony Kroch and now thoroughly modeled by Charles Yang.[16] While plausible, that situation is by definition not the one we were considering: changes happening in isolation. To verify this idea, one cannot go back to Central Africa one hundred thousand years ago, and situations of tribal isolation, among the hundred or so inaccessible communities that still exist in our world today, are virtually impossible (and surely unethical) to track. That said, the point of principle is clear; one may even try artificial language experiments to test the hypothesis that a surface change can "trickle down" to the language core after some generations.

Our model also makes a prediction that we already alluded to in chapter 2, which we can add a further nuance to now: the acquisition path by infants may well be affected by these structural differences. If true, this may be found in the lab, in ways that Lila Gleitman and Ken Wexler have been suggesting for decades,[17] but which others like Stephen Crain have been skeptical about.[18] If maturation of the language faculty seriously exists, to some extent that brings back some of Piaget's points, albeit probably much earlier than he ever thought (not so much in puberty, but perhaps all the way back to situations in utero).[19] We now know that children use hearing information before birth,[20] so as to come out with a certain prosodic profile. It is conceivable (though this is speculation) that such a profile might help set core parameters in a dark way, prior to meaningful exposure to words. Moreover, it seems as if directionality parameters are already on track from the moment children start producing their first two-word combinations, which occurs around eighteen months or even earlier for some infants.[21] At the other extreme, accents, idioms, and neighborhood peculiarities are easy to acquire well into adolescence, perhaps more passionately then, even.[22] So that part of the process seems active past the maturational years, perhaps during the time that we have argued in chapter 1 the child is, for all acquisitional purposes, a "generative semanticist." Alas, at some point—except if one is called Ken Hale,[23] perhaps—much of this stops for most of us, so we generally keep our accents for the rest of our lives.

Last but not least, we need to mention that, as a point of principle, it is also relevant to begin to ask what happens in situations of language breakdown, aging, drug-induced states, or, more tragically, genetic anomalies. We ourselves have no idea, but the research program is clear: the more superficial a variation feature is, the more it may remain when other aspects of language are all but gone. It is easy to observe, for instance, people with Broca's aphasia who have an almost complete syntactic breakdown but perfectly fine phonemics. It would be most interesting to test some of these ideas in domains that range from specific language impairment to dementias associated with age or altered states of various kinds. If linguists are invited to participate in relevant experiments, we can provide nuanced ways of testing these central questions. Again, it is of little practical consequence if any of this is right or wrong in its every detail: it would be a more informed way of relating to patients and subjects of all kinds, in terms of notions that are of obvious relevance to the working linguist. We return to the matter shortly.

5.2 Likes and More in Language and Elsewhere

In this section we take a broader view to reflect on the primitives that appear central to theorizing about linguistic structuring, with an eye on whether machine learning can presently spot such primitives. There have been many situations in this book in which we have talked about or implied identical items: token symbols in a looped finite-state structure, nonterminals in a phrasal projection, indices to match in a binding context, chain occurrences. It is hard to do structural linguistics without the ability to consider two symbolic elements, thereby to determine whether they are the same. Curiously, some syntactic dependencies have to be stated well beyond identity. Consider for instance:

(1) a. *John loves his children and Mary does too* [*love his children*].
  b. *John loves his children and Mary does too* [*love* ***her*** *children*].

The ellipsis in (1), presenting the so-called *strict* reading of the elided pronoun, is straightforward: the elided *his children* can be thought as literally identical to the antecedent in the first sentence, and thus Mary in this instance is taken to love John's children. But a *sloppy* reading in (1b) is also possible for some speakers—and for that the (boldfaced) elided pronoun cannot be *his*. It is either *her* or some abstract element that is not coding for gender.[24] The point is that the parallelism for elliptical purposes is more elaborate, or at any rate weaker, than mere identity.

Identity failures can be more dramatic, with the similarity more distant than implied in strict elliptical readings. Observe these contrasts from Fiengo and May (1994:218):

(2) a. **Mary admires John*$_1$*, and he*$_1$ *does, too.*
  b. *Mary admires John*$_1$*, and he*$_1$ *thinks Sally does, too.*

If the elliptical material in (2a) is *admires John*, the ungrammaticality of (2a) follows, for the elided *John* is bound by *he* in violation of Condition C of the Binding Theory. But Fiengo and May argue that such a conclusion is too narrow, given the grammaticality of (2b). If the elliptical material is *admires John* in this instance too that would still be a violation of Binding Condition C, because that requirement is not sensitive to local domains (and the pronounced *he* c-commands the material in the VP it is the subject of). It is because of processes of just this sort that Fiengo and May propose the mechanism they dub "vehicle change." Without going into their technicalities, the idea is that the antecedent in these kinds of elliptical situations can change in its syntactic form so as not to be represented as the name it elides. If what is "reconstructed" in the elliptical site in (2b) is not *John* but, effectively, (some abstract version of) the pronoun *him* instead, the relevant LF should be no less grammatical than the one for (3b):

(3) a. **Mary admires John*$_1$*, and he*$_1$ *admires him*$_1$ *too.*
  b. *Mary admires John*$_1$*, and he*$_1$ *thinks Sally admires him*$_1$*, too.*

In that form, the contrast is predicted: the elliptical *him* reconstructed in (3a) still violates Principle B of the Binding Theory. The reason Principle B is not violated in (3b) relates to the "syntax of silence"—plus further nuances: if the elided material is under the scope of *Sally admires . . .* , then that portion of the structure will shield *him* from being obviative with respect to *he*, because the two pronouns are in different binding domains. Now "vehicle change" implies some form of *similarity*: between what is elided and what antecedes it.

There are other somewhat drastic nonidentities in ellipses, as illustrated in (4) (similar examples have been discussed all the way back to Klima [1964]):

(4) *John doesn't have any money, but luckily Mary does . . . [have some money].*

Any requires polarity licensing by a negative element, missing in the ellipsis—the entire point of the continuation is that Mary does have money. But the meaning of having any money, if grammatical in isolation, would not be what is implied in (4), which entails that what is elided has to be abstract enough to range over *some* and *any*. Bottom line, in all these instances we lack formal identity, involving something like similarity.[25]

There are situations in linguistics in which it would seem as if categories have to be in some sense entirely distinct, also. One such can be described as in (5) and (6):

(5) *John might have been acting silly.*
   a. [*Might* [*John* [__ [*have* [*been* [*acting silly*]]]]]]?
   b. *[*Have* [*John* [*might* [__ [*been* [*acting silly*]]]]]]?
   c. *[*Been* [*John* [*might* [*have* [__ [*acting silly*]]]]]]?

(6) *Peter has said who saw what.*
   a. [*Who has* [*Peter said* [__ *saw what*]]]?
   b. *[*What has* [*Peter said* [*who saw* __]]]?

Considerations implicit in (5) go back to Chomsky (1957, 1995), although in (5) the examples are analyzed as in Emonds (1978), involving auxiliary movement of the sort discussed in chapter 2, and in terms of Travis's (1984) Head Movement Constraint: the displaced auxiliary verb cannot move over another auxiliary—hence the ungrammaticality in (5b) (where *have* is moving over *might*) and (6c) (where *been* is moving over *might* and *have*).[26] One way to speak of the ungrammaticality in (6) is as discussed in Rizzi (1990): in the ungrammatical instance in (6b) a Wh-phrase like *what* is moving over another Wh-phrase like *who* in its way to the clausal periphery, whereas in the grammatical (6a) the Wh-phrase *who* does not move over another Wh-phrase. In these instances, the Wh-phrase obviously moves over other elements, like the auxiliary *has* or the NP *Peter*. So "like" elements (Wh-phrases vis-à-vis other

Wh-phrases, auxiliaries vis-à-vis other auxiliaries) interfere with one another's displacements, but "unlike" elements (like a Wh-phrase with regard to an auxiliary or even a regular NP) do not. This is why Rizzi *relativizes* his minimality condition (preventing a transformation when a more local transformation is formally possible) to *types* of grammatical elements. In the negative (no movement can involve two items under these conditions), this situation does not add anything conceptual to the preceding discussion: in none of these instances is it mere identity that counts. In some sense, similarity (the factor in the minimality relativization) matters instead. But in the positive, considering the grammatical displacement paths in forming relevant chains, it appears as if it is lack of identity that matters between a displaced element and each and every c-commanding element in its categorial path toward the target of movement.

There is an even more nuanced case to study in relation to domains of rule application, when two different rules can apply in a given context. Abstractly, consider a situation as in (7), in which (7a) applies whenever the more specific (7b) does too:

(7) a. $R: E \rightarrow I$ b. $R': E \rightarrow B / \_C$

Intuitively, R in (7a) is the equivalent of asking some element E (say, an embryo) to turn into an element I (an individual), with no particular restrictions in the process; R' in (7b) is more concrete in its requirements: the process can only take place in some context C (say, from embryo E to a butterfly B, in the context of a cocoon C, in the metaphorical example). When faced with this sort of rule operation disjunction, grammars could apply either rule unpredictably, attempt to apply both rules, or use some other principle to order the rules. In contrast, following ideas already in Chomsky and Hale (1968), Kiparsky (1973) argues that (at least phonological) rule disjunctions of this sort arise only if governed by a requirement dating back to the Sanskrit grammarian Pānini, which Kiparsky dubbed the Elsewhere Condition. This restriction forces the operation of a given rule R to be overridden by the application of a more specific rule R'; so in (7), (7b) trumps (7a). This is because R applies when the string XEY is encountered for X and Y arbitrary variables; in contrast, R' applies in a narrower set of circumstances, when the more specific string $XECY$ is encountered, where the latter is a subcase of the former.[27]

The Elsewhere Condition is so-called because it obtains whenever grammatical ambiguity arises if a process relevantly applies *elsewhere*—in which case the more specific possibility wins. Chomsky (1955:101) already presented context-sensitive rule pairs, the first of which has a context stated and the second avoids the cumbersome and unilluminating listing of all contexts except that in the first, by describing that situation as "else." In connecting to the Pāninian tradition, Kiparsky (1973) effectively rationalized the condition in terms of learnability considerations, as emphasized ever since Chomsky (1965). For an example of this approach, Berwick (1985) postulates a Subset Principle amounting to learners guessing the smallest possible language compatible with the evidence received.[28] In a sense, learners are daring enough to come up with possibly new structures, which is the central Chomskyan approach to Cartesian creativity. But at the same time, even creative learners have to be, in a related sense, conservative, particularly inasmuch as we also assume they are incapable of processing direct negative instructions. The issue here is for a learner not to make the wrong guess in situations of putative process ambiguity, as in (7). The beauty of syntactic rules is that they apply beyond the narrow confines in which they are first encountered, but that is also their risk: we do not want the creativity to take the learner to a place where only a negative instruction would correct a guess that does not correspond to what the grammar actually sanctions, because that would create a learning paradox. A learner who goes with the most specific option is not taking any risks with regard to the domain of the rule application: should the guess be wrong (the particular grammar, in fact, allowing the less marked structure), positive data directly allow an extension to such a super-case. We must then reflect on how the more specific subcases are generally ascertained.

Actual situations in which the Elsewhere Condition applies can be even more interesting than the somewhat obvious *XECZ* counting as a subcase of *XEZ*. Key to the condition is the inactivation of a process *P* on the basis of a property of the rule system *S* that *P* instantiates, together with a crucial logical entailment that a process *P′* also instantiating *S* applies whenever *P* does, but not the other way around. It does not really matter for this logic whether the processes are morphosyntactic or anything else: they could be phonological, semantic, or whatever is rule-based, if the general learnability logic obtains. For instance, a classic instance is the comparative *-er* or superlative *-est* blocking in English alternatives with *more* or *most* for (roughly) bisyllabic predicates. This is why we say *larger/largest* (instead of *more large* or *most large*) but the semantically comparable *more* or *most sizeable* is fine. The morphologically simpler form, if grammatical, outranks the more complex one. Lasnik (1981) presents a comparable account of "*do*-support" in English; Zeevat (1995) raises the condition in the context of idiom formation; and similar considerations apply elsewhere. But the reason we raise the matter now has to do with a somewhat curious application due to Horn (1972), having to do with paradigms of the general form in figure 5.1. We need not be exhaustive now, as we are simply asking what it means to be in the presence

a.

+	–
or	*nor*
and	**nand*

b.

+	–
possible	*impossible*
necessary	**innecessary*

c.

+	–
healthy	*unhealthy*
sick	**unsick*

d.

+	–
happy	*unhappy*
sad	**unsad*

e.

+	–
pretty	*unpretty*
ugly	**unugly*

Figure 5.1
Partially lexicalized paradigms

of a grammatical paradigm. Horn's treatment of case (a) involved the exclusion of *nand* on the basis of the more specific *or* and *nor.*

There are three steps to the reasoning. First, whatever satisfies coordinator *and* (e.g., *authorities lie **and** authorities tax*) also satisfies coordinator (nonexclusive) *or* (*authorities lie **or** authorities tax*); so *pq* entails *p or q*, for *p* and *q* unrelated propositions. Second, the "lexical space" of negating *and* (what *nand* is intended to mean) is equivalent to the logical combination of the weaker *or* and negating that as in *nor*; that is, a word meaning "not and" would have to cover the more specific instances of what *or* describes (in particular, *exclusive* or, a subcase of ordinary *or*) or the also more specific instance of negating that—so the putative *nand* is less specific than either (exclusive) *or* or *nor.* Third, relevant concepts live in the same formal space, what may be thought of as a "paradigm." If all of those circumstances obtain, the elsewhere word *nand* is blocked by the existence of the more specific notions.[29] The exact same logic obtains for case (b), involving modal expressions, and similar analytical expressions—which we leave as an exercise for readers to verify.[30]

Matters are subtler for the other examples in figure 5.1, because it is not logically the case that situations in which sadness, ugliness, or sickness obtain apply whenever happiness, prettiness, or healthiness does not. Need a person who is not sad (ugly, sick) be happy (pretty, healthy)—but not the other way around? Logic does not seem to yield an obvious answer, although a cognitive analysis might. Our own intuitions differ, to be honest, and are not particularly robust. Which is all to say that subcase situations can be quite subtle, not a matter of simple subsets in a set-theoretic sense, logical entailment, or anything like that. With that caveat, the rest of the Elsewhere Condition seems to apply, possibly for the same general reason. If your mind works in such a way that you take sadness to be the elsewhere case, then happiness is a marked situation—and then your safe bet as a learner is to maximize that lexical space, in detriment of the space of "sadness." We are only making a cognitive (and learning) point here. For creative learners with only access to generalized positive data, it makes sense to proceed conservatively, at least in situations for which a risky bet could not be safely corrected.

In our view, it should be clear that notions like identity, or even similarity, play no obvious role in understanding paradigms as in (7). Instead, one certainly needs Boolean notions like negation or complement conditions, perhaps entailment—though we say that with caution, inasmuch as we also saw how perhaps mere implicatures count, with a broad cognitive base that we have little to say about. Our only point is more modest: the structural circumstances under which certain combinations are possible go well beyond statements about like categories, into surely more arcane sorts of formal dependencies, whatever those turn out to be.

5.3 Features, Similarities, and Beyond

One approach to the difference between identity and similarity is in terms of features. *Who* and *what* are different words, but they share the same Wh-feature. The push toward making features relevant to the computation was anticipated already in Chomsky (1955) (e.g., in the implicit system of categorial features in the appendix to chapter 4 there, which was absent from the 1975 version) and is quite apparent in Chomsky (1995:chapter 4), and more generally in Chomsky (2000) with the introduction of the notion of Agree. This is a dependency between feature attributes of the same kind whose value is locally calculated within a given domain. Features are also a central component of the BPS proposal in Chomsky (1995:chapter 3), which defines categorial projections in terms of the feature system in Muysken (1982). That distinguishes ±*min* and ±*max* projection features to get the three types of combinations attested in language: heads (+*min*, −*max*), maximal projections (−*min*, +*max*), intermediate projections (−*min*, −*max*). The system crucially assumes that there is no such thing as a (+*min*, +*max*) category. For that to be the case, the ±*min* and ±*max* features must be privative (not binary) and the marked value plus (as opposed to the default value minus, indicating absence of a value) must lead to a specification that is in some sense contradictory when applied to the *max* and *min* attributes. That situation is common in arithmetic. If a scalar is positive that ipso facto entails that it is not negative, and vice versa; a scalar cannot be both positive and negative. But just as arithmetic becomes complex as we invoke imaginary numbers—and such numbers are not incompatible with real numbers, leading to complex numbers or vectors—so too other features are not privative. We saw this, for example, in our discussion in chapter 4 of segmental (consonantal vs. vocalic) and categorial (verbal vs. nominal) features, which are binary and compatible in all combinations. This is how Chomsky (1974) predicted *four* types of major "parts of speech": nouns [+*N*, −*V*], verbs [−*N*, +*V*], adjectives [+*N*, +*V*], and prepositions [−*N*, −*V*].[31] We ourselves made central use of this sort of formal system when separating types of bistrings. Which is all to say that, aside from identity and similarity statements, the grammar makes use, also, of notions like inverse (for privative features) and orthogonal (for binary features).

Before reflecting on the matter more generally, and to emphasize how these issues are not arcane in the rigorous functioning of the system, consider one more situation:

(8) a. [*Who were* [*house representatives asked* [*whether to impeach* __]]]*?*
b. [*Why were* [*house representatives asked* [*whether to impeach the president*]]]*?*

Example (8a) is along the lines presented in Ross (1967:29) to argue that Chomsky's Wh-Island Condition is too strong.[32] Here we are interested in contrasting it with a version involving movement of *why*, of the sort systematically studied in Huang (1982). The first example involves an argumental gap (as explicitly signaled), whereas the second does not, as it involves adjunct extraction. As Huang noted for comparable examples in Chinese, there is no way that *why* can modify the embedded event (the impeaching) across *whether.* Contrasts as in (8) were central to the approach to locality in Lasnik and Saito (1984, 1992), which serves as the basis for the Minimalist treatment in Chomsky (1991) and Chomsky and Lasnik (1993) (chapters 2 and 1, respectively, of Chomsky [1995]). The idea is to capitalize on the "uniformity" of the adjunct *why* chain as compared to the "nonuniformity" of the argument *who* chain. The former is uniform in that the Wh-phrase never starts in an A-position (being an adjunct) and it stays an Ā (that is, non-A)-dependency given that it is integrated into a Wh-chain. This uniformity cannot be relevant for argument *who* because it starts in an A-position and then displaces to an Ā-position. One can then argue that uniform chains are sensitive to intervening material like complementizer *whether*, whereas in nonuniform chains there is a way to bypass that stricture.[33] What matters now is the distinction between A and Ā sites, which is crucial to the reasoning. There are various other differences between these, which were touched on in chapters 3 and 4, when we alluded to the dissimilar behavior of chains of the A and Ā sort. In particular, we are interested in both the idea that A-positions are *like* other A-positions, or Ā-positions *like* other Ā-positions—in ways that seem to be distinct from how A-positions are *unlike* Ā-positions. So here too the grammar seems to be making use of some elaborate notion to state the uniformity of an A-chain and an adjunct Wh-chain, as compared to the lack of uniformity of an argument Wh-chain. There is nothing "similar" about these, beyond the fact that they are chains. Or to put this more positively: whatever similarity may exist in the system treating these objects as chains (e.g., in terms of putative "collapses" in the sense of chapter 4), the system cannot ignore the differences that allow us to treat the objects as behaving in predictably distinct ways.

We are going into these matters here because we consider them to be central to syntactic structuring and what a grammar must capture. From a machine learning perspective, if one wants a system to seriously abstract out these elaborate structures from a data corpus, it will not do so with an algorithm that identifies only like elements. In principle, it could be that a century of linguistics, dating back to Ferdinand de Saussure, is all wrong: the features, the categories, the phrases, the chains, the derivations, their interactions, and all. That is always a possibility in empirical science. But if anything is even remotely on track—as we have tried to argue in this monograph—then it is strange to expect it all to fall into place by tracking stuff that is similar to whatever can be spotted without any (or very weak) priors. If the system's priors contain some interesting organizing glue (a formal equivalent to the features, the words, phrases, etc.), then success may happen. But we would argue that, then, the Devil is in the priors: call those "innate" and we can all go for a stroll in the forest.[34]

Because we are trying to be positive with the exercise, we would like to end this section considering a would-be machine that learns differently from the ones we are accustomed to. Let this be a thought experiment, having little to do with machines limited by present-day technology. It was quite a feat, already, to move from machines only recognizing identities to others capable of understanding similarities. Success in that is not alien to linguistics or the cognitive sciences. Howard and Juan are not identical, and many devices can recognize that. But clever devices could start breaking us into smaller predicative bits, for example, signaling our love for syntax, fondness of our teacher Noam, appreciation of music, and so on. Those are among many of the features we share in common, just as we have other features not in common: for example, Howard is slightly taller than Juan, and Juan is slightly younger than Howard. Track our features and you can in principle see where we differ and where we don't, and the same could be done about our siblings, parents, children, friends, and so on. The apparatus that one needs for that strikes us as present, in some sense, in our lexicons, so we are not surprised that success can happen in cognitive analyses extending such metrics of similarity by friendly statistical tools. All music to our ears. But not enough—is what we are saying.

Now imagine another device that, in addition to reasoning by similarity, can also ascertain what we have been pointing out for syntactic features: opposites, orthogonalities, perhaps inverses in some more general sense and within some algebraic space. It does not much matter to our point, yet, what extra power such a hypothetical device would have, so long as we are willing to understand that it needs to go beyond similarity. Moreover, let's idealize, just as we did with the bee-dance example. Before we go into the incredible complexity of human language, consider a simpler arithmetical exercise, which we will also propose in the form of another friendly challenge for our electronically inclined friends and colleagues.

First let's present the simple formal facts:[35] Imagine a world that only has zero and as many natural numbers as we wish or have the power to represent. For expository simplicity, suppose we use the familiar Arabic digits, although one could state our problem in any notation or numerical system. The device we are imagining has very few priors: it can add any two numbers and can compare results.[36] We are imagining that the algorithm has the ability to see "likes," in both number and digital representation: it can find out (by averaging the results of many sums) that 4 is more "like" 2 than 3, or 9 more "like" 3 than 5, and so on. We realize that this would be trivial if the device knows how to multiply, but we are explicitly trying to assume that the device has not been programmed with anything that complex. In fact, for this device it is also the case that some arbitrary number like 314 is in some sense "like" 314314 (a mere repetition of the random combination of numbers) or like 314314314 and so on—a fact that, as such, may lack mathematical significance. In other words, the device is no mathematician. The question is how much this device can learn about the number system by letting it play with the random combinations it starts with and can combine by addition, if it is allowed to examine them in terms of arbitrary many iterations of dumb searches for "likes."

We have something else in mind. Consider the obvious arithmetical fact in (9), still using the 314 combination (or any other random combination readers wish). Because of how multiplication works, if were we to multiply 1,001,001,001 times 314, the result could be organized as in (9a). We will not prove this now, but we think it is easy to see that so long as the number of 0s and 1s in the first multiplication factor is the same as the number of random combinations of digits in the second factor (here three, for 314), and we always start that sequence with a 1 and follow it with only 0s—finalizing the repetitions with another 1, so long as we stick to repetitions of that pattern—we will have the general geometry in (9b). As a result, the product will amount to a periodic repetition of the digits in the second factor, whatever they happen to be. While this has, so far as we know, no mathematical importance, it may be computationally interesting in that it provides a simple way to numerically relate a random series *N* of natural numbers (or 0 meaningfully placed, not to the left in familiar conventions) to another number whose numerical representation "cyclically" repeats *N*, as in *NN*, *NNN*, and so on. This is the sort of string N^n that finite-state loop recognizing string *N* produces by iterating *n* times. The object that relates *N* and N^n is of the form $[100\ldots]^n1$ (still using the superscript notation in the Markovian sense).

(9) a.

$$\begin{array}{r} 1001001001 \\ \times 314 \\ \hline 4004004004 \\ +1001001001 \\ +3003003003 \\ \hline \mathbf{314}\mathit{314}\mathbf{314}\mathit{314} \end{array}$$

b.

$$\begin{array}{r} [1\ [000\ldots0]_{n-1}\ 1\ [000\ldots]_{n-1}\ 1\ [000\ldots]_{n-1}]^{m-1}\ 1 \\ \times [p\ldots qrs]_n \\ \hline [s\ [000\ldots0]_{n-1}\ s[000\ldots]_{n-1}\ s[000]_{n-1}]^{n-1}\ s\ldots\ldots\ldots_1 \\ [r\ [000\ldots0]_{n-1}\ r[000\ldots]_{n-1}\ r[000]_{n-1}]^{n-1}\ r\ldots\ldots\ldots_2 \\ [q\ [000\ldots0]_{n-1}\ q[000\ldots]_{n-1}\ q[000]_{n-1}]^{n-1}\ q\ldots\ldots\ldots_3 \\ \vdots \\ [p\ [000\ldots0]_{n-1}\ p\ [000\ldots]_{n-1}\ p\ [000]_{n-1}]^{n-1}\ p\ldots\ldots\ldots_m \\ \hline [\quad [p\ldots qrs]_n\ [p\ldots qrs]_n\ [p\ldots qrs]_n\ p\ldots[p\ldots qrs]_n]\ m \end{array}$$

So what? Well, this game is easy for humans to play. The first question to ask is whether a current machine learning device can already generalize something along the lines of the pattern in (9), if it is encouraged to seek "likes," basically inducing this:

(10) If one adds any given series of random numbers *N* to itself a total of *m* times, for *m* a number of the Markovian form $[10^{d-1}]^k1$, where *d* is the number of digits in *N* and *k* is arbitrary, then the result is another number of the Markovian form N^m.

So for instance, if you add 314 to 314 1,001 times, you get 314314 (or in Markovian terms, as a string of characters, 314^2); if 1,001,001 times, 314314314 (i.e., in the same terms, 314^3); if 1,001,001,001 times, 314314314314 (i.e., 314^4); and so on.[37]

Any middle schooler can do more than that, given the game we have proposed. For example, they can reason: "So if adding 314 to itself 1,001 times

I get 314314, that must also mean that, if I do the opposite, taking away 314 from 314314 a total of 1,001 times, I eventually end up with the very element I am subtracting." Thinking in terms of opposites comes very naturally to middle schoolers—we know by experience! We have no idea how they do it, but they are especially keen to try such a gimmick if it happens to be the contrary to what a parent says. If they have the time and inclination to keep asking questions—as tends to be the case—they can furthermore start puzzling over what would happen once we have reached 0, whether we could continue taking away 314 from nothing. Or if we could perhaps pack the process efficiently so that adding 314 to itself can be done more rapidly, and once that is achieved, whether one cannot do the opposite of that, and so on. We are sure readers have had similar experiences playing by themselves or sharing with others on the puzzlement that arises with numerical expressions like these, which only get more interesting as they deepen: What would it mean to do the inverse of packing a sum into a multiplication? Does it have any meaning to pack multiplications too? Is there an inverse of that? Does that putative inverse have any meaning?

For a linguistic being, it seems impossible not to go into such questions, which presuppose the sorts of "unlikes" we saw as necessary for syntactic analysis: inverses and comparable creatures. Can we imagine a mechanical device capable of trying some of these inverses, even in the simple arithmetic exercise? To be sure, such a device can be programmed to do that in instances of the sort we have sketched; we are not saying these are not computable tasks. But the challenge is to have the device come up with the inverses out of its own iterative behaviors, in whichever way we care to let it "go wild," as our children do. We mean that part of the challenge in total innocence and with serious hope; we are willing to celebrate in admiration if one makes progress with such a purely mechanical device. If not, we can always invite our more philosophically inclined friends to tag along for a reflection on what this might all mean. We ourselves have no idea. While understanding that having inverses, orthogonals, opposites, and so on be cognitively innate deepens the mystery, the fact that nature somehow figures them out reminds us that nature may be smarter than one can imagine. Judging from the behavior of electrons, protons and neutrons, that probably should not surprise us. We hope there being "room at the bottom," in Richard Feynman's celebrated phrase, implies more than physical room for tiny stuff to happen. Perhaps there is room also for the explanatory apparatus that some of this innate stuff would seem to require. All we are saying is that machine learning either does or does not "see" beyond the surface relations in (9). If it can without being programmed to do so or presuppose the entire numerical edifice where such algebraic twists are represented (the number line, plane, and so forth), we ought to see that device at work. It should prove useful to have it work with such simple puzzles, before worrying about defeating Garry Kasparov at chess or Chomsky at linguistic analysis.

5.4 A Sketch of the Dynamical Model

We hope we have proposed two entertaining machine learning challenges, involving the evolution and acquisition of bee waggle-dances and the discovery of algebraic patterns in random combinations of natural numbers. The third and final challenge will be less of a puzzle than an even friendlier suggestion to collaborate. While we cannot see how machine learning could induce the sorts of structures we find in language (and nature more generally) with simple (e.g., connectionist or Bayesian) mechanisms as proposed in the literature, we suspect devices of the right sort may be able to help us find dark data, as they do in physics and economics. This is, in other words, an invitation to seek funding together. We can, and do, compete and let agencies adjudicate. But the world may well be a more interesting place if we work together.

We see this monograph as an extended argument for structure. We won't repeat it now: it is just what we and our colleagues do for a living. But we have tried to be candid about the ways our system can be pushed toward a deeper understanding. We have focused on some of these matters in the speculative chapter 4, where we were clear about areas in which we know there is still obscurity—for example, for A- and Ā-positions—but it is an open matter what the relevant definition should be, given Minimalist considerations. When facing such internal challenges, we have pointed in an analytical direction based on what we understand to be the program and the problems that arise. For example, we proposed bistrings as a way to articulate information files that are clearly sensitive to potentially global syntactic specifications while keeping track of NPs as special syntactic categories. There may be better alternatives, but our formal proposal is explicit enough to be evaluated and criticized as relevant. Meanwhile, we have gone into the implications of the system we have been sketching, particularly inasmuch as it is sensitive to various levels of an FLH. For us chains are real enough to make into single bistrings (just as super-chains may exist too, leading to entangled structures across bistrings). At the same time, simpler phrases are equally real, even if they are not chains. Moreover, even simpler (flat) collections of words seem real too, even if they are not phrases. "Being real" simply means that the interpretive components (phonetics and semantics) interact with the syntactic entities, which results in something that makes it "to the airwaves" and is structured "internal to minds."

To be explicit, our system needs to recognize at least the following object types:

(11) a. ***Many many many*** *scientists* ***work hard, think deep, and write carefully.***

b. ***Convicts kicked the bucket*** (**so that rulers could boast that the bucket was kicked.*)

(cf. *People paid taxes so that rulers could boast that taxes were paid.*)

c. ***Which picture of himself*** *did John say* $^{\textit{which picture of himself}}$ *Peter liked* $_{\textit{which picture of himself}}$.

d. *Mary* ***admires John's critics***$_1$, *and he*$_1$ *thinks Sally does* $^{\textit{admire his1 critics}}$ *too.*

In (11a) we see iterative and possibly flat structures as discussed in chapter 1. If all one found were word-level iterations as in (11a), one could argue that such structures can survive to the LF component and be interpreted in some noncompositional fashion.[38] But this is harder to see for iterated phrases (*tons upon tons upon tons of lies*) or phrases flatly conjoined. On one hand, we want a Markovian syntax to ensure the relevant flatness with the consequences discussed in chapter 1; on the other, the phrases are still real. We return shortly to the implications of such a fact. Example (11b) shows how the idiomatic interpretation for *kick the bucket* is lost on passivization (as in the parenthetical). It is interesting whether theta-roles more generally, not just idioms, require a purely phrasal or configurational interpretation, as in the theory proposed in Hale and Keyser (2002). Either way, at least some structures with an idiomatic shape must be interpreted in some phrasal fashion, their integrity being lost on transformation. In (11c) we simply show a complex chain as is amply seen in chapter 3, whose collapse can be in different contexts depending on the anaphor's antecedent. Clearly a chain like this is not a configurational object, but a super-configurational combination that ranges over the contexts (or occurrences) that the chain can collapse as. Finally, in (11d) we show what amounts to a super-chain, or collection, this time, not so much of configurations, but entire chains. Note that in this vehicle-change situation what entangles across domains is *admires John's critics*, which contains at least the chain formed on displacing the theme *John* within the nominal (the critics are *of John*). In addition, as we saw per Fiengo and May's (1994) argument, the elided chain cannot contain *John*, but instead the chain presents an abstract pronominal version. It is still somewhat unclear under what conditions these super-chains are licensed, beyond elliptical parallelism, although structure is certainly relevant, inasmuch as c-command is presupposed.[39]

In sum, lists, phrases, chains and entanglements have to be structurally recognized, in some form or another. Interestingly, perhaps, just as entangled super-chains appear to be chain collections, so too chains themselves seem to be super-phrases, or configurational collections. Configurations too were classically seen as list collections, although that depends on exactly how Merge works within a BPS system.

In addition, one cannot simply and statically wait until the end of the derivation to process this collection of richly articulated structures. Observe (12) to begin with, which is ambiguous in too many ways for us to list them all without going off on a tangent:

(12) *No man's fans within his clan, no woman's allies from her clique, or respective relatives ever like to fight each other.*

The meaning that interests us to make our point is one in which the antecedent of *each other* is the collective, so the putative fighters are taken to be not just the fans and the allies, or the allies and the relatives, and so on, but rather the entire plurality that aggregates all fans, allies, and relatives. If we follow the argument we provided in chapter 1 for such structures, the conjunction must coordinate its members *without phrasal structure*. But two of the conjuncts in (12) include the licensing of the bound variables *his* and *her*, which the quantifiers *no man* and *no woman* must bind so as to provide a distributed reading of the man's fans and the woman's allies. So the flat structure can only arise *after* the binding. The only way this could happen is if the system is "cyclic" enough for chunks of interpretation to be processed all the way into an LF dependency while, at the same time, dominating phrases can still be taken by the system in simpler ways, prior even to being considered in a configurational fashion.

A similar argument can be made without invoking the finite-state considerations emphasized in chapter 1, by considering a contrast as in (13):

(13) a. *They threw the president's critics to the lions.*
b. *They threw a bone to the president's critics.*

Clearly *throw to the lions* and *throw a bone* are idioms. Also, in one instance the idiomatic phrase has a variable open for the theme thematic role (*x to the lions*) whereas in the other there is a variable for the goal role (*a bone to x*). This will be important for the argument, as we see momentarily. It is also clear that the phrase *the president's critics* has undergone a transformation internal to the NP, with the theme in a specifier position. In other words, an expression like *the president's critics* is no longer a mere phrase—it contains a displaced item within, making it (contain) a chain. Linguists have argued whether ditransitive constructions involve a theme structurally lower than a goal or it is the other way around, with the goal structurally lower than the theme. This is why it is significant for us to have idioms, with the same verb *throw*, of the form in (13a) or (13b). In at least one of those constructions, for X a verbal argument, it will not be the case that *throw* + X constitutes a phrase. It is not important now whether it is *throw a bone* or rather *throw to the lions* that is not a phrase—it is even possible that in neither case do we have a phrase directly involving *throw* and one of its arguments.[40] The point is that, in one of those cases (or perhaps both), after having entered the transformational component, the grammar must somehow derivationally return to a more basic structure so as to reinterpret it idiomatically, for it never existed before as a phrase that could be directly interpreted in such a way. The situation is analogous to the one discussed for (12), in the sense that, after having entered the phrasal component, the system must return to a structure and somehow provide a flat interpretation.

These "returns" to the derivation would have been impossible in the P&P system of Chomsky (1981),[41] although they seem very much in the spirit of the equally dynamical system of Chomsky (1955). Whether they are possible in the current Minimalist Program depends on how precisely one formulates the derivation. We will not undertake this exercise now, beyond sketching what we believe is necessary and possible within current models. Just to review matters from that perspective, the system is generally assumed to start on a lexical array (often called the *numeration*, as in Chomsky [1995:chapter 4], though that is just one implementation) of lexical tokens constructed from the lexicon.[42] A selection process Select allows us to place a pair of items in the active derivational space Δ, so that Merge can start producing phrases. As a given phrase K is assembled within Δ, Select keeps bringing other heads out of the numeration, arbitrarily and monotonically extending K. The extension is assumed to be at K's root. We will not delve now into issues that may arise in terms of Merge being mediated by featural dependencies, although that matter arises (at least) when (long-distance) agreement is invoked. Bear in mind that Merge produces phrases, whereas it is assumed that the numeration is a mere list of disconnected items. This thus poses an interesting issue, regarding the Markovian structures emphasized in chapter 1.

A way to obtain such flat structures is by pulling token lexical items out of the numeration and placing them in Δ, our derivational space, *without merging them*. In other words, if we want to generate a list of sins like *pride, lust, anger*, and so on, to form the sentence in (14a), we start by pulling these elements out of a numeration as in (14b) and place them in Δ as in (14c), with literally no merger whatsoever,[43] then to pull *pillory* out of the numeration and having this verb merge *with the list* as in (14d). For that, we need to determine what it is to merge *to a list*:

(14) a. *Priests pillory pride, lust, anger, etc.*
b. {$Priests_1$, $Tense_1$, $pillory_1$, $pride_1$, $lust_1$, $anger_1$, $etc._1$}
c. Δ: *pride lust anger etc.*
d. Δ: {*pillory*, {*pride lust anger etc.*}}

Merging to a list may be just that: a binary relation between some word like *pillory* and another object, which happens to have no structure beyond having been placed in Δ. Some may balk at that prospect, but we see no reason to. Remember, we argued for phrases in chapter 1 under certain circumstances. Our arguments were based on constituency tests and, ultimately, structurally ambiguity resolutions that presuppose semantic compositionality. But this is squarely what is missing in the list. So far as we can see, then, nothing prevents such a weak derivational commitment as merely (randomly) placing items in Δ, thereby operating *with that*. One can preclude that by definition, but we see no reason to add such a stipulation, particularly if the unstructured list is interpreted as an unstructured list. Occasionally a cigar is just a cigar.

Readers may perhaps be still worried about how to linearize the items in the totally unstructured list, because depending on our definitions (in particular of exactly how it is that the list merges further up as in (14d)) they may all actually c-command the others (in particular by being dominated by all the categories that end up dominating the list). So the items in the list cannot be linearized (by Chomsky's [1995] version of Kayne's [1994] LCA). But note first how the method in (14) will work only for words that we pull out of the numeration. It is enough to recall (12) to see how many lists are composed of complex phrasal objects—a problem we have left open. We can address both this problem and the LCA issue just raised by allowing the derivation to (i) spell-out multiply when linearization needs arise, and (ii) *renumerate* items that have been placed in Δ. The renumerating idea is discussed in Johnson (2002). It amounts to taking a derivationally derived item and placing it back into the numeration, for further derivational use *as a lexical unit*. Nothing short of that would seem to resolve the idiom concerns we've raised. For concreteness, suppose derivational states arise as in (15) and (16), with object shift to the *v*P periphery and ignoring verb raising (as in Lasnik 1995) or the structural details of the double object construction (here modeled on Chomsky and Lasnik's [1993] proposal):

(15) a. *They threw the president's critics to the lions.*
b. [$_{TP}$ *They* [$_{vP}$ [*the president's critics*] [$_{VP}$ ***threw*** [[$^{the\ president's\ critics}$] [***to the lions***]]]]]

(16) a. *They threw a bone to the president's critics.*
b. [$_{TP}$ *They* [$_{vP}$ [*a bone*] [$_{VP}$ ***threw*** [[$^{a\ bone}$] [*to the president's critics*]]]]]

The important point is that we have, by hypothesis, a chain involving *the president's critics* in (15) and *a bone* in (16), so that we may assume the DOWN occurrence in the first instance, and the UP occurrence in the second, to be ignored, with that chain collapsing UP or DOWN so as to leave behind whatever is necessary for the idiom, boldfaced in each instance.[44] Now we are not done yet: some component of the grammar must take care of interpreting both [$_{VP}$ ***threw*** [[$^{the\ president's\ critics}$] [*to the lions*]]] and also [$_{VP}$ *threw* [[$^{a\ bone}$] [(*to the president's critics*)]]] as the idioms that they are. While allowing the early spell-out of the idioms is a step in the right direction, the phrases then treated as a PF unit, that in itself says nothing about interpretation. Johnson's renumeration, however, could do just that, if elements in the numeration are effectively tapping the lexicon directly. That is, if we think of this lexical array as "placing the lexicon on call," in such a way that if an item is derivationally placed in the numeration, our lexical memory of it is set in motion—and we can interpret that item as a concept. In turn, if we are allowed to renumerate items like idioms, we see no reason to prevent an exercise of this option with lists as in (14c) and (14d). Recall that we have no LCA way of linearizing *pride lust anger etc.* But if we can renumerate it in whichever order it had been placed in Δ, then we would freeze the list and, thereby, be able to interpret it that way. Renumerating the list in either order may have the basic effect of linearizing it in morpholexical terms,[45] subsequently to be interpreted in the relevant order, if that makes any (e.g., stylistic) difference, which is often the case.

An interesting issue is how to generate looped structures like *never, never, never* and the like. Clearly, we have no way of telling whether there even is any order among the repeated items, all being literally the same. Are these real token elements or, instead, occurrences of the same formal sort as we get in chains? An argument about the objects being mere occurrences is the fact that we can pronounce them multiply. Then again, it is not clear that we are decoding each in its own right, as opposed to some aggregate which the system interprets as intensity or emphasis of some sort—and in that sense may be equivalent to syllabic elongations as patent in expressions like *neeeeeeever!* If the latter is the way to go, perhaps there is a single item in the numeration, initially, and we loop it into multiple items by selecting into Δ, self-merging it as many times as one wishes, thereby creating multiple occurrences of a trivial (head) chain, then to renumerate the entire sequence of said occurrences into an iterative structure. Having multiple occurrences would prevent a compositional interpretation (assuming that the chain is a unique item). Perhaps the iterative externalization is only one among possible ones, including a more holistic externalization by placing emphasis on the stressed vowel.[46] For us, this is important now only inasmuch as it separates derivational stages involving selection, merger, linearization, and renumeration. We will not elucidate how these interact with one another; we are simply posing the matter as an interesting exercise to resolve.

We would like to also briefly ponder what it means to be part of a syntactic object, in general. In graph-theoretic terms, of the sort for instance in Ginsburg and Partee (1969), disconnectivity is akin to semantic irrelevance: there cannot be a compositional semantics to items that are not part of the same graph. But this is not a problem in the present framework in two different respects. First, we are not seeking a compositional semantics for the items in a list; quite the opposite, for relevant items we are suggesting that compositionality is at best irrelevant and at worst it yields the wrong results (recall note 38). Second, we are not and have never been committed to graphs as syntactic representations. Indeed, Lasnik and Kupin (1977) explicitly argued even against set-theoretic PMs generated by Post rewrite rules of the sort introduced in Chomsky (1955) (which have a direct graph equivalent, as can be proven in the terms of Partee et al. [1990]); this was in favor of more streamlined objects that are *not* naturally generated by phrase structure rules. As we saw in chapter 4, there is a way to streamline said objects even further: via our R^3PMs, where bistrings live. In the relevant algebraic objects, we see no reason to prevent portions without any significant structure, so long as this is derivationally contained in a sort of formal "bubble" that continues to merge on its own, per the renumeration mechanism.[47] The idea makes no sense in E-language terms, because a formal language is based on string or graph definitions that presuppose connectivity. We are not doing E-language, however, but pondering the putative properties of I-language, within the biolinguistics enterprise. We are prepared to admit that something we are not considering rules out this proposal with total lack of connectivity for certain items; we are simply unclear as to what that something would be, and meanwhile we take the null hypothesis to be the possibility that the items in the list are "just there." Frankly, we see no way to avoid something like this for sentences like (14a), which present portions that would seem to behave very much the way texts do at a different level: with only very indirect relations between the separate items that are just placed side by side.

There is one more general topic we want to return to, as it was raised already in chapter 4: the situation emerging whenever a monotonical merger extending the root of PM K by adding further heads to it has to go into a halt, so as to start merging another phrase L, eventually to merge L as a noncomplement extending K. Technically, we execute that next step by placing K on a memory stack S, so as to continue working with the merger of L within Δ. There are interesting issues noted in chapter 4 that arise when connecting whatever x is in Δ and whatever y is on S, as well as how information within each Δ and S works with regard to one another, if connectivity exists. The entire motivation behind the MSO proposal is that only material that is active in Δ can be operated on, including linearization mechanisms like the LCA. Agree relations also take place within an active Δ, from features within a head (the probe) at the root of the PM and into the complement domain. The creation of chains as seen throughout this monograph apparently starts in domains first signaled by agreement, then to "pied-pipe" phrasal structure dominating the item probed into (the goal).[48] Matters of phasehood and related domains can then be stated on these probe-goal relations. The only thing we have added to that architecture (aside from biting the bullet of disconnected items) is Johnson's possibility of renumerating phrases as lexical items, for the reasons discussed involving idioms, with consequences, also, for "flat structures."

We also showed in chapter 3 many situations that cannot reduce to simple phases and extend beyond so long as c-command obtains. This was our motivation behind exploring reduced PMs in the sense of Lasnik and Kupin (1977) as constructed from relating BPS objects generated by kinds of (external and internal) merge to strings of words. It is an interesting question precisely when in the derivation that, in our terms, *tensor product* is to take place. It has to be early enough for the ensuing objects to feed the LF component, in which binding and other licensing conditions are checked. But late enough for linearization conditions to have been executed already, for instance, so as to determine which chain occurrences are to be pronounced. That suggests that our proposed tensor product is part of the transfer process itself, at the point in which the system creates semantic representations on the basis of what we called reduced RPMs, which still allow us to keep enough information to establish the major scopal and construal dependencies in LF on its way to interpretation. It is worth noting, also, that for our R^3PMs to have global significance, we must be able to aggregate the fragments emerging in association to a given phase to a subjacent phase, arbitrarily many times. The fact that our bistrings are vectors integrated into matrices allows us a simple matrix addition to result in the extended objects, although sorting out the specifics of such an additive procedure (and how it may relate to the transfer mechanisms and phasal dependencies, particularly in situations of transfer halt as alluded to at the end of chapter 3) is something that we will not pursue beyond this programmatic sketch.

That is roughly the invariant part of the system, presuming a variety of locality, uniformity, and other conditions that make derivational steps necessary only as a last (derivational) resort (see Chomsky [1995] for the classical statement). It is, in that regard, a squarely Minimalistic proposal, only extended beyond the usual phasal confines and into the bistrings that, when collected, allow the information components of the system to keep open active referential files. Presuppositional structure is presumably encoded that way: a system along these lines is centered along referential possibilities, which add content to denotations by way of whatever information happens to be asserted and presupposed in given syntactic uses, each of which lexically activates said concepts. In this view the lexicon is operational all the time, syntax navigating on the formal ocean of its putative connections. Some realize into concrete thoughts that materialize in the form of sentences, or better still derivational spaces built from lexical arrays, which enter in and out of activity with the computational progress of any given derivation.

Variation in that system, which learners have to acquire to navigate particular conceptual regions of this mental space that coalesce into a given I-language, apparently arises within places in which the structure is not fully specified, especially as interactions ensue. For example, in the linearization interactions, general word orders are witnessed, as per Kayne (1994), especially in the Chomsky (1995) variant (though see also Fukui and Takano 1998; Abels and Neeleman 2012). Depending on which portions of chains systematically collapse UP or DOWN, "timing" possibilities effectively take place: a language whose chain occurrences are generally linearized UP will exhibit "overt" movement, as compared to a language systematically acting otherwise, generally in the spirit of Fox and Pesetsky (2005). Various other possibilities could occur, also, contingent on how processes actually deploy; for example, whether they favor head-to-head dependencies or, instead, they materialize as phrasal-to-head possibilities (all of it relating to works too numerous to mention, from Baker [1996] to Snyder [2016] at least). We are agnostic about which other possibilities may emerge across languages, for there is nothing in our system that favors some options over others (for example, our proposal is consistent with Sheehan et al. [2017]). Finally, at a more superficial level, aside from arbitrary choices for words and cultural selections (what is idiomatic in one language need not be in the next), it is possible that languages differ on what other renumeration ranges they permit and when, that too being arbitrary. It is known, for instance, that some languages realize plural morphemes by repeating the singular form: in Malay *rumah* means 'house' and 'houses' is *rumahrumah.* Neither marking plural by the reduplication nor doing it by a morpheme like *-s* seems deeper than the other (and see note 46), which we take as manifestations of microvariation—for example, in the sense of Brandner (2012).

5.5 In Search of Dark Variation

All of that said, while microvariation seems easy enough to spot, and in our view related to the flat possibilities that associate to renumerations and morphological dependencies in general, a harder question is what forms of macrovariation may arise. Up to now the way to proceed in that regard has been to pay attention to the work of typologists and to hopefully generalize it beyond their initial observations. That is how linguists came up with putative parameters—and what keeps being challenged too. This kind of "discovery procedure" approach leads to some postulation or other,[49] which the next language over either verifies or not. Usually that means that, given counterexamples, all proposals have had to return to the drawing board. Our hope is that new technologies will allow us to do better—therein lies our third and more practical challenge. In our view it necessarily involves at least two steps, which can run concurrently.

Step one only involves experimentalists to test the veracity of our model. In a nutshell, if there are forms of at least micro- and macrovariation (or possibly more within the latter category), there should be observable effects for our psycho-physiological devices to pick up. It does not matter much, to us at least, whether the observation is made behaviorally or neurologically, or even cleverer methods could be used to test the matter. From our perspective, the issue boils down to the following. Consider:

(17) a. *Have they any time soon?* [a′. *Do they have any time soon?*]
b. *Go they any time soon?* [b′. *Do they go any time soon?*]

In brackets in (17) are two grammatical sentences of American English. Obviously the other sentences in (17) are not grammatical in this dialect, although to native speakers (17a) sounds less unacceptable than (17b).[50] We do not know, by the way, whether the difference between (17a) and (17b) is one of micro- or macrovariation, but this is the kind of situation that may allow us to test the matter: whether violations of macrovariants are worse to one's ear than violations of microvariants are.[51] The hope is that some serious experimental technique is more reliable, whether in the particular contrast in (17) or in others that we can all easily construct. We understand that we would be comparing hypothetically ungrammatical sentences for how bad each is, but we suspect that this issue can be controlled by a clever experimental setup, for example, telling our subjects that the task we are after is having them examine the sentences of a foreign friend trying to learn their language, which the token utterances in (17) are examples of. The subjects could then be given some task to keep them focused while accepting that not everyone learning a new language speaks with the same ease—for instance, having them suggest alternative phrasings—all while the experiment is actually measuring reactions to the hypothetical ungrammatical environment (e.g., in tracking eye movement, watching event-related potential or magnetoencephalography readings). We have nothing deep to say about the experimental nuances, beyond commenting on the relevance of experiments along these lines, in a sense seriously testing "degrees of grammaticalness."[52]

Step two in our challenge goes beyond the community of linguists who can help with ascertaining the differences between micro- and macrovariation, as noted. Suppose we convince ourselves of the reality of that prospect and we start cleaning up some central corpus in a language of choice, so that we have a sufficiently parsed material beyond what already exists in electronic repositories. By that we mean not just that words are appropriately tagged with their syntactic category—however we achieve that already nontrivial task—but furthermore that significant chunks of the corpus are parsed into at least elementary trees. We understand that parsing our R^3PMs will not be achieved any time soon, because we are just proposing them. But significant parsers already exist even for standard Minimalist models, at least for English. To be sure, said parsers, as is necessarily the case for any engineering device, implement whatever theory was in the market at the time of their design, which we may have quibbles with of the sort exercised throughout this piece.[53] But some structuring is generally better than no structuring, even if we may need to go into a passionate dispute over the proposed analyses. At any rate, that is what we have, and we are perfectly content with that. Here comes the punchline: We believe that machine learning analyses of those parsed structures could be a useful way to determine whether there are unexpected correlations at that structural level, between portions that have been structurally parsed and for which we give the devices similarity metrics and other such mechanisms to find "likes."[54] We mean garden-variety algorithms that match correlatives according to some (e.g., featural) metric.

Admittedly, that is meant as a fishing expedition, but aren't all machine learning explorations just that? Also admittedly, we don't want that expedition to spontaneously give us phrases out of words or chains out of phrases, with the clever machine doing for us what decades of theoretical linguistics is struggling with pinning down. Rather, we want the sophisticated algorithms to work *with* us, guided by our educated guesses—for example, about what features matter to the system. We know, say, that grammars care about such features as tense, number, case, and so on, instead of color or loudness. Color features are easy enough to spot, even in lexicons, and loudness is obvious even in speech, separating screams from whispers. No matter, if a machine learning algorithm is actively seeking those easy-to-spot features, it would probably be wasting time and resources in ways that, we wager, would be less obvious for what we take to be "grammatical features." The same is true about many of the other phenomena we looked at in this book. We have emphasized, for instance, how NPs are special. A machine attuned to seeking correlations among NPs will be doing something more useful than one seeking correlations among prepositional or adjectival phrases. It may seem to nonexperts that this is just common sense, but it really is not. There is nothing commonsensical about relevant relations of construal being sensitive to c-command strictures or about head-complement relations being more central to the system (e.g., in defining theta roles or domains of probing in agreement circumstances) than specifier-head relations are. It may take a lifetime for an algorithm to figure that out, just as we suspect that the algorithm exploring the numerical relations in (9) is not going to do very well beyond finding repeating identical patterns. But the combined effort of one such powerful algorithm and a team of linguists seeking long-range correlations or testing for macrovariations could be rather powerful. If others are ready to sit at the table to discuss the matter in roughly these terms, then we are too.[55] We find that useful, although we are willing to be agnostic even about those parameters that we ourselves have worked with over the years. If the matter is articulated in some version of the program we are sketching now, we are prepared to encounter parametric correlations that would not have even occurred to us, especially as the class of languages to examine grows every day.

5.6 Tentative Conclusions

In this chapter we have considered language variation, the underlying cause for needing to acquire different languages. We have separated what we believe may well be *three* different types of variation, each progressively deeper in structural terms: (i) statistical microvariation, (ii) parameters arising in elsewhere (subcase) conditions, and (iii) dark macrovariation. While variation as in (ii) has been considered for a long time within generative grammar, and as in (i) is the driving force for connectionist approaches first and then Bayesian models, our proposal in (iii), though admittedly a shot in the dark, is also meant as more foundational—and certainly possible within our "mixed" system.

We have argued throughout for a deep transformational component, together with a less complex phrasal system that generative grammar shares with structuralism. In addition, from chapter 1 on we have argued that even the surface system of essentially flat structures has an important role in grammar. So the architectural question boils down to whether variation is possible in all three of those structural divisions, and if so, of what kind it is. Putative variation in an unstructured system should be superficial, geared more by data-driven statistical considerations than variation in the more convoluted domains of the grammar. Conversely, if such a serious transformational component exists, it is natural to ask whether it even has any variation; it may not. Then again, we are prepared to raise the question of what it would mean for the system to vary at its very foundations; if it does, then variation of that kind ought to be as profound as the one arising in architecture, for example, depending on whether a building's foundations are set on granite or a swamp: the New York skyline, rooted on the Manhattan schist, would not have been possible in the Washington, DC, Mall, which had to conquer the Potomac waters.

Aside from allowing us to rationalize otherwise hard to understand linguistic data patterns, our mixed system is natural in a biological system. For instance, immunity has two distinct components: the archaic so-called *innate* immune system and the much more modern (in evolutionary terms) *adaptive* immune system. Organism physiology is the result of a complex interplay among three familiar factors: biochemistry, chance, and still poorly understood third factors relating to complex dynamic systems; the ensuing systematicities work well enough to survive and prosper at evolutionary scales. Until a pandemic hits or a contextual circumstance (like the climate) changes, and then all bets are off. Because we think of language as a natural system, we expect all three factors to be playing significant roles in the ensuing system. As a consequence, we believe it too optimistic to expect the system not to present the sorts of nuances that any other physiological system would, from deep (and hard to spot) architectural correlations to relatively superficial contextual emergences.

In our specific proposal, we see human language as presenting at least three different developmental stages, in a sense akin to a metamorphosis. First an axial organization that could even be seen as prelinguistic (whatever such terms mean at this level of abstraction) in that it may take place prior to a baby's babbling stages. Second, acquisition proper, more or less in the traditional sense. Third, a mature atomistic state, in which children are active members of a community that they take pride in being part of. Needless to say, these could vary from individual to individual in different ways. For instance, a baby may babble a little earlier than others, just as they can start walking at slightly different moments and with different initial strategies; similarly for when a child starts idiomatizing expressions. In a different sense, these divisions are somewhat fluid; thus, our admired Ken Hale apparently kept the ability to acquire a second (or fiftieth in his case!) language with the tools we believe a baby uses, while most of us cannot. But even for normal human beings, there is such a thing as "talent" in acquiring other languages as grown-ups, which possibly means having some access to the abilities of a child. And most of us are, to some extent or another, multilingual, which forces us to also think on how we switch from one language to another, and whether that is a comparable process as children or grown-ups. While we do not have answers to these questions, our point is that a theory about a physiological system ought not to be too dogmatic in establishing its methodological boundaries.

Science must idealize, which is why Saussure set aside diachronic linguistics when pursuing his structuralist system, or Chomsky concentrated his early work in Hebrew or English. As progress is made, however, it is reasonable to ask whether certain idealizations are too strong and it is better to try something else, none of which can be determined a priori. In our case, our argument for the developmental system was proposed in chapter 1 as an attempt to address what we dubbed Jackendoff's puzzle. Our view is that, early on, toddlers acquiring language proceed like generative semanticists: letting syntactic conditions interact with the acquisition of lexical items. By "generative semantics" we don't mean the exact systems proposed in the 1960s with generative tools of the time, as much has changed since then. We mean any system imposing computational restrictions on this task, like the Distributed Morphology project (and others in the literature that fit the present bill). Our point is that toddlers use such devices not just to form words, but also to acquire new ones, this being why they are so good at it. However, that slows down before puberty, as we start acquiring idioms and become aware of certain ways of saying things that mark our group identity. That seems like a system transition.

We have no idea why that happens, whether it is driven by hormonal changes of the sort culminating in puberty or that the sheer dynamics of group formation settles into these patterns for some reason. To us, the important point is that, from that point on, children start acting like atomists, taking words as units of sorts that lack internal transparency and with less open-minded creativity to expand vocabularies—or at the very least depending on group acceptance for certain creative uses to become the norm. All of that obviously requires statistical analysis and can profit from the tools that our colleagues in those areas of the field have aptly explored. In that sense, it is not surprising, we think, that philosophers analyzing language should see it exhibiting lexical properties lacking systematicity, productivity, or transparency. Such is the case for the adult language, which in our terms starts pretty much before puberty. But if, in contrast, one studies what toddlers do as *also* language, even if still being acquired, properties fit the generative semantics bill much better.

It may seem strange to think of what toddlers have as language, if it is being acquired. Although by that metric, who really has a language, if we can always add a new expression to it? Obviously, we all continue to expand our lexicons, with more or less fortune, until death or mental decay prevents us from learning anything new. But from the beginning we have said that we take our structural study to be one of I-language, understood as a mental procedure. In that sense, a toddler with under one thousand words is as much a language user as Shakespeare; all we are really saying is that young language users may be deploying syntactic tools, which lack the atomistic emphasis that becomes patent later in life, for some reason, when all the core parameters of their language are set and what's left is to set identity-determining microvariations.

This way of seeing things leaves us with a nontrivial puzzle, especially in those toddler years. Again, we are happy with, say, a Bayesian approach for the atomistic phase of the system, with all the consequences. We are also prepared to consider some sort of epigenetic basis for the very early stages of acquisition, prior to even babbling or fixing eye-gaze in babies. We have often joked privately about macroparameter setting as akin to getting a key protein through nutrition or the microbiome, with consequences as drastic as this has for a bee larva becoming a queen or a worker. We have no idea how that would work in the case of language, but we see no reason to rule it out and would go as far as to say that something that momentous may well cut the otherwise daunting problem of language acquisition in half (or as many portions as macroparameters of that ilk may exist). With those two, early epigenetic and late atomistic, stages as boundary conditions, the real problem is left in between, as it were, babbling and puberty. Those are the years in which toddlers turn into running kids, and somehow in the process they are acquiring just about any language they are exposed to.

We call that a "problem" and not a "mystery" because our hope is that a serious understanding of whatever "generative semantic" devices result in acquisition (whether as Distributed Morphology or anything else) might become a promising enterprise. But that said, it is also perplexing how to conceive of that period in which "children are like sponges" if what happens before is a form of, basically, growing, and what happens after is clearly learning, what in between growing and learning is in the middle? We don't know. We have a hard time understanding the nature of data in this stage or whether it is even data in the sense that we recognize for the learning, final, stage. That particular puzzle starts earlier, because—jokes or metaphors aside—we also do not know what sort of epigenetic conditions lead to fixing a macroparameter. Is that even information? Does it relate to brain biochemistry? No one knows, which also leaves the in-between stages somewhat in the dark: what needs to be set are phasal structures of some sort (with heads first or last, categories pronounced or elided, and so on). But we really have no idea yet even whether what children are paying attention to are words (whatever that means at an early stage) or higher-order cues, whether phrases or Boolean generalizations over something or other. It is easy enough to speculate, and we know of several speculations, but for now, all of it is grounded on relatively little beyond attempts at asking ourselves what it all could possibly be, barring fairly obvious impossibilities such as negative instructions.

If all of that sounds like an admission of ignorance, that is exactly how we mean it. We find that more profitable than pontificating about one particular approach over the others, in customary nature-versus-nurture mantras. (Is it all a Language Acquisition Device setting marked options? It is all statistical generalization?) To us the answer to whether it is nature or nurture is a resounding yes. Which won't be saying much until we figure out what each of the approaches yields and how (in our own approach) the process transitions from mainly nature to mainly nurture, in only a few years.

Thus, we do not see our colleagues doing machine learning, of different kinds, as opponents. Quite the opposite, we see a lot of potential for profitable collaboration, and in that spirit we posed three friendly challenges to their community, which we would be happy to collaborate in solving. The first comes from our own preference to start with modest and tangible goals; studying the case of bee waggle-dance, which has fairly well-understood structural conditions and where radical experiments with the model organisms are possible, seems to us like a great opportunity. The second stems from our attempt to separate linguistic predicates in terms of identities, similarities, and beyond (with different mechanisms to capture each: a formal system with identity conditions, featural division, and orthogonal/inverse conditions); just as the field has explored mechanical devices to induce "likes," it would be important to ask ourselves whether such an approach is possible, to begin with, for theoretical *inverses*, in a formal sense. Finally, part of the reason we remain friends with our machine learning colleagues is, frankly, because we have a hard time seeing how we, on our own, could find genuine macroparameters.

We said this already but will repeat it again: it is very possible that none of the parameters ever proposed in the last four decades is a genuine exemplar of what we are thinking of as a dark parameter. Still, the fact that one hasn't found yet a dark parameter (just as we don't quite understand many other "dark" entities out there, some of which seem crucial to our modern syntheses in many sciences) doesn't mean they are missing. For us, these elusive entities of open-growth programs may well exist very early on in the process of language acquisition, when for all we know the language experience may even be purely prosodic or holistic (we ourselves can't tell). But should they exist as we suspect, searching for dark parameters in annotated corpuses of languages across cultures could be a fun exercise. Let alone a way to help preserve our cherished linguistic diversity, which is being tragically lost as we write.

6 Conclusions and Future Research

In this monograph we have reviewed the main arguments for the existence of structure in language, from the lowest levels of the FLH up toward "context-sensitive" territory where the fun is. But not *all* the fun, in our view. In chapter 1 we argued that just as the existence of transformations does not invalidate phrasal relations, so too the existence of the latter does not invalidate "flat" relations either. Language is complex and, to capture its nuances, we believe one needs mixed computations with at least finite-state, context-free, and (mild?) context-sensitive correlations. Humans also run bipedally, which combined with almost complete alopecia apparently made us phenomenal long-range hunters. But that did not mean we ran all the time or for we lost all our hair. Similarly, ellipses, construals, displacements, and all the wonders that make our thoughts as powerful as they are, do not mean we cannot hold a dead child in our arms—possibly with the same pain as any other ape would have—exclaiming "No, no, no, no, no!". Giving a compositional analysis to such an expression seems to us less reasonable than asking what is the relevant structure of the sequence.

Throughout this book we have taken a biolinguistics, or even Evo-Devo, approach to language as a natural object. It is from that perspective that, while formal considerations seem central in attempting precision in the analysis—which we have fully embraced—there also ought to be room for initial physiological constraints, growth considerations, attention to learning restrictions if direct negative instructions are essentially useless, and so on. Much of that is over and above statistical considerations of the sort central to classical conditioning and, in revamped form, machine learning and other such neo-associationist takes on the problem. It would be irrational to deny any role to that sort of machinery and therefore to statistical analysis more generally. The issue is whether all there is to language can be reduced to inducing regularities from data or instead the other (physiological, developmental, acquisitional, performative, etc.) conditions end up loading the statistical dice with "priors" in the relevant computational devices modeling the phenomenon. In effect, we are issuing our monograph as a friendly challenge to our statistically minded friends and colleagues: roughly (at least) something like what this book presents is what needs to be given an account. How much "emerges" from interactions on a trivially tensorized network with no priors, and how much will require elaborate such preconditions to yield anything coherent, is something we all ought to benefit from studying. We are agnostic in this regard: it will be interesting no matter what, and we should present the enterprise as a collective effort.

One example of this collaborative spirit we are aiming for is our suggested treatment of what we have presented as Jackendoff's puzzle. Much ink and some blood were spilled over the basic idea in the sad form of the so-called Linguistic Wars. That is precisely the kind of situation we're trying to avoid, for civil wars have always been the most uncivil. Generative semantics had great descriptive and analytical contributions to make; some of the best linguists of all time have been generative semanticists—and they were shortchanged in the course of history. In our view, the Minimalist Program as presently pursued would have been unthinkable without their contributions. Interestingly, many of the arguments against their radical decompositions of lexical items (where the rubber met the road) still hold against current decompositionalist approaches, often without even an awareness of this fact. It continues to be true that sublexical relations are not systematic, productive, or transparent—and (those being the hallmarks of a computational system) one ought to ponder what that means. Our own modest proposal has been not so much eclectic as nuanced, or so we hope: just as tadpoles or caterpillars radically grow into frogs or butterflies, so too we have suggested that learners grow from "generative semanticists" to "atomists." Then researchers can have their cake and eat it too: at the early stages we do expect sublexical computational properties in the very acquisition of new words, yet as the system stabilizes, atomistic considerations settle in, resulting in an opaque system that is good for syntactic processing.

Aside from being conciliatory, our idea is certainly testable—more on this shortly.

The rest of the monograph proceeded in similar terms. In chapter 2 we tried to clarify what is meant by "structure dependence," in the technical transformational sense that is often not paid attention to. This is important again these days, because new powerful algorithms attempting to extract structure from data corpuses, so far as we can tell, come short of abstracting out such structural dependencies. The best systems we are aware of seem capable of recognizing that a phrasal structure already present in a data set *is* actually there. This is not trivial. Older algorithms, without present-day capabilities for distance-metrics and other analyses of similarities, were not capable of that much. At the same time, language is more than that, and until someone shows us an algorithm capable of dealing with long-range structural correlations, we remain skeptical as to how those kinds of structures could be extracted from the data. In addition, it should be clear that a very nontrivial issue is how structure "got there" to begin with—if some algorithm is going to spot it. Even if the computational sciences end up producing a future-generation algorithm capable of abstracting structural-dependency (in the technical sense), the language sciences more generally still need to explain what it is about said correlations that makes them part of the relevant data sets.

In the same general vein of presenting structure in detail, in chapter 3 we went from standard conditions on transformations and rules of grammar to long-range correlations (that is, reconstruction "superpositions" and cross-chain "entanglements"). Many of us pay our bills doing these sorts of analyses, and it is important for other fields to gain at least some understanding of what has been achieved. We may be biased, but we find this remarkable. We encourage anyone interested in language to make an effort to understand how these are not arcane or cabalistic considerations: they are very real properties of language after language, their universality being the main reason to take them seriously. We also urge our own colleagues not to oversimplify. Many such relations do not, possibly cannot, follow from local considerations. That *all-you-need-is-merge* mantra has got to stop, because, desirable as it may have been, it's false. It serves no purpose to shortchange ourselves in such a central topic.

In chapter 4, we attempted a formalism to carry the computational system beyond local derivations *by phase*: what we described as R^2PMs, or string matrices including syntactic labels. We went there because this is a formal system we know, so we plead familiarity in our defense. But we have tried to be fully explicit, so our idea should be easy to prove wrong. In the process, we think we came up with some new and interesting observations about the overall system, for example, its insistence on constraining noun-noun dependencies. We have no idea why that is, by the way, and it is all too easy to blame this on cognitive speculations. But *that* the grammar holds nouns (NPs, names, pronouns, construals among those, etc.) as central seems very hard to deny. We were cornered into that by our formalism, curiously.

Finally, we tried to wrap things up in chapter 5, where we studied what we take to be the main theoretical predicates (from identity to inverses and other such notions) in determining syntactic structure. Very interestingly, interactions among structures for which such theoretical constructs are central actually vary from language to language. We find that remarkable, for a cognitive system, particularly when the resulting forms must be acquired by new generations of learners with mainly positive exposure. Solving that wonderful problem has always been at the crux of generative grammar, and we think it continues to be the cornerstone of the edifice. Our idea has been to suggest that, just as structure is not uniform and computations are mixed (going "up the FLH"), so too variation is different depending on how central it is to the structural edifice. Some will be peripheral and some will be core; moreover, learning each type of variant may be an entirely different process.

This is yet another place where our cooperation across the language sciences seems central. First, because we actually suspect that current connectionist or Bayesian systems (and similar such algorithms) may well be all that is needed to capture peripheral variation, often referred to as microvariation. Paul Smolensky's Harmony Grammar, for instance, has already made progress in that regard. At the same time, we suspect core variation, sometimes referred to as macrovariation, to be of a different kind. Then again, taking that idea seriously requires two different arenas in which cooperation and attention to one another's work seems key. First, our very divide among types of variation is something that ought to be tested in neurolinguistic, psycholinguistic, and other experimental arenas. If we are right, different kinds of ungrammaticality, arising from using structures "of the wrong language" in a dialect whose structural distance can be controlled for (neighboring vs. distant variants), ought to give different results in speakers. Ideally, we would see different "markers" (of brain events, eye-movements, etc.) depending on the micro- versus macro-variable. Second, to even measure structural distance, or *find* distant variations that are hard to spot even for experienced typologists, the work of machine learning devices would be priceless. Here the collaboration would have to go both ways: relevant algorithms could not just search on raw databases; rather, the relevant corpuses would have to be structurally annotated—by structuralists.

In a more technical fashion, and to wrap up this final summary, we have also made some interesting progress in pure syntactic terms. For example, we argued in chapter 4 that what we called "bistrings," depending on whether they are anchored on nominal projections or on orthogonal verbal projections, present portions that the interpretive system "sees"—is able to put that in a file buffer—and also what remains within the hidden computation interactions. We suggested in passing that this creates the equivalent of a *computational stack*, if information in construal files is to be parsed, separating what is computed in general from what is, in a narrower sense, specifically interpreted. We attributed the interest of grammars in constraining relations involving NPs or *among* NPs precisely to this division of labor. It is conceivable that this kind of architecture is behind a fundamental capacity that humans have associated to their language system: their ability to parse syntactic structures.

The entire parsing phenomenon is literally at right angles to the derivational construction of syntactic structures. The latter are presumed to work "bottom-up," starting in the deepest, noun-anchored, embedding, for reasons that we will not rehash. But obviously readers are parsing these sentences from *this* word to the *next*, so linearly and normally starting with information that for the most part has little, if anything, to do with deep thematic dependencies articulating verbal events. This is the main reason why human parsers need to be of the analysis-by-synthesis sort, also for reasons that we are presuming now, as we have throughout the book. If nothing else, such a clever way of "dividing and conquering" the syntactic representation—a fortiori implying structural "chunkings" like phases/cycles in the task—presupposes both (i) a nontrivial memory for structure, and also (ii) the ability to "turn structure on its head," so that it can be recognized not just in the form it was produced, but in some "inverted" guise too.

One may have a sophisticated structural mental system without an associated parser, as may well be the case in other apes or animals more generally. Such a creature may be extremely smart in relevant regards (computing, for instance, individual ways of navigating the world or analyzing it to some extent or another) and even somehow be expressive about it all. And yet the creature in point could be solipsistically "trapped" within the mental confines of that possibly very personal world. It should be easy to see that endowing such an organism with even a rudimentary parser (for at least some of the high-level structures that conspecifics express) would have an enormous value for a social species, helping it articulate groups of some sort. But we will not speculate on the nature of such a parsing mechanism beyond noting the needs that articulated structure imposes. The orthogonality of bottom-up syntactic structuring versus left-to-right linearity in speech is well recognized, but there are other orthogonalities we have touched on in passing, particularly if syntactic structure goes into context-sensitive territory, allowing for long-range correlations (of the agree, bound-variable, or construal sort). One needs a sophisticated memory buffer to parse a subject associating to a predicate coming thereafter, but the memory needs to be much more articulated when involving antecedent relations over arbitrary stretches of structure. It is in this context that semantic files seem crucial, and we have provided some formal representations (the bistrings of chapter 4) to let us talk about their structural nuances, in terms of c-command, identity, similarity, orthogonality, inverses, and so on. We are only scratching the surface of these bistrings here, to note that they (or something like them) must exist to capture relevant structural dependencies, as we saw even into "the syntax of silence."

Another potential space for collaboration among fields, within the language sciences, stems from fleshing out the details of a maturational approach like ours. If one argues for a transition from a "toddler state" to a "child state" in language acquisition, one owes an explanation of what it is toddlers do differently from older children, and for how long. Descriptively, we have at least a sense of (i) this happening (for most people) only until the onset of puberty, when second languages get harder to acquire, and (ii) it correlating with the tendency to atomize structures that we have related to the prevalence of idiom formation. For us, the issue is the same that arises for a child over-regularizing the English **goed* over the irregular **went*—a stage that doesn't last into adulthood. We essentially claim that the cognitive mechanisms allowing a child to "retreat" back to *went* are of the same general sort that allow a child to interpret, say, *boil down to* as "reduce," over and above a literal compositional interpretation of that phrase involving ebullition.

Although we haven't developed this here, we are forced into the following logic. First, we must grant to the baby, bootstrapping language in syntactic terms, the ability to cast a syntactic net of hypothesized relations over to-be-acquired lexical items. The acquisition itself being dynamical—in the sense that it has to start somewhere, and it will be partial until at least all open parameters are set—the actual priors a baby may be deploying in the acquisition task may change from day to day. The child is literally building the airplane as she flies it. Still, the general approach of this early learner will be to apply whatever syntax she can muster, at the relevant acquisition time, to the best possible parse of incoming data, generalizing from that in her production. One such baby may have successfully parsed tokens like *Daddy baked cookies* or *Mommy asked questions* to induce from those and similar tokens a past-form assigned to morpheme *-ed*, thereby attempting *Doggy goed away* by direct deductive generalization. For such a baby, we must find a way to assume either that she doesn't even process *Granny went away* or if she does that she still for some reason prefers saying *Granny* ***goed*** *away*. Clearly, in the baby's grammar, the latter token must somehow override the alternative.

That baby at some point, in the toddler-to-child years, generally retreats back to the adult *Doggy/Granny went away*, which must mean that particular analysis is for some reason preferable *at that juncture*. Our conjecture is that the force behind that transition relates to whatever allows the child to even get the point of idioms, something that was not there from scratch. In our own technical terms explored in chapter 5, this presupposes what we called a *renumeration* of a phrasal construct, so that its component parts are lexically bagged as compound elements or morphemes of a complex sort. In some sense too, the suppletion *went* is, vis-à-vis the regular **goed*, a way of bagging all relevant lexical items (the substantive *go*, the grammatical *-ed*) into a single word, which we could require a renumeration to specify: the grammar has to generate something like *go*+*-ed*, but if we allow for renumeration of irregular forms, we could allow the process to accept *went* thereafter. The narrow point, now, is that babies start systematically renumerating only after parameters are essentially set and, consequently, large chunks of the lexicon have already been successfully acquired.

Aside from questions about the time it takes for a system to make such a transition (and whether it is hormonally regulated or, instead, its specifications stem from system-internal considerations), the immediate issue that such an approach poses is why it is reasonable for learners to even follow such differing strategies. If the ability to renumerate is at stake, why is that ability not there, or being systematically used, from scratch? In the terms we have sketched in chapter 5, several performance possibilities arise, from considerations about working derivational memory (which may increase with age perhaps) to issues about attention span (ditto). We will not attempt to settle the matter now, but it is important to place it in context, as it raises concerns dating back to Chomsky's earliest work on the so-called Evaluation Metric, to choose among alternative grammars given some primary linguistic data (Chomsky 1951, 1955, 1964b).

Such metrics were central to Chomsky and Halle (1968), for instance, when evaluating rules in terms of the inclusiveness of their application context: the rule with context takes precedence over a competing rule without; this was understood as a learning strategy. It is an interesting question to analyze whether, and if so how, such considerations extend to systems without rules, as was customarily assumed for syntax within the generative tradition since Chomsky and Lasnik (1977). To start with, it should matter much what the exact comparison set happens to be and whether it is potentially infinite; in general, comparisons among infinite sets are tricky if one doesn't have a definite intensional way of characterizing the relevant domains. This is the reason Lasnik (1981), following the essentials in Dell (1981), only considered finite (indeed, very small) sets of comparable morphological alternatives, as arising in paradigms for the regular **go-ed* versus the suppletive *went*. This is also why we keep taking morphological paradigms seriously, for in their very finiteness (triviality in size, really), they raise learnability issues that are entirely different from those arising for open-ended syntactic alternatives.

To illustrate, consider optional processes, like whatever stylistic mechanisms allow *I read a book about syntax yesterday* alongside the "NP-shifted" *I read yesterday a book about syntax* or the "PP-extraposed" *I read a book* *yesterday about syntax*. Even if some of these may be more marked than others (depending on unclear factors), they all seem possible. Moreover, it isn't obvious that such processes involve specific semantic or morphophonemic features gearing whatever underlies each variant. Now, it should be easy to see that, while morphophonemic comparison is by definition limited to cases like the one already illustrated (e.g., *stood* vs. **standed*), in the realm of sentence grammar there is clearly an infinite set of possible situations like *reading a book* (*an article*, *a magazine*, etc.), *about syntax* (*semantics*, or for that matter *recursion involving sentences*, etc.), it being *yesterday* (*the day before*, and so on). The way comparison works, it must be among elements that are *like* one another; for example, while *stood* may relevantly compete with **standed*, it does not with **goed* (*went* does, instead). The problem is that, in terms of first-order data, the only way to ask whether *I read a book about syntax yesterday* outranks alternatives is by going into that mouthful—which can get arbitrarily complex. One could try to make the comparison in terms of higher-order (e.g., parsed) data like $[[[\ldots]_V[[\ldots]_N[\ldots]_{PP}]_{NP}][\ldots]_{ADV}]$, but that presupposes a different level of analysis. A learner going there must have already reached enough stability in the system to compare such elaborate structures, not to speak of the memory or attention span presupposed in the task. Alternatively, the learner would not even enter that slippery slope, simply leaving the constructions as open options for their grammar to execute—unlike what we witness for limited morphological variants of the suppletive sort.

That essentially negative conclusion would limit the use of the Pāninian Elsewhere Condition, in general, to the acquisition of *morphological paradigms*. In recent years, some researchers in the Bayesian tradition have tried to go beyond that, because in those inferential terms there is a statistical price to pay the broader a hypothesis is, so a narrower hypothesis is more likely when attempting to approximate a data set. Stated from a Bayesian perspective, there is a tension between the cost of going with a more general possibility and the specificity of a narrower, though less probable, alternative. This may well be how to state a learning preference in nonextensional terms, once an I-language is assumed. Although classical Bayesian systems do not seem to care much about I-language in our sense and concentrate instead on corpora analysis. To us, it may be more interesting to consider, in addition, the specific intentional conditions leading to given learning choices, if they are even practically stateable. That would be in the spirit of Chomsky's original Evaluation Metric, although this is surely not the program current Bayesian approaches seem concerned with. Indeed, to the extent that studies of prior conditions in the system approximate the results of generative grammar, one often finds attempts to make such priors part of general theories of learning or cognitive capacities, which have nothing to do with Universal Grammar proper.

That said, one must admit also, that the role of Universal Grammar has been restricted within the study of syntax, to so-called first factors (of "language design"). As mentioned in chapter 3 and elsewhere in this book, second factors are supposed to be mostly haphazard or historical, while still unclear third factors, instead, are seen to follow from general biophysical and/or computational considerations. The tension is then direct if the latter are not supposed to be "domain-specific." In that regard, it is interesting to note how Yang's (2017) Tolerance Principle (or its corollary the Principle of Sufficiency) is explicitly taken to be one such (statistical) third factor—and yet it is presented as specific to language learning. In any event, whatever way theorists find to successfully instantiate something like Chomsky's original metric (with current statistical tools and within a nonextensional characterization of an I-language) ought to be of relevance to the maturational approach that we have explored in the present context.

Implicit in the logic of our proposal is the idea that a generative semanticist learner (broadly construed as using *some* syntax) may retreat to an atomist position later in life. While the reasoning is clear, it has learning consequences, for a child analyzing a structure as a generative semanticist is arguably presuming something *more specific* than a child going with an atomistic analysis is. In particular, the "syntactically principled" child is deploying a hypothetical network of relations, including the decomposition of items like a verb (say, *boil*), depending on whether it is being used intransitively (*the soup boiled*) or transitively (*Pat boiled the soup*), in the latter instance as something with the import of cause(-to-)boil. An older atomist child would treat cause(-to-)boil, instead, with all its thematic valences, as an atomic *boil*, homonymous with its transitive variant—with perhaps enough of a residual semantic structure to understand that if *Pat boils the soup* then *the soup boils* (Pietroski 2005, 2008). In a similar vein, for us a toddler facing *the idea boils down to nothing* is incapable of interpreting that as anything but a

Table 6.1
Development of atomism

↓ →... ...	Prelinguistic stage(s)	Decompositional toddler stage	Atomistic child stage
go	??	*go+ed*	*went*
boil	??	*the soup boiled (down)*	*the idea boils down to...*

compositional structure, bizarrely involving some boiling and some idea. What we seek to understand is how at some point the idiomatic interpretation gets to be the default—which adults only rarely interpret literally.

Thus, we see a transition needing to explicate the following developments: The vertical arrow in table 6.1 is meant to represent the open-ended space of a lexicon, while the horizontal arrow stands for developmental time. The decompositional toddler transitions to the atomistic child, in the process (according to us) retreating from *go+ed* to *went* and from the literal meaning of *boiling* (*down*) to the idiomatic one. Empirically, we know that the majority of children do the first kind of transition faster (by the time they go to kindergarten or earlier), while children may continue to be confused about adult idiomatic interpretations until later—although by puberty they seem to embrace them with gusto. It is unclear exactly what that means in developmental terms, and we will not be able to resolve it now; our point is simply that we would be happy partners in elucidating such details, which seem complex enough even in the abstract.

With the acquisition process organized as in table 6.1 (where we are not choosing to represent prelinguistic stages that, to us, are present too), it is not difficult to see different biophysiological demands at each developmental stage. Setting aside the earliest stage (in which children may latch onto patterns for nonlinguistic reasons, like emotions or sheer social bonding), by the time the learner is treating linguistic information as just that, two very different tasks await. Early on, the child needs to ascertain a system—any system that works with the input data. In contrast, as some system is already in place, the child uses it for whatever language works (thinking, expressing, communicating, lying, and so on). Our hope is that these very different needs cater to distinct learning and use strategies. To be clear, in both instances the system is being learned *and* used, but the emphasis differs at each stage. It is probably not a coincidence that during the early years, in the "explosive stage," a toddler acquires over a dozen words a day, which amounts to over twenty thousand by the time they enter primary school. They continue acquiring many words into puberty, though not so fast thereafter. By the time they start seeing idioms and liking to have their own, their grammar is adult-like—though they may still continue to acquire rhetorical devices. At that stage, idiomatization seems to be part of a trend to "make language their own," or more generally their group's, when they start laughing at parents not quite *getting it*.

For us, the technical issues to explore are how renumeration caters to the atomization and precisely when it gets to be systematically deployed. Even though it seems to be a strategy of choice by the time a fundamental syntactic scaffolding is in place, it does not seem near as rampant early on when the elements of the scaffolding are being established. Is this because the learning strategy shifts? Could it be that while the early learner is conservative, in the "elsewhere" sense we have been discussing, the late learner becomes daring and prefers to gamble with riskier hypotheses? There are ways of expressing all of that in statistical terms, whether Bayesian or of other sorts; we all shift strategies as we invest in our retirement funds, based on what goals we want to achieve: whether to grow our portfolio or make it last for a long time. We will not presume a technical analysis now beyond what we have already said, regarding the mechanism of renumeration. But it should be clear that a collaboration with learning theorists could test our hypothesis and, if it holds, push its boundaries as needed.

We cannot end without at least mentioning language decay, having concentrated on its emergence within the human mind. We ourselves feel close enough to those ages in which inevitably, and in apparently nonrandom ways, structures begin to crumble, and very curious things happen. We have seen our loved ones, for instance, "retreating" to what we thought were long forgotten childhood expressions, as if they came in the same package as long-term memories of those very years. Could those be "in a different space" or "guarded in different memory systems," having been acquired earlier? We don't know, but we do feel all of that is fair game, especially given another poorly understood architectural question: whether what we think of as different languages (which some of us appear to carry in our heads) involve literally different lexicons or portions of a single macrolexicon. That also touches on what this extraordinary system seems to do to our social constructs, which our lexicons must be, at least in part. We say this in the spirit of showing how a well-known divide—between those of us studying matters cognitively and others approaching the problem socially—also need not be as much of a chasm as it often seems. We hope it is hard to deny the sophistication of the structural nuances we have reviewed. By way of the mechanisms we have proposed (and specifically our bistrings within R^3PMs), it is easy to see how articulated syntactic codependencies, stating correlations between arbitrarily (syntactically and semantically) distant notions, can be represented. One may then literally bring into the same representation not just apples and oranges, but apples and any bizarre chimera one cares to think about.

As scientists we know how difficult it is for novel ideas to crystallize, but the point is that the linguistic system offers us the possibility to at least try. Our bistring way of representing long-range correlations is, in principle, stable enough to be able to make it into one's mental lexicon in the form of recorded presuppositions, in the hope that it may stabilize into someone else's too. That "coregistration" has the potential of creating not just one's own repository of informational idiosyncrasies, but also a network across individuals; in other words, a culture. We ourselves have little to say about how such abstract entities (comparable to economies perhaps) emerge, grow, stabilize, decay, and so forth. But we are suggesting that our structural mechanics allow them to *start*. If these initial conditions seem trivial to proponents of "social intelligence" and similar such concepts, we would be happy to compare our proposal to others out there on how to even initiate such supra-individual entities. We think the exercise could be useful.

Notes

Chapter 1

1. Strictly, there are no "grammaticality judgments." Linguists use judgments of *acceptability* from native speakers of a given language. Each of those judgments is a small psycholinguistic experiment. Nowadays judgments can be tabulated in careful conditions involving small populations, or be "directly" observed in terms of techniques to measure brain reactions to experimentally modified specifications. But ultimately a theorist must hypothetically decide whether to interpret a given observation in terms of "grammaticality" (as opposed to a host of orthogonal factors pertaining to a speaker's performance, for example).

2. As is well known, the Turing architecture involves a countable number of steps, but there are an uncountable number of sets of natural numbers (i.e., of subsets of N) (basing his approach on Georg Cantor's famous Uncountability Theorem, Gödel (1934) establishes the basic proof that eventually leads to the familiar computational architecture). Langendoen and Postal (1984) attempted to build an argument that there are an uncountable number of sentences in a natural language, English, but their sketch of a proof was based on artificial English examples. The matter remains open.

3. This book is adapted from many pieces written over the decades so typographical differences within the examples (e.g., the use of varying abbreviations) reflect different styles.

4. An operation is associative if the way in which its terms are grouped does not affect the result. For instance, multiplication is associative: so $(2\times3)\times4=2\times(3\times4)$.

5. For trivia fans, the "i" of fame from the 1998 iMac and other Apple products is often attributed to Ken Segall. *Internet* is supposed to be what it represents, though Steve Jobs also had the *i* stand for "individual." The Internet is thought to have been established in late 1988; its commercial use beginning in mid-1989. Chomsky (1986b:22) refers "to this 'notion of structure' as an 'internalized language' (I-language)." It is clear that he also means his (capital) "I" as *intensional* (generated by a grammatical procedure) as opposed to extensional. From the discussion, it is also obvious that Chomsky used the "I" as a mnemonic for "individual," which seems close in spirit to what Jobs intended a decade later for his devices.

6. Even that is already abstract: it presupposes the invariants of universal phonetic transcription. In chapters 3 and 4 we return to these foundational matters, some of which hide profound insights.

7. A *Markov process* is a random procedure with prerequisites in the transition from one state to the next. Future probabilities for any state s_i of the system depend solely on its most recent values (where "most recent" is a finite amount); see, e.g., Papoulis (1984). Markov processes play a central role in information theory (see, e.g., Cover and Thomas 2006). In the 1950s, such elementary processes were assumed to be playing a key role in language and behavior more generally.

8. A *Markov source* generates something as intricate as its states and interrelations among them. This, however, can be converted into a linear string by assuming associativity among the network elements.

9. A string rewriting system over strings from an alphabet defines rewrite rules as in the examples, with a string at the tail of the arrow being rewritten as the string at the arrow's head. Originally Post (1947) used these systems to solve so-called word problems posed for string rewriting systems in Thue (1914).

10. It is also easy to introduce other symbols in between the *a*'s and the *b*'s:

(i) Σ: S
F: $S \rightarrow aSb$
$S \rightarrow aCb$
$C \rightarrow \cdots$
$C \rightarrow$ [*relevant terminals, in between a and b, including the null string*]

The reason the number of *a*'s and *b*'s remains identical is because each of these elements is introduced as part of the same rules. If among the rewrites of *C* (the dots in the expansion of the rule) there is a different number of *a*'s and *b*'s, then that identity can be altered, arbitrarily.

11. This is useful terminology. Technically, iteration is also a form of recursion, but of a weaker kind. It is also called "tail" (or "head") recursion, in that the indefinite recurrence takes place at one end of the rewriting string. Full recursion (in normal parlance, recursion without qualifications) presents a recurrence that goes beyond these limited situations, as seen in the example.

12. This has immediate consequences for learnability considerations of the sort we raise in chapter 2 and return to in chapter 5. For example, Berwick's (1985) Subset Principle is of little use as originally stated, if one abandons a set-theoretic notion of language. As we see later, what is at issue in relevant discussion is the comparison of language portions that are more or less structurally specific—with generally the subset portion being more specific. Notions of specificity ought to carry over from formal languages to devices generating them, but the transition is far from direct or even obvious.

13. That is, an element whose antecedent for referential purposes must be grammatically determined. We discuss anaphoric relations in much detail in chapters 3 and 4.

14. We say that *A* c-commands *B* if all nodes (crucially within a *phrase marker*) that dominate *A* also dominate *B*. This is perhaps the most important structural notion within generative grammar, and it shows up across domains. We return to the matter throughout, especially in chapter 4.

15. The relevant literature is vast, but Baker (1988) is a source with much relevance to our concerns.

16. Readers can compare (21) with (12). While (12) can be straightforwardly generated with a [Σ, F] grammar, capturing (21) in those terms is less straightforward and leads to loss of generality.

17. It seems fair to refer to these formal objects as "new," because they were Chomsky's genuine contribution. They relate intuitively to objects discussed in Harris (1952), and more formally to constructs explored by Thue (1914). But their specific import within language description (for example, to capture auxiliary dependencies or the phenomenon of "voice") is due to Chomsky.

18. There is a certain reconstruction of history in interpreting the introduction of transformational rules as posing issues of context-sensitivity. In a narrow technical sense, context-sensitive rules were considered though rapidly discarded (in favor of transformations) in Chomsky et al. (1956), although Chomsky (1975)—in the published introduction to his 1955 classic—does claim (not obviously) that original lexical insertion rules were "context sensitive" rules of the phrase structure component (quotes in original). In the end, this all depends on what one means by (syntactic) "context," in particular whether context is just the left or right portions of any string in traditional systems or, in a narrower sense, the terminal string instead. An even broader use is presumed in the nonformal notion of "mild context-sensitivity," which we will not go into here.

19. For implicitly negative adjectives, anything but flatness yields the wrong kind of structure. Thus, we want to say that a *fake, fake gun*; a *lousy, lousy argument*; or a *phony, phony aristocrat* are normally understood as really fake, lousy, or phony exemplars. If the adjective took scope over a phase denoting unreal or bad exemplars in each instance, the negative character of the new adjective would result in the relevant denotation reversing in polarity (in that sense a fake [fake gun] could be seen as a real gun). So at the very least we need the flatness in addition to the more elaborate phrasing.

20. One such relevant rule for (25) would be something like (i):

(i) a. *Pred* → *ADJPred*
  b. *Pred* → BooleanADJ
  c. *ADJ* → *old, tall, tired, friendly . . .*
  d. *Boolean* → *not, and, or, but . . .*

The right-recursion rule is (ia), which is weakly equivalent to iteration as described for the examples in (4) and (5). Arguably the hierarchical structure that (ia) yields is too rich; see note 18.

21. A GT maps separate phrase markers *K* and *L* into a single phrase marker *M*. In this they differ from singulary transformations, which map a phrase marker *K* into a modified version *K′*.

22. The point can be made also with structures as follows, quoting the Google repository:

(i) a. *The comments are going to come* ***thick and fast and furious****, pro and con.*
  b. . . . *troubles will surely come, oft-times* ***thick and fast and furious****.*
  c. . . . *so* ***thick and fast and furious*** *have been the deadly encounters . . .*

The idiom *thick and fast* can be read to mean "abundant," while *fast and furious* can be read to mean "very rapidly." A bracketing as in (iia) for (i) predicts the idiomatic meaning to be "abundant and furious" and that in (iib) to mean "thick and happening very rapidly." A flat bracketing as in (iic) predicts, instead, an arguably more likely meaning such as "happening abundantly and very rapidly":

(ii) a. [[*thick and fast*] *and furious*]
b. [*thick and* [*fast and furious*]]
c. [*thick and fast and furious*]

23. It is interesting to note that the sort of artificial "sentence" constructed by Langendoen and Postal ([1984], as alluded to in note 2 for the purposes of challenging the denumerability of linguistic objects) involves coordination in its attempt to construct an infinitely long linguistic token.

24. If a complex structure can be spelled out as a unit, the system could arguably treat it as a compound of sorts, in the sense of Uriagereka (2012). Concatenation could then proceed over the derived object. We discuss this matter in more detail in chapter 5.

25. With the perspective of history, a more guarded way to say this is that, historically, the study of weak generative capacity arose in parallel to the study of generative grammar, and conceptually it constitutes an extension of the study of generative grammar that may be less central to the biolinguistic perspective.

26. Everett (2005) claims otherwise, citing as evidence his study of the Pirahã language. According to Everett, the syntax of this Amazonian language presents no recursion. For skepticism regarding such a claim, see Nevins et al. (2009). The debate goes on, as seen in Everett (2017) and the reply in Lobina and Brenchley (2017).

27. For example, Weir and Joshi (1988) observe a close relation between so-called linear indexed rules and the combinatory rules of categorial grammar. In formalisms of this sort, it is possible to get linguistic information to pass along in a phrase marker, by coding it in terms of a higher-order symbol whose purpose is basically to store nonlocal information. However, a system with lower-order symbols and nonlocal operations seems abstractly equivalent to a system with higher-order symbols and local operations.

28. So that every string in the language is longer than the next shorter string by at most a constant.

29. This is parsing of a sort solved in deterministic polynomial time—in contrast with exponential time, which would be computationally intractable.

30. Notions such as "head movement," "head parameters," "internal" and "external merge," "extraction," "relativized minimality," or "sideward movement" are not central to the conceptual point being raised: i.e., that grammars proposed to deal with such phenomena converge into the same computational space.

31. They are attempting to capture the familiar "headedness" of phrasal projections; that is, the fact that a VP must contain a verb, and NP a noun, and so on.

32. The Subjacency Condition, introduced in Chomsky (1973), states that a long-distance dependency is possible across certain domains (classically called "bounding nodes," nowadays referred to as "derivational phases") only if it proceeds in "successive cyclic" stages, from one such domain to the one immediately containing it. "Subjacent" refers to this form of internal adjacency between wholes and their parts.

33. Although, as Noam Chomsky (personal communication) points out, Humboldt, like Descartes before him, was concerned with the creative aspect of language *use*, which generative grammar (the study of the *mechanisms* that enter into this creative phenomenon) has had relatively little to contribute to so far.

34. Thus some systems are "agglutinative" (e.g., Quechua), others are "isolating" (e.g., Chinese), and intermediate cases exist as well. We will not go into issues posed by signed languages.

35. We know that the first two of these sentences do not sound natural and that the third does not quite mean the same as the other two. In the end both of these concerns will undermine the theory we are discussing, a matter we return to shortly. But for now let's ignore this fact.

36. Chomsky's (1970) specific argument was mostly concerned with Lee's (1960) transformational analysis of derivational morphology.

37. In that model having the same initial representation basically meant having the same logical form and therefore ultimately corresponding to the very same thoughts.

38. Chomsky is not moved by this argument, as he takes the lexicon to be finite and essentially memorized (points that Jackendoff disagrees with). While it is hard to prove the matter one way or the other, the fact remains that gaps of the sort under discussion exist, and they may well be relevant to the task of lexical acquisition by simply eliminating certain hypothetical words from consideration by the child. So the issue boils down to establishing this empirical point, a matter that we are presupposing in the present exercise.

39. We are thinking of the Lexicon Project (crystalizing into Hale and Keyser [2002] and subsequent works), and the closely related Distributed Morphology paradigm (e.g., Halle and Marantz 1993; Marantz 2005).

40. Chomsky has never agreed to this way of putting things. For him the meaning of a word goes beyond language, touching on cognitive systems too numerous to mention. Bringing neuroimaging results to bear on this discussion, when lexical access is at issue, diverse brain regions light up, connecting areas that, for example, would be invoked had individuals experiencing given words been actually using the objects they denote (to put the matter in deliberately provocative terms). This is in sharp contrast with the localized activity often related to narrow syntactic considerations, as argued by Friederici (2017).

41. Fodor and Lepore (1998) discuss the general problem in terms of lexical paradigms that are different from the one Jackendoff originally used, but so far as we can see, Jackendoff's structural concern remains.

42. This doesn't seem true about analytical notions such as *bachelor*, which does seem definable as *unmarried adult male*. However, few words are truly analytical, and even for those it is far from obvious that further definitional intangibles shouldn't be invoked. Thus Lakoff (1987) famously observed that the Pope (necessarily an unmarried adult male) hardly seems like a good exemplar of a bachelor. This is just part of a devastating attack on this decomposition of "bachelor" by Winograd (1976). Winograd's point was that this is as close to a good definition as we get, and it is still rather horrible.

43. Gleitman (1981) explicitly likens language learning to metamorphosis, a point that Borer and Wexler (1987) pursue further, as do other chapters in Roeper and

Williams (1987). The argument we are about to present can be seen in this light, within a more contemporary perspective on epigenetic processes.

44. These transitions are never straightforward, in growth processes in general, but the idealization as such is clear enough. Although a language learner is also a language user, and a language user, to some extent, continues to be a learner for life, there is a natural acquisition stage and a natural usage stage, which may in the end even have significantly different structural conditions (see Townsend and Bever 2001).

45. Reversals are possible, for instance, in children overgeneralizing **goed* instead of the irregular *went*, who nonetheless settle on the adult form. For situations of this general form, involving a finite (indeed small) set of choices, Lasnik (1981) argues for indirect negative evidence: in the absence of confirmation of a hypothesized default form, and presence of a marked form, the Elsewhere Condition has the effect of unlearning. We discuss this condition in detail in chapters 2 and 5.

46. Expressive idiom sharing is often the sociological mark of a group, as argued in Holt (1991).

47. What we have been discussing is not so much whether something is syntactic (whatever that means) as whether it is computational in familiar ways. Jackendoff (2002) would probably be willing to grant computational characteristics to conceptual structure as well, although that poses issues of whether there are multiple computational emergences in the evolutionary history of humans.

48. One possibility to explore in this context is second language acquisition past the critical age—and whether (or to what extent) it may involve Universal Grammar. This is a complex topic, as shown for instance in Flynn et al. (1998). We have no axe to grind on the topic, but elucidating it may provide some clarity on the different implementations of the hypothesis we are exploring now.

49. If we allow for developmental treatments, the class of analyses that this allows is larger than if we do not. It is customary to try and constrain theories so as to make learnability considerations plausible. At the same time, it seems as if Jackendoff's problem poses a significant impasse for the system as it stands. If accounts arise that do not require what amounts to a maturational treatment, we would be happy to consider them. We simply do not know of any yet.

Chapter 2

1. The qualification stems from the fact that the last few decades have revealed a powerful role of mechanisms that are not purely genetic (the classic notion of innateness in the twentieth century), but that arise from epigenetic interactions among genomes, proteomes, microbiomes, and possibly more. The classic POS argument as such is at right angles to any of this, so long as one considers structures that learning generalizations cannot induce from data sets alone.

2. Chomsky (1957:39) has an explicit characterization of the C element in (3), his (29i). The C stands for "component" or, more accurately, "long component," as discussed in Chomsky (1955:168, 232, for example). Long component phonemic analysis was systematically studied in Harris (1944), and it is behind the sorts of long-range correlations

implicit in (1), which lead to the rule in (3). Curiously, Chomsky (1955:232) specifically suggests that C "carries the long component of number." Then he notes how this element "has the peculiar feature that the verb is 'singular' when the subject is 'plural,' and *vice versa*" (234). In other words, if the subject is the plural *they*, the verb is the "singular" *run*; whereas if the subject is the singular *he*, the verb is the "plural" *runs*. Quite aside from whether that morphological observation is ultimately tenable, what is important for our purposes is the long-range dependency, here between a characteristic of the subject and a reflex in the verb, which can be arbitrarily separated from that subject, in linear terms at least. The structuralist long components have had an effect on other formal analyses of prosodic dependencies, including those that resulted in Optimality Theory (Prince and Smolensky 1993), e.g., via McCarthy (1981). The idea is also behind the current notion of Agree in the Minimalist Program (though in this framework the correlation is reversed: the Probe is in T or *v* associated to the verb, while the Goal is in the subject or similar such agreeing phrases, again arbitrarily separated from the Probe—within limits relating to Phase Theory).

3. It is an interesting computational question exactly what those "adjunctions" (in a particular direction) happen to be and how they relate standard syntactic processes with morphological specifications. This is not our focus here, but we do regard the matter as both important and ultimately somewhat unsettled, at least within the Minimalist Program.

4. In this quote Chomsky mentions sentences as being derived from other sentences (in the spirit of Zellig Harris's [1952, 1957] notion of transformation)—although the parenthetical and the formal statements in the monograph clearly mention *underlying strings*. The difference between transformations in the Harris and the Chomsky senses is significant. For Chomsky the structural analysis and structural change relate to strings (ordered sets), not to sentences as they do for Harris. In a sense, Harris's theory can be seen as part of discourse analysis (of sentence analogues), what European structuralists called "transposition" (see the discussion in Tesnière 2015 [1959]:386ff.)

5. In the ensuing paragraphs a slightly different grammar is assumed than that in Chomsky (1957), but in ways irrelevant to the issue at hand.

6. Chomsky (1968:56fn28) adds a comment: "More properly, to a string of minimal linguistic units that may or may not be words." This relates to our note 4.

7. Chomsky (1968:54fn10) states: "when I speak of a sentence as derived by transformation from another sentence, I am speaking loosely and inaccurately. What I should say is that the structure associated with the first sentence is derived from the structure underlying the second. This relates to our note 4."

8. For somewhat analogous reasons, it is meaningful to ask whether a married person happens to be bigamous, but it is meaningless to ask whether an unmarried person is.

9. Again, Chomsky's POS argument, like almost all such arguments, is based on the *unacceptability* of certain conceivable sentences, not their acceptability. This is so because there is little evidence that children are generally corrected for syntactic errors, or that such correction would be efficacious. Putnam's argument is nothing like that.

10. For example, the ability for a horse to win a race might be related to such factors as the horse's breed, its level of training, body weight, age, and so on. Then using

Bayes's theorem, such factors could be used to assess the odds of a particular horse winning a particular race, affecting its handicap or bets for and against, as compared to the probability of betting without any knowledge of such factors.

11. It is the equivalent of (dis)proving action-at-a-distance through strictly local relations: that won't do, because at-a-distance *means* nonlocal; if one redefines at-a-distance to mean local, one is playing games.

12. Although these grammars are not in the published version of the paper, we have taken them from an online version (http://www.mit.edu/~perfors/cogsci06/archive.html; accessed in 2006) that is unfortunately no longer available.

13. This is not a speculative remark: there are theories such as Williams (1981), and several others thereafter, introducing nontransformational rules that do just that, for example via the "slash notation" of categorial grammar. In such systems, designated categories effectively carry with them a grammatical context, notated in the symbol itself, which gets matched against other designated categories (such as gaps). Surely such systems are also restricted—for example, to "passing the slash" under c-command conditions, not otherwise, or other such structural limitations. It is an empirical question precisely how to constrain such systems, but it seems as plausible to constrain them in terms of some analogue of structure dependency in Chomsky's sense (now applied to the slash notation or whatever else is necessary to capture the long-range correlation that it is modeling) as it is to constrain transformations in such terms.

14. At least if the analysis is to fulfill Chomsky's goals of descriptive and explanatory adequacy for linguistic theory (thus providing us with an insightful analysis of paradigms like (1), which can be described in terms of grammatical systems that human children can reasonably acquire with merely positive exposure).

15. Lest this be confusing, children are not receiving a percentage of 7% (i.e., 0.07 in decimal notation) of relevant utterances. Rather, they are receiving 0.07% of said utterances (i.e., 0.0007 in decimal notation).

16. The average person speaks about 100 words per minute, or 6,000 words per hour speaking nonstop. Unrealistically (assuming the average sentence is 3 words in length, as most verbs are transitive), that would be a maximum of some 2,000 sentences per hour, again speaking nonstop. No one speaks or listens nonstop, so let us arbitrarily say that about 200 sentences per hour is an effective amount a toddler can pay attention to, which comes to about 2,000 sentences a day (assuming the child sleeps some fourteen hours on average since birth until the kindergarten years). Such a child would hear one or two relevant examples (of the sort in (18)) every day. By comparison, structures that seem to be normally acquired on the basis of generalizing from data, within those same general parameters, would require some 140 exemplars.

17. Berwick's argument was couched in E-language terms, in the sense discussed in chapter 1. It is worth pondering whether the same general argument can be reproduced in I-language terms.

18. We say "generally" because, although it is obvious that, say, Romance languages descend from Latin, it is unclear, for example, what language the Nicaraguan Sign Language that Kegl and Iwata (1989) studied descends from—its speakers (children who were deaf and living in near isolation during war conditions) apparently having invented the language from scratch.

19. It is debatable whether stable conditions for humans involve external pressures from other languages in the course of life (as opposed to linguistic conditions, mono- or multilingual, being roughly constant). Note that dialects are shaped up to the late adolescent years, but are harder to shift thereafter. Theories of language change (as classically sketched by Lightfoot [1991], Kroch [2001], or Yang [2013]) presuppose cross-generational variation behind the change, as opposed to anything internal to the language. In other words, variation in those terms is coupled to real learning, not natural selection.

20. Recall, for example, Stabler's (2013a) reflections reported in section 1.4.

21. In other words, one may need to index, type-lift, or go into context-sensitive transformations as seen in this chapter, to instantiate the + in the CFG+ algorithm, the formal details being irrelevant to the argument.

22. Strictly, an L-system is not a (Chomsky) formal grammar, as it does not generate formal languages. This is a consequence of the L-system lacking Chomsky's restriction preventing rules from applying simultaneously—indeed, in L-systems all applicable rewrite rules must execute their instruction as applicable. Uriagereka (2018:chapter 10) shows how cross-serial dependencies of sorts can be generated in this fashion, although it is unclear what this entails if the relevant outputs are not languages.

23. Fractality is a measure of a curve's roughness (thus, the idea that, ultimately, the curve's length entirely depends on the measuring yardstick's length), as discussed in Mandelbrot (1975). A subclass of fractal constructions is self-similar, in that its general shape recurs at any scale that one may use to observe the formal object. It is this particular subclass of fractals that independently analyzed L-systems can model, with consequences that may well be relevant to the study of grammar. See Uriagereka (2018:chapter 10) on this.

24. The issue is contentious because other theorists, notably Berwick et al. (2011), have argued that bird songs can be modeled on finite-state terms. The matter is empirical and hard to elucidate, because we humans have not found a reliable way to test whether birds exhibit phrasal structures in their behaviors. Obviously, the standard way to establish our own structural nuances (e.g., running constituency-analysis tests based on semantic considerations) are irrelevant at best.

25. When we asked Randy Gallistel about his opinion on whether other animal behaviors (whether they are related to expression and communication, e.g., in navigation or similar domains) can be modeled in finite-state terms, he responded (personal communication, February 16, 2018): "Remember one definition of a finite state machine is a Turing machine that cannot read what it has written to memory. There is no question that ants and bees both write to memory (the cognitive map, which includes location vectors and landmark and horizon snapshots) and read from it."

26. In this piece (164ff.) the idea is emphasized that language may have evolved for internal (thinking) purposes having little to do with communication. Berwick and Chomsky (2015) do not specify concrete mechanisms that could be relevant in this regard (although it seems compatible with neurophysiological ideas in Friederici [2017]).

27. As Randy Gallistel (personal communication, February 27, 2018) tells us, regarding the "push-down stacks" presupposed in the recognition of context-free languages, these "are only for storing intermediate results. A cognitive map in a vector space, where the location vectors give access to snapshots, is not something that can be done

with a push down stack." Basically, something like the pixels of an image would be very inefficiently stored in a push-down stack.

28. For instance, in rewrite terms, something like "once constituent *X* is invoked, do not rewrite *X* as anything involving *X*, and do not rewrite *X* as any *Y* such that any further rule down the derivation rewrites as *X*."

Chapter 3

1. Specifically the "chopping" (deletion) aspect, as Ross decomposed movement into copying and chopping.

2. Roughly, if *X* asymmetrically c-commands *Y*. We will return to the origins and development of c-command.

3. The Principle of the Cycle was first introduced in phonology, in Chomsky et al. (1956).

4. The first such systematic parallelism between sentences and NPs dates back to Chomsky (1970).

5. In the simplest instance, a specified subject is lexical. But, depending on what the antecedent is, Chomsky also considered specified an "empty category" (whether trace or PRO), a matter that continued to be discussed into the 1980s (see Lasnik and Uriagereka 1988). In a very abstract way, the issue is still live as we see at the end of this chapter.

6. For which there is a Minimalist approach via the Minimality Condition (see Lasnik and Uriagereka 2005).

7. Remember that the cyclic node for Chomsky in 1973 was what he labeled S, what we now call CP.

8. A situation where the Wh-phrase "escapes" an equally tensed clause with an equally specified subject. Chomsky (1973) recognized this problem and stipulated what was at the time called a "Comp-to-Comp" exemption for the purpose of sanctioning (26).

9. Combinations of obligatory and optional rules posed learnability difficulties (see Williams 1974; Lasnik 1990; and Lasnik et al. 2000 for perspective). The cycle in the sense, for instance, of Chomsky and Halle (1968) implied a sequence of rules applied within a given domain, and then again in the next such domain, and so on. That particular notion becomes moot if transformational rules may apply freely.

10. Descriptively, complementizers that allow movement "across" can be deleted:

(i) a. $[_S$* (*that*) $[_S$ *the principal would fire the teacher*] *was expected*].
 b. $[_S$ *it was expected* (*that*) $[_S$ *the principal would fire the teacher*]].

Complementizer *that* is optional in (ib) and, correspondingly, its domain allows the intermediate movement in (29b) that bypasses a Subjacency Condition violation. In contrast, *that* is obligatory in (ia) and, correspondingly, its domain prevents an intermediate movement as in (29a), resulting in violation of the Subjacency Condition. This reasoning extends to other domains in which complementizers are not optional:

(ii) a. *I regret* *(*that*) *controversies create enemies.*
 b. **What do* $[_s$*you regret* $[_s$*that controversies create* __]]?

11. Under some assumptions, the effect of Ross's Coordinate Structure Constraint as in (10) could also be predicted: if coordination requires sentential coordination (the classic Conjunction Reduction analysis, as revamped in Schein [2017]):

(i) a. *The nurse [polished her trombone] and [computed her tax].*
b. [$_S$ [$_S$ *The nurse polished her trombone*] *and* [$_S$ *the nurse computed her tax*]]
c. *Whose tax did* [$_S$ [$_S$ *the nurse polish her trombone*] *and* [$_S$ *the nurse compute* __]]

From this perspective, in (ic) the displacement of *whose tax* is arguably across two S bounding nodes.

12. Similarly, one wondered (when the Transformational Cycle was relevant) why NP or S should be the cyclic nodes or later on why complements to lexical heads cease to be barriers.

13. This is in the spirit of the "generalized transformations" of Chomsky (1955), as are other ideas that we discuss in this chapter.

14. Our term "derivational space" (first used in Uriagereka 1997:120) should not be confused with the much narrower term "workspace", e.g., as used in Chomsky (2019) or Chomsky et al. (2019). While the latter notion is compatible with ours, it restricts what we are calling the "derivational space" to accessible Merge terms.

15. Uriagereka (1999) sought not to complicate a "base" statement as in (45) with an "induction" involving noncomplements—but to let (45) apply as many times as needed to linearize these c-command units.

16. The clause-mateness follows from the SSC preventing operations across subjects, the structurally highest verbal dependent in a clause, with the TSC freeing up possibilities in untensed domains.

17. The completed coreference table for a sentence was subject to a consistency condition, so that if two NPs are marked as coreferential, their denotations must pick out the same individual in the semantic domain.

18. Already in Chomsky (1973:254n33) it is suggested that, when the subject is raised a "trace" is left behind, or "the rule of wh-Movement leaves behind a trace" (270), and more generally, "we might then stipulate that every rule that moves an item from an obligatory category (in the sense of Emonds [1970]) leaves a trace" (Chomsky 1973:269n49). This sketchy notion of trace, however, is broader than what Fiengo develops, for example allowing traces to emerge after deletion, and in some instances (ibid.) representing an intrinsically ungrammatical element in certain structural conditions: "the trace is *, in which case the sentence will be blocked as ungrammatical unless the position with * is filled by some subsequent rule." The latter idea recalls the "repair by ellipsis" analysis reviewed in section 3.3.

19. This is at the core of the unified treatment in the P&P model, which leads to interesting ideas like the PRO Theorem that we cannot go into here (but see Lasnik and Uriagereka 1988:48, 92).

20. The notion "accidental coreference" is technical for Lasnik (1976). At issue is whether NPs *A* and *B* in phrase marker *K* may happen to refer to the same individual, and if so whether that is mediated by the structural relation between *A* and *B* (whether c-command is at stake). In Lasnik's view, in essence, if *A* c-commands *B* and *B* is a

name, then *A* and *B* may not overlap in reference as a consequence of a rule of grammar. Lasnik's actual structural relation was precede and kommand, where the latter was an extension of Langacker's command from just S to both, then assumed cyclic nodes, S and NP. Reinhart (1976) showed that command is empirically almost indistinguishable from Lasnik's precede and kommand.

21. In the relevant reading, *who* and *what* form a complex Wh-operator exhaustively ranging over pairs (of individuals *x* and *y* such that *x* thinks Mary bought things *y*, see Higginbotham and May [1981]).

22. "Taking scope" is normally understood in terms of c-command by the quantifier/operator, for reasons discussed in Larson and Segal (1995) and Heim and Kratzer (1998). Simply put, a quantificational expression may be seen as a predicate of sorts, which takes as its argument the rest of the sentence where the quantifier originates and creates a variable as an "open expression". As the predicate that it is, the quantifier has to be phrasally related to that open expression, also called its scope. Compositionality expectations require the quantifier and its scope to be LF sisters.

23. Data as discussed in Pica (1987), Battistella (1989), Cole et al. (1990), and Huang and Tang (1991).

24. Chomsky's examples in English are more local than one can witness in Chinese. This has received much attention, as in Chomsky (1986b), Pollard and Sag (1992), Runner et al. (2006), among others. It is also controversial whether the Chinese anaphor *ziji* is monomorphemic, as discussed by Reuland et al. (2020) based on observations in Chief (1998), which may have consequences for the locality of the relation.

25. An example like (57c) is also degraded for some, suggesting that epithets introduce further requirements.

26. Given the following data discussed or implied in Postal (1966a), we are skeptical about such treatments.

(i) a. *I saw myself.*
  b. **I like me.*
(ii) a. *We like ourselves.*
  b. **We like us.*
(iii) a. **I like ourselves.*
  b. **I like us.*
(iv) a. **We like myself.*
  b. **We like me.*

When the subject and object of *like* are coreferent, the first person pronoun and corresponding anaphor are in complementary distribution (with caveats for (i), clearly for (ii)). But Postal notes that when the subject and object overlap in reference (the plural referent including the singular), the complementarity falls apart. Madigan and Yamada (2007) show that "inclusive reference" varies across languages: for instance, the equivalent of (iiib) is not bad in many variants (as in the Tiësto song *i like us better when we're wasted*), and even (iiia) seems possible in Kuching Malay. Be that as it may, any treatment that sanctions a pronoun when an anaphor is impossible predicts the contrasts in (i) and (ii), but it also predicts (iiib) and (ivb) to be grammatical, which is less straightforward in many languages, and in some it seems contrary to fact.

27. In particular when it is at the phase of the embedded clause, *Mary not likes you.*

28. Although it is an open question how idioms are to be interpreted (or whether they all are in the same way), Chomsky (1995:210) argued that these elements involve "base generated" sites, as do theta-dependencies more generally. It is unclear how (derivationally when) "base" positions are to be interpreted.

29. The reason it makes sense to use three levels of embedding as in (63), rather than the simpler structure in (i), is that we want to test the interpretation of chain occurrences. Consider:

(i) *No criticisms of each other's theory appear to any two linguists to be without merit.*

For a sentence like this, one could sanction a derivation as in (ii):

(ii) a. [*appear* [*to any two linguists*] [[*no criticisms of each other's theory*] *to be without merit*]]]
b. [[*no criticisms of each other's theory*] *appear* [*to any two linguists*] [[*no criticisms of each other's theory*] *to be without merit*]]]

In (iia), while satisfying its thematic configuration, *no criticisms of each other's theory* is in a position for the anaphor within to be licensed by *to any two linguists.* Even if we are forced to further displace the subject so as to license *any* in the experiencer phrase, per the reasoning in the text that, and only that, may be the chain occurrence to survive the derivation. In contrast in (63) we are forcing two chain occurrences.

30. We have not been able to find an example like (63) involving a single, atomic, item (that cannot be disaggregated into more than one chain), but which involves two separate interpreting requirements both of which are to be satisfied locally. It would have to be an element like the nonexisting **eachever*, one of whose parts is a polarity item and the other a distributor—to be placed in a context in which the polarity licensor and the distributive licensor are separate. One example that comes close is (i):

(i) a. *They seem to each appear to wonder whether the other is right.*
b. *They* ^{each} *seem to* ^{they} *each appear* $^{they\ each}$ *to wonder whether the other is right.*

Suppose, following Sportiche (1986), that the floated *each* actually forms a thematic/predicative unit with the displaced *they*, so that it is *they each* that is base-generated as the subject of *to wonder*, then to displace upward. We know since Lasnik and Fiengo (1974) that *each* has to be local to what it distributes, in this case *they.* We also know that *the other* has to be c-commanded by *each.* Alas, the relationship between these two need not be local, as (i) shows (observe how it happens across an island). But that, then, does not force us to "pin down" *each* in a position different from where it already is in (ib)—that is, local to *they.* To test a chain uniqueness requirement, we would want to find a phenomenon like (i), but where the equivalent of *the other* is also in need of being local to *each*, and the only way this could happen is if there is an *each* DOWN (in the vicinity of *the other*) while still having another *each* UP (in the vicinity of *they*).

31. This paradigm goes back to Higginbotham (1980) and is more systematically pursued in Heim et al. (1991).

32. This is a modification of an idea in Kratzer (2009), reminiscent of P&P proposals postulating "anaphoric" or even "government" features that depend on an antecedent

(see Lasnik and Uriagereka [1988] for a summary). Chomsky (1955) had already proposed that bound pronouns are lexically different from free ones, which these proposals presuppose.

33. Grano and Lasnik (2018) develop the suggestion of H. Kitahara (personal communication, October 24, 2014) that if a bound pronoun starts with defective ϕ-features, those cannot value ϕ-features on T—which is taken to trigger phase transfer.

34. It is worth noting in that regard that the phenomenon of clitic climbing, alluded to in (72), is notoriously speaker-specific. It used to be thought that it is never allowed out of a finite clause, but now it is known that this is not the case in either Slavic (Stjepanovic 2004) or even Romance variants (Terzi 1996). Terzi's paradigms are especially apropos, inasmuch as she shows how the domains in which long-distance clitic climbing in Brindisi Salentino is possible all involve bound pronouns. Importantly, though, these authors also report significant individual variation in the licensing of these structures.

35. Kayne (1984) discussed many examples of the relevant sort, which led Chomsky (1986a) to a proposal explicitly invoking a version of the Subjacency Condition based on "barrier" specifications. Note also:

(i) ??*Which book did you shelve* __ *after you wondered why no one read* ***e***?

For some, an example as in (i) degrades (this time around with the parasitic gap inside a Wh-island). From the G&L perspective, the issue might again be, in this instance, in the intervening *no one*.

36. Compare:

(i) [*John is likely* [*t to pass the exam*]]

Here the trace in subject position can be anaphoric on the c-commanding and nearby *John*, across no intervening element. Obviously in (83a) *anyone* intervenes in the relevant sense.

Chapter 4

1. See in particular Citko (2005), pursuing ideas that, as Larson (2016) shows, have a long tradition within generative grammar. So far as we understand these proposals, in them chain uniqueness stems from there being a single element that merges multiply. But we still do not understand (i) how interpretation, in point of fact, can be distributed (e.g., θ-dependency in a given configuration and scope A-dependency at a different one) and (ii) how the realization for PF and LF can be at different occurrences. For what it's worth, multidominance operations are ruled out by Chomsky's (2019) notion of a "workspace."

2. A derivation consists of a series of lines. The first follows from (1a); to proceed from one to the next, we replace one symbol by the symbol sequence it can be rewritten as, until there are no more symbols that can be rewritten. This yields the terminal string.

3. This formalism predicted that rewrite rules are not ideal to characterize syntactic relations, predating Stowell (1981), which shows empirically how these rules are redundant with lexical information presupposed by phrasal dependencies. An RPM, a subset of a PM, could be constructed by generating a PM and eliminating everything except

the terminal string and the monostrings. In contrast, L&K built RPMs formally from scratch, asking what it is to be a construct of the relevant sort. For them, any set of strings is an RPM so long as it meets conditions as discussed in this chapter.

4. We are simplifying and adapting the presentation to current models. Example (9) is significantly different from the statement in L&K, but it could be easily relaxed depending on the facts. The issue gets complicated in light of what counts as a "terminal," particularly in Distributed Morphology.

5. Although the underlining, as such, is merely notation and not part of this particular formal statement.

6. Recall that the LCA maps a terminal α c-commanding some structure K as preceding the terminals within K.

7. A tensor product is an operation standardly defined within linear algebra, which can be thought of as concatenating the elements within a matrix. Smolensky and Legendre (2006:chapter 5) use an operation with these particular mathematical properties, albeit starting from rather different presuppositions and tracking the parsing of binary trees. We are interested, instead, in combinatorially constructing related objects, though not quite such graphs (but, rather, set-theoretic entities of a weaker sort). For ease of exposition, we will be using the Dirac notion $|y\rangle$ to denote a vector y.

8. It will be an interesting exercise to determine whether this ordered set has only information that is syntactically relevant, for example, in the derivational sequence of operations that is implicit in it.

9. Evidently, with more additions there could be "tristrings" or "*n*-ary-strings" also, which we return to.

10. For Kayne (1994) the relation between c-command and precedence is a general property of PMs. As we mentioned in chapter 3, Chomsky (1995) takes a different view: linearity is taken to be a sensorimotor property, which obtains only as the system is shipped to the external interface (so presumably not at LF). Uriagereka (2012) shows how, when reduced to a biconditional relation between c-command and precedence, Kayne's axiom can be turned into a theorem, given certain assumptions of the general sort discussed in section 4.3. That statement of linearization does not extend beyond head-complement relations, however, which entails that the system must go into multiple spell out in relevant extensions, with interesting consequences as already explored in chapter 3 and which we return to in chapter 5.

11. We will not go into how precisely the explosive parsing complexity is connected to a learnability claim, as that would take us too far afield and because we ultimately have no axe to grind on this.

12. Reinhart (1983) makes a proposal of this kind, based on the idea that, if a speaker intends coreference, bound anaphora must be used, unless there are apparent reasons for avoiding it. Lasnik (1991) notes a problem with the reasoning, posed by an exchange along the following lines:

(i) A: *Charlie Brown talks to his dog.*
    B: *My neighbor Max does too* $^{\textit{talk to his dog}}$.

Clearly the elided constituent has both a strict and a sloppy reading. However, the strict reading should not be possible according to Reinhart's theory. By hypothesis, A intends coreference and there is no reason for A to avoid bound anaphora. There is also no reason for B to assume that A had a reason for avoiding bound anaphora. The conclusion is thus that B cannot intend by his utterance that Max talks to Charlie's dog, because the elided material must include a bound variable.

13. The attribute V stands for "vocalic" and C for "consonantal". Without trying to be technical about this, the ±vocalic feature can be seen as allowing syllabification around (with the vocalic element counting as the syllabic nucleus), whereas the ±consonantal feature involves air obstruction in the articulation.

14. Alison Brooks, whose child learned a San language in the Kalahari Desert, recently told us how apparently San children start their bootstrapping with pointing (of the sort in signed languages), while their first words are typically verbs. She attributes this remarkable fact to the equally surprising one that the famous "clicks," unique to the phonology of these languages anciently separated from the rest in human history, are less common in verbs than in nouns, where they are rampant. If these facts generalize, the children would seem to resist lexical bootstrapping on nouns-with-clicks. From our perspective, we would argue that even such children are cognitively anchoring their sentential projections on the deictic pointing, whose nature we would presume to be nominal.

15. This is not central to our concerns, but see for instance Nespor et al. (2011) for details of how languages differ regarding their stress versus syllabic timing, in both instances around vocalic nuclei, all of which is acquired by native speakers. See also the phonological implications of note 14.

16. If we were able to operate simultaneously on both objects in (32) we would arguably be able to perform many more computations than seem possible in human languages. This also bears on the workspace considerations in Chomsky (2019) and Chomsky et al. (2019), though that narrows things down even further.

17. We review other such claims in chapter 5, as they extend to the uniformity of chains and beyond.

18. We need not emphasize now that, for any syntax one can provide, there is a mapping to a semantics that one either asserts or presupposes. So-called phrasal axioms are routinely assumed in the literature, although their details depend in part on the nature of the semantic representations, which differ significantly from one semantico-pragmatic theory to the next. While none of that is our domain of expertise or concern at this point, what we are doing in this chapter can be seen as imposing restrictions on possible syntax/semantics mappings. Axiom (17) is one such restriction, and condition (35) should be assumed in the same light. Surely similar considerations arise for the syntax/phonology mapping, for example, in terms of linearization as already discussed.

19. Again, we are concentrating on the sort of transitive structure that a matrix like (26) stems from, which all of the examples in (39) and (40) instantiate (including long-range variants across clausal boundaries). To be sure, there are many other PMs with crazier internal relations, where in principle we could also find uniform bistrings within. It is unclear whether such expressions (e.g., one that violates thematic restrictions or a different one that violates Case conditions) converge on a valid LF that, thereby, can be shipped to interpretation in terms of the sort now being examined. Logically, it

could be that one such representation is in some sense interpretable but not syntactically convergent.

20. For some, a correferential expression is slightly better in the format in (39a) or with emphasis:

(i) *Will* [*only* ***his***$_i$ *friend*] *recognize* [***John***$_i$***'s*** *mother*]?

21. Covariance also arises locally so long as the variable is a reflexive, as in (i):

(i) *Will* ***no one*** *recognize* ***himself***?

22. As we saw in note 20, a variant with a reflexive is perfect in the local conditions in (i):

(i) *Will* ***John*** *recognize* ***himself***?

23. Following Postal (1966b), we may take *he* to be a shorthand for "the one" (or "the man"), *they* for "the ones" (or "the men"), etc.; thus, pronouns can be treated as incomplete definite descriptions.

24. To be totally parallel to (39b′) with topicalization, the relevant example would have to be:

(i) ???***No one's*** *mother* (*in the costume party*), *do I expect* [*his friend*] *to recognize.*

This seems worse than (41), possibly as related to the quantifier being inside the topicalized phrase.

25. Per Postal's (1966b) treatment of pronouns in note 23 we are assuming that the relevant structure is as in (i):

(i) ?*Will* [***his*** [***=the man's***] *friend*] *recognize* [***John's*** *mother*]?

There is a uniform bistring for this object of the form ⟨0, *the-man*, 0, 0, 0, *John*, 0, 0⟩, in whose construal file *John* is the referential anchor, but it does not precede its anaphoric recollection. At the same time, it is common for narratives to have the form in (ii), the opening lines to Ernest Hemingway's *Old Man and the Sea*:

(ii) HE was an old man who fished alone in a skiff. . . . In the first forty days **a boy** had been with him. But [then] **the boy**'s parents had told him that THE OLD MAN was . . . unlucky, and **the boy** had gone at their orders in another boat. "SANTIAGO," **the boy** said . . .

While the introduction of the boy's character, marked in bold, satisfies the F/NC, that of the old man's, marked in caps for referential uses, does not seem to. Which indicates there are further nuances to this sort of requirement that we cannot go into, and which may well relate to how comfortable speakers are with (i).

26. Culicover (1976) independently reaches very similar conclusions, along comparable structural lines.

27. They are easy to find in the Google repository in their nonadjectival version, though we have not found any examples for the adjectival nominal versions, perhaps due to the oddity of repeating the noun.

28. Just as the orthogonal 1/*i* were found by William Hamilton to stand in orthogonal relations to two other elements usually termed *j* and *k* (yielding the quaternions), and

those in turn "rotate" into twice as many "octonions," and so on—ad infinitum, always rotating orthogonal systems into doubly complex ones. In general, orthogonality will formally depend on a specific frame of reference.

29. Recall that precedence is taken to be a property of words, not phrases.

30. In contrast to what we are saying, Chomsky (2005:14) offers the following judgments:

(i) a. * $[_{CP}$ *Of which car*$_i$ *did* $[_{TP}$ *[the driver* $t_i]_j$ $[_{v^*P}$ t_j *cause a scandal*]]]?
  b. $[_{CP}$ *Of which car*$_i$ *was* $[_{TP}$ *[the driver* $t_i]_j$ $[_{vP}$ *awarded* t_j *a prize*]]]?

We have difficulties with this contrast, which may be influenced by the fact that preposition stranding is the natural option in English. When we pointed this out to Chomsky through personal communication, he conceded that the facts with preposition stranding are as reported in (47) in the text, though he also suggested that the stranding may be a confounding factor. We are unsure why, given Chomsky's example in (ii), which he extensively discussed in Chomsky 1973:

(ii) $[_{CP}$ *Which car*$_i$ *did* $[_{TP}$ *you* $[_{v^*P}$ *see [a picture of* t_i]]]]?

So clearly more empirical work is needed, in English and other languages.

31. The embarrassment is even greater when (as is now customary) one assumes the VP internal hypothesis, which entails that *no* specifier of TP is ever a potential θ-position.

32. At least not in terms of justifying the movement to a head in terms of a morphological property of that head that effectively constitutes its trigger.

33. In this instance, globality was understood as taking place within the scope of the displaced operator, in the sense that crossover effects could be detected within such an unbounded domain.

Chapter 5

1. Of the twenty-thousand odd known species of bees, only some 10% are even social. Of those roughly two thousand species, only a couple of dozen are known to present the dance, and there is no evidence, to our knowledge, that nondancing species show more interest in the dance than chimpanzees do in language.

2. For example, we found Barron and Plath (2017) an interesting mechanistic model of the right sort, although as they point out "we still know very little about the neurobiological mechanisms supporting how dances are produced and interpreted." These and similar models could be tested in machine learning terms.

3. We have in mind the sort of proposal studied in Reggia et al. (2001) for more neutral agents and the (attested) emergence of communicative strategies—evidently with more state-of-the-art algorithms.

4. We saw some relevant examples in chapter 2 that we will not review again, but even more modest attempts (for example, the sorts of challenges that Emmanuel Dupoux and colleagues at L'Ecole des Hautes Etudes en Sciences Sociales have been posing), focusing on phonetic and lexical representations, seem quite ambitious to us. This is particularly so when, whereas putative findings for bees could be immediately

tested in neurophysiological terms, the same is far from obvious for putative human conditions.

5. Although see Kohl et al. (2020) for remarkable recent evidence that there are significant variations.

6. The first genes that seem implicated in language have been discovered after 2001, the first relatively clear brain circuits are presently being unearthed, and a putative science of complex dynamic systems is still in its infancy, as is the math presupposed to understand them seriously.

7. For instance, and aside from Chomsky's works cited throughout (but without trying to be systematic or exhaustive): Ross (1967), Perlmutter (1968), Bresnan (1972), Jackendoff (1972), De Rijk (1972), Fiengo (1974), Milsark (1974), Postal (1974), Kayne (1975), Emonds (1976), Lasnik (1976), Reinhart (1976), Chomsky and Lasnik (1977), May (1977), Baltin (1978), Platero (1978), Rouveret and Vergnaud (1980).

8. We are thinking here of Lightfoot's (1991) so-called cues or Fodor's (1998) "treelets," the sort of abstract information that is supposed to set a parametric option in some particular direction, ideas all related to the influential Dresher and Kaye (1990) for the acquisition of metrical patterns in phonology.

9. And bear in mind that epigenetic stuff ranges from temperature to an actual encounter with conspecifics of a given sex, epigenetic cycles of development vary dramatically from early stages—even at gestation—to postpartum conditions, and by now it is hardly debatable that how immune systems react to microbes affects both evolution and development.

10. The specific role of third factors is unclear, whether Chomsky's strong(est) minimalist thesis holds, how to relate the program to neurophysiology and molecular biology, and so on.

11. We mean this comment in the broadest sense: in our view, even classical generative systems effectively presented the equivalent of parametric options in terms of how rule systems are stated. The point is not one about a narrow formulation, but about a general architectural consideration.

12. This may be an understatement, as discussed for instance in Broussard's (2018) aptly titled *Artificial Unintelligence* (on how computers misunderstand the world). All of this would be simply interesting from an intellectual perspective, if a variety of business experts were not already applying such mindless devices not just to speech recognition or other engineering feats—but also to "optimizing" working hours for part-time employees (so as to reduce costs for the management and keep them under the number of hours that trigger federally protected health insurance). This is probably just the beginning.

13. For example, there appear to be differences in interpretation between "hit and run" and "run and hit," and the iterative "dancing and dancing and dancing and . . ." clearly denotes an extended and continuous, open-ended, dancing, a generalization that extends to other such iterations.

14. Dunbar (1992) famously speaks of there being cognitive constraints on network size for social species, perhaps as related to neocortical neurons limiting information processing capacity. The fact seems to be that early modern human groups comprised

roughly between one hundred and two hundred individuals and apparently started splitting beyond such sizes. It is natural to speculate that language diversification could have contributed to these dynamics. See, for instance, Lou-Magnuson and Onnis (2018) for recent simulations in that general regard, as well as references.

15. Lightfoot (1991, 1999) has presented this so-called catastrophic view of intergenerational change.

16. See, for instance, Kroch (1989) or Yang (2000).

17. See Gleitman (1981) or Wexler (1990), among several other contributions.

18. See, for instance, Crain (2012).

19. We thank Dave Lebeaux for raising this matter with us, in relation to his 2000 model (see also Radford [1990]). The matter might be relevant, also, for models suggesting that evolutionary scenarios may track the Chomsky hierarchy: Zuidema (2005), Hauser et al. (2007), Balari et al. (2011), among others.

20. See, for instance, Mehler et al. (1988), and much subsequent work from Jacques Mehler's lab.

21. See Berk and Lillo-Martin (2012) for a useful perspective that includes signed languages.

22. Prinz (1983), among several others, showed that children take quite a long time (up to puberty in some instances) to systematically acquire idiomatic interpretations; thereafter, such expressions are central to adolescent talk, for reasons of the sort discussed in Labov (2001).

23. The late Ken Hale is rumored to have spoken some fifty languages, most acquired as an adult.

24. Speaker variation is clear for the sloppy reading, which is even more patent in the following examples:

(i) *Mary loves her children and John does too.*
(ii) *John loves his children and the Smiths do too.*

The fact that some speakers find the relevant ellipsis hard in these instances suggests that there are nuanced ways of structuring relevant features in terms of defaults (e.g., masculine vs. feminine, plural vs. singular), from which apparently the licensing is possible in the direction of the marked setting, but not conversely.

25. In chapter 3, note 25, we saw how coindexation for the purposes of Binding Theory cannot be mere identity either, but some form of set inclusion or some such is necessary.

26. Actually, that way of describing the phenomenon is debatable: it may be that the relevant English rule obeys Tense Fronting only, not Auxiliary Fronting, in which case the possibility of fronting an auxiliary other than the one associated to the tense morpheme would not even arise. Rizzi (2001:93) discusses other possibly relevant examples, involving Italian untensed (gerundival [Rizzi 1982] and participial [Belletti 1981]) clauses in which a nonfinite verb fronts leftward as in (5), but the participle cannot move across the gerundival auxiliary, as that would violate the Head Movement Constraint.

27. All structural conditions describable by *XECY* are describable by *XEY*, just as any dish describable by ingredients meat, potatoes, and carrots is also describable by

ingredients meat and potatoes, the latter being less specific. Several linguists (including Anderson [1969]; Dell [1973]; Aronoff [1976]; Lasnik [1981]; Zwicky [1989]) have invoked this condition in phonology, morphology, and some aspects of syntax.

28. It is an interesting issue, which we will not elucidate now, exactly what "smallest possible language" means in I-language terms of the sort currently assumed in the Minimalist Program or other P&P models.

29. A well-known logic gate in the building of a digital circuit is NAND (intended to describe a situation of an AND gate followed by a NOT gate, whose output yields a "false" value only if both inputs are "true" and yields "true" otherwise). There is nothing illogical about such an operator. Observe:

(i) *p*	*and*	*q*	*p*	*nand*	*q*	*p*	*or*	*q*	*p*	*nor*	*q*
F	**F**	T	F	**T**	T	F	**T**	T	F	**F**	T
F	**F**	F	F	**T**	F	F	**F**	F	F	**T**	F
T	**F**	F	T	**T**	F	T	**T**	F	T	**F**	F
T	**T**	T	T	**F**	T	T	**T**	T	T	**F**	T

Horn's point is not one of logic, but of (learning a) grammar: as the highlights in the truth tables show, the logical space of *nor* and (exclusive) *or* cover the same ground as that of *nand*, so a conservative learner (as described in the text) goes with the condition that leads to no unlearning based on negative data. Building digital circuits poses no such issues, so it is perfectly appropriate to give them whatever logical gates are useful (typically, these also include such gates as XNOR, or exclusive nor, with true outputs only for identical, true or false, inputs). To the best of our knowledge, that particular operator does not arise in natural language, but not because of it being illogical.

30. The word *unnecessary* is possible in English, but notice that this is part of a different paradigm (the one that negates *possible* involving negative *in* (with phonological assimilation) instead of negative *un*).

31. In a feature system of this sort, the [–*N*, –*V*] element is like V in one respect (being—*N*) and like N in another respect (being—*V*). That is not, however, how Chomsky talked about P categories at the time, and thus for instance in Chomsky (1974 (e.g., page 2 of lecture 3) Ps are arbitrarily separated from Ns, Vs, and As (which is called "lexical" even in Chomsky [1981:48]).

32. Ross's actual example was:

(i) *He told me about a book which I can't figure out where to obtain.*

Ross notes that, for unclear reasons, extraction from embedded sentences with an infinitive is better than with a finite verb. A possible account of the grammaticality of this example was given in section 3.7.

33. The treatment, via deletion, is too elaborate to go into here (see Lasnik and Uriagereka 2005:chapter 4).

34. Where innate may reduce to genetic, epigenetic, proteomic, connectomic, molecular, physiological, or whatever could possibly matter that is not specific to the learner.

35. Perhaps mathematicians have pointed this out; apologies in advance for coming up with this as a game.

36. Although it is already a nuanced computational matter what one means by "comparing."

37. It should be obvious that the superscript notation for the looping string has no connection to the power notation. In other words, in our terms 314^2 is meant as 314314 and not 98,596.

38. In a famous sentence, Churchill admonished the British to *never, never surrender—never!* Obviously, Churchill did not expect his people to never engage in the act of never surrendering, which is what a compositional semantics would yield for *never never surrender*. Another famous quote, this time by Shakespeare, has King Lear, his daughter Cordelia dead on his arms, lamenting *"No, no, no, no, no!"*. Again, while one can give a compositional meaning to *no no* (negating the negative), what Lear means is an emphatic "No!," which cannot be achieved compositionally. See Uriagereka (2008:chapter 8) for discussion. It is interesting to note that the quarto version of the play has Lear say *"no,"* whereas in the folio version the quote is *"Never never never never never,"* as in the Churchill sentence, raising the same issues.

39. Recall the pair in (73) and (74) in chapter 3, repeated now:

(i) A: *JFK's mother liked his children.*
B: *Pat did too* [*like his* (*JFK's*) *children / like her* (*Pat's*) *children*].

(ii) A: *JFK's mother liked his children.*
B: *Pat's husband did too* [*like his* (*JFK's*) *children /*like her* (*Pat's*) *children*].

For a sloppy reading to be licensed, even in this cross-discourse elliptical context, the antecedent for the silent variable must c-command this variable, as in (i).

40. That is actually (in some form—and there are many variants) the current prevalent analysis, going back to Larson (1988) and Kayne (1984), both of whom argue, in different ways, for ditransitive verbal dependents (theme and goal) entering into some sort of clausal relation.

41. In that model, D-structure was supposed to code thematic dependencies and only those, while displacement operations yielded LF (a set of chains in some formulations) and other further adjustments eliminating brackets and emphasizing stress and intonation contours produced the PF representation. Each level was responsible for each kind of information, which the Minimalist Program has questioned—radically so in a system with derivational phases.

42. The numeration cannot be a subset of the lexicon if the lexicon is a set of lexical types and the numeration presupposes lexical tokens, which is the reason why it is called a numeration in the first place (in the formulation in Chomsky [1995], a multiset of lexical items associated to a number indicating token count).

43. A literal idea along these lines was proposed in Uriagereka (1998:section 4.4). Chametzky (1994) proposed a similar possibility, concentrating instead on a label-less merge. These various strands led to proposals for label-less adjunction, for example as in Hunter (2010) or Hornstein and Nunes (2008), and the fully disconnected possibility was explored in Uriagereka (2008).

44. For ease of exposition, we are not bothering to specify now that *to the president's critics* in (16) ought to also be "out of the way," presumably in some even further (indirect object) *v* position.

45. Chomsky (1995:337) is forced to conclude that morphological linearization follows its own rules, which are different from the LCA (or he could not linearize merged heads). It is worth bearing in mind observations that go back at least to Jakobson (1960), to the effect that expressions like *fish and chips* have a different flavor than variants like *chips and fish* do. This goes beyond mere usage percentage: *chips and fish* is certainly not ungrammatical, and it clearly has the figure/ground effect of the user expecting more chips than fish, for example (similarly with *butter and bread, roses and wine*, *run and hit*, and other such reversals).

46. In other words, externalization may be possible either in phonological terms, with a feature spreading over the relevant category as an elongation/intonation, or in morphological terms, with the feature, instead, being bundled into actual morphemes with separate pronunciations.

47. This is the equivalent of an organism containing another element within, and leading a healthy existence; eggs, for example, are not connected to their bearers, which carry them for life with various consequences; similar points can be raised about interrelations of organisms with the microbiome and more.

48. This is yet again another one of those topics that Ross (1967) first studied, and which continues to be central to minimalist considerations, for example, as discussed in Chomsky (1995:section 4.4.4). Chomsky states his proposal in that piece in terms of his rule of Move F (feature), but the ideas remain entirely central to Agree-based systems of the sort he first proposed in 2000 as well.

49. Language *L* allows the dropping of arguments, or multiple overt Wh-movements to the same domain, or adjunctal dependents that double agglutinative morphemes directly associated to the verb, and so on.

50. The first sounds like someone speaking British English, whereas the second sounds like a German speaker who does not know much English trying to get by in Chaucer's language. Actually, at that time the equivalent of (17b) would have sounded natural, much more so than the American English variant.

51. Ellen Lau (personal communication, 2019) points out to us that the examples in (17) may yield measurable effects for irrelevant reasons. For example, the sequence *have they any* may be more common to American speakers than the sequence *go they any*. That said, Doug Saddy (personal communication, 2020) offers the possibility of running relevant experiments with "Jabberwocky" lines, as already tested in Moro et al. (2001). We set the issue aside now, inasmuch as it is unclear to us whether verbs like *have* (which can front in many English dialects) ought to be treated as functional elements of the sort "Jabberwocky" leaves unchanged.

52. The notion is central to Chomsky's ([1955] 1975) discussion in chapter V is devoted to the general idea.

53. Several minimalist parsers seem relevant to the task, among them Stabler (2013b) or works in the public domain by Jason Ginsburg (http://www.osaka-kyoiku.ac.jp/~jginsbur/MinimalistModeling.html) and Sandiway Fong (https://sandiway.arizona.edu/mpp/mm.html). Fong (1991) remarkably came up with a parser to deal with all 335 example sentences in Lasnik and Uriagereka (1988). One should bear in mind that our examples were grammatical and ungrammatical (the parser needs to determine that), and we were not planning our book as a friendly text where the test cases relate

to the content in a direct way, as in any meta-linguistic exercise: the book was about grammar and so the examples were basically more or less nasty tests for that grammar, as elaborate and challenging as a class of graduate students can come up with. In addition to dealing with the principles that the book explored, Fong's parser was published a couple of years after the book, so we are reasonably hopeful even for the kinds of proposals we have made in the present book, at least the ones that we have been explicit about.

54. In this instance we are not even trying to get the machine to look for inverses or anything fancy as discussed earlier in this chapter. Simple correlations could do, if they were systematic enough.

55. As we read and understand his project, Giuseppe Longobardi is attempting to do just that, presupposing parameters from the P&P literature (see Longobardi and Guardiano 2011, for example). We are agnostic, however, about any correlation between (population) genetics and parametric differences—the only point we are emphasizing now being the machine learning aspect of this approach.

References

Abels, Klaus, and Ad Neeleman. 2012. "Linear Asymmetries and the LCA." *Syntax* 15:25–74. https://doi.org/10.1111/j.1467-9612.2011.00163.x.

Ajdukiewicz, Kazimierz. 1935. "Die Syntaktische Konnexität." In *Polish Logic 1920–1939*, edited by Storrs McCall, 1–27. Oxford: Oxford University Press.

Anderson, Stephen. 1969. "West Scandinavian Vowel Systems and the Ordering of Phonological Rules." PhD dissertation, MIT.

Anderson, Stephen. 1970. "Two Notes on Split Antecedents." *Linguistic Inquiry* 1:545–547.

Aronoff, Mark. 1976. *Word Formation in Generative Grammar*. Linguistic Inquiry Monographs. Cambridge, MA: MIT Press.

Bach, Emmon, and George M. Horn. 1976. "Remarks on 'Conditions on Transformations.'" *Linguistic Inquiry* 7 (2): 265–299.

Baker, Mark. 1988. *Incorporation: A Theory of Grammatical Function Changing*. Chicago: University of Chicago Press.

Baker, Mark. 1996. *The Polysynthesis Parameter*. New York: Oxford University Press.

Balari, Sergio, Antonio Benítez-Burraco, Marta Camps, Víctor M. Longa, Guillermo Lorenzo, and Juan Uriagereka. 2011. "The Archaeological Record Speaks: Bridging Anthropology and Linguistics." *International Journal of Evolutionary Biology* 2011 (1): 382679.

Baltin, Mark. 1978. "Toward a Theory of Movement Rules." PhD dissertation, MIT.

Bar-Hillel, Yehoshua. 1953. "A Quasi-Arithmetical Notation for Syntactic Description." *Language* 29:47–58.

Barrie, Michael. 2005. "Control and Wh-Infinitivals." In *New Horizons in the Analysis of Control and Raising*, edited by W. D. Davies and S. Dubinsky, 263–279. Studies in Natural Language and Linguistic Theory 71. Dordrecht, Netherlands: Springer.

Barron, Andrew B., and Jenny Aino Plath. 2017. "The Evolution of Honey Bee Dance Communication: A Mechanistic." *Journal of Experimental Biology* 220:4339–4346. https://doi.org/10.1242/jeb.142778.

Barss, Andrew. 1986. "Chains and Anaphoric Dependence: On Reconstruction and Its Implications." PhD dissertation, MIT.

Barss, Andrew, and Howard Lasnik. 1986. "A Note on Anaphora and Double Objects." *Linguistic Inquiry* 17 (2): 347–354.

Battistella, Edwin. 1989. "Chinese Reflexivization: A Movement to INFL Approach." *Linguistics* 27:987–1012.

Belletti, Adriana. 1981. "Frasi Ridotte Assolute." *Rivista Di Grammatica Generativa* 6:3–33.

Belletti, Adriana, and Luigi Rizzi. 1988. "Psych-Verbs and θ-Theory." *Natural Language and Linguistic Theory* 6 (3): 291–352.

Berk, Stephanie, and Diane Lillo-Martin. 2012. "The Two-Word Stage: Motivated by Linguistic or Cognitive Constraints?" *Cognitive Psychology* 65 (1): 118–140.

Berwick, Robert C. 1982. "Locality Principles and the Acquisition of Syntactic Knowledge." PhD dissertation, MIT.

Berwick, Robert C. 1985. *The Acquisition of Syntactic Knowledge*. Cambridge, MA: MIT Press.

Berwick, Robert C., Gabriël J. L. Beckers, Kazuo Okanoya, and Johan J. Bolhuis. 2012. "A Bird's Eye View of Human Language Evolution." *Frontiers in Evolutionary Neuroscience* 4 (April). https://doi.org/10.3389/fnevo.2012.00005.

Berwick, Robert C., and Noam Chomsky. 2015. *Why Only Us: Language and Evolution*. Cambridge, MA: MIT Press.

Berwick, Robert C., Kazuo Okanoya, Gabriel J. L. Beckers, and Johan J. Bolhuis. 2011. "Songs to Syntax: The Linguistics of Birdsong." *Trends in Cognitive Sciences* 15 (3): 113–121. https://doi.org/10.1016/j.tics.2011.01.002.

Berwick, Robert C., and Amy Weinberg. 1984. *The Grammatical Basis of Linguistic Performance*. Cambridge, MA: MIT Press.

Berwick, Robert C., and Kenneth Wexler. 1987. "Parsing Efficiency, Binding, C-Command and Learnability." In *Studies in the Acquisition of Anaphora*, edited by Barbara Lust, 45–60. Studies in Theoretical Psycholinguistics. Dordrecht, Netherlands: Springer. https://doi.org/10.1007/978-94-009-3387-3_3.

Boeckx, Cedric. 2008. *Bare Syntax*. Oxford: Oxford University Press.

Boeckx, Cedric, and Juan Uriagereka. 2012. "Minimalism." In *The Oxford Handbook of Linguistic Interfaces*, edited by Gillian Ramchand and Charles Reiss, 541–574. Oxford: Oxford University Press.

Borer, Hagit, and Kenneth Wexler. 1987. "The Maturation of Syntax." In *Parameter Setting*, edited by Thomas Roeper and Edwin Williams, 123–172. Dordrecht, Netherlands: Springer.

Brandner, Ellen. 2012. "Syntactic Microvariation." *Language and Linguistics Compass* 6 (2): 113–130.

Bresnan, Joan. 1970. "On Complementizers: Towards a Syntactic Theory of Complement Types." *Foundations of Language* 6:297–321.

Bresnan, Joan. 1972. "Theory of Complementation in English Syntax." PhD dissertation, MIT.

Broussard, Meredith. 2018. *Artificial Unintelligence: How Computers Misunderstand the World.* Cambridge, MA: MIT Press.

Browning, Marguerite. 1987. "Null Operator Constructions." PhD dissertation, MIT.

Chametzky, Robert. 1994. "Chomsky-Adjunction." *Lingua* 93 (4): 245–64.

Chief, Lian-Cheng. 1998. "Mandarin Intransitive Reflexive Verbs and the Unaccusative Hypothesis." *Language, Information and Computation* 12: 48–59.

Chomsky, Noam. 1951. "Morphophonemics of Modern Hebrew." MA thesis, University of Pennsylvania.

Chomsky, Noam. 1955. "The Logical Structure of Linguistic Theory." Ms., Harvard University and MIT. [Revised 1956 version published in part, 1975, New York: Plenum; 1985, Chicago: University of Chicago Press].

Chomsky, Noam. 1957. *Syntactic Structures*. The Hague, Netherlands: Mouton.

Chomsky, Noam. 1959. "Verbal Behavior." *Language* 35:26–58.

Chomsky, Noam. 1961a. "On the Notion 'Rule of Grammar.'" In *Proceedings of Symposia in Applied Mathematics 12: Structure of Language and its Mathematical Aspects*, edited by Roman Jakobson, 6–24. Providence, RI: American Mathematical Society. [Reprinted, 1964 in *The Structure of Language*, edited by Jerry A. Fodor and Jerrold J. Katz, 119–136. New York: Prentice-Hall.]

Chomsky, Noam. 1961b. "Some Methodological Remarks on Generative Grammar." *Word* 17 (2): 219–234.

Chomsky, Noam. 1964a. "Current Issues in Linguistic Theory." In *Structure of Language*, edited by Jerry A. Fodor and Jerrold J. Katz, 50–118. New York: Prentice-Hall.

Chomsky, Noam. 1964b. "The Logical Basis of Linguistic Theory." In *Proceedings of the Ninth International Congress of Linguists*, 914–1008. Cambridge, MA: Mouton and Co.

Chomsky, Noam. 1965. *Aspects of the Theory of Syntax*. Cambridge, MA: MIT Press.

Chomsky, Noam. 1968. *Language and Mind.* New York: Hancourt, Brace, and World.

Chomsky, Noam. 1970. "Remarks on Nominalization." In *Readings in English Transformational Grammar*, 184–221. Boston: Ginn.

Chomsky, Noam. 1971. *Problems of Knowledge and Freedom.* New York: Pantheon.

Chomsky, Noam. 1973. "Conditions on Transformations." In *A Festschrift for Morris Halle*, edited by Stephen R. Anderson and Paul Kiparsky, 232–286. New York: Holt, Rinehart, and Winston.

Chomsky, Noam. 1974. "The Amherst Lectures." University of Paris VII.

Chomsky, Noam. 1975. *Reflections on Language*. New York: Pantheon Books.

Chomsky, Noam. 1976. "Conditions on Rules of Grammar." *Linguistic Analysis* 2 (4): 303–351.

Chomsky, Noam. 1977. "On Wh-Movement." In *Formal Syntax*, edited by Peter W. Culicover, Thomas Wasow, and Adrian Akmajian, 71–132. New York: Academic Press.

Chomsky, Noam. 1980a. "On Binding." *Linguistic Inquiry* 11 (1): 1–46.

Chomsky, Noam. 1980b. *Rules and Representations*. New York: Columbia University Press.

Chomsky, Noam. 1981. *Lectures on Government and Binding*. Dordrecht, Netherlands: Foris.

Chomsky, Noam. 1982. "A Note on the Creative Aspect of Language Use." *Philosophical Review* 91 (3): 423–434.

Chomsky, Noam. 1986a. *Barriers*. Cambridge, MA: MIT Press.

Chomsky, Noam. 1986b. *Knowledge of Language*. New York: Praeger.

Chomsky, Noam. 1991. "Some Notes on Economy of Derivation and Representation." In *Principles and Parameters in Comparative Grammar*, edited by Robert Freidin, 417–454. Cambridge, MA: MIT Press. [Reprinted in Chomsky, *The Minimalist Program*, 129–166.]

Chomsky, Noam. 1994. *Bare Phrase Structure*. MIT Occasional Papers in Linguistics 5. Cambridge, MA: MIT Working Papers in Linguistics.

Chomsky, Noam. 1995. *The Minimalist Program*. Cambridge, MA: MIT Press.

Chomsky, Noam. 2000. "Minimalist Inquiries: The Framework." In *Step by Step: Essays in Honor of Howard Lasnik*, edited by Roger Martin, David Michaels, and Juan Uriagereka, 89–155. Cambridge, MA: MIT Press.

Chomsky, Noam. 2001. "Derivation by Phase." In *Ken Hale: A Life in Language*, edited by Michael Kenstowicz, 1–50. Cambridge, MA: MIT Press.

Chomsky, Noam. 2005. "Three Factors in Language Design." *Linguistic Inquiry* 36:1–22.

Chomsky, Noam. 2007. "Approaching UG from Below." In *Interfaces + Recursion = Language?: Chomsky's Minimalism and the View from Syntax–Semantics*, edited by Uli Sauerland and Hans-Martin Gärtner, 1–29. New York: Mouton de Gruyter.

Chomsky, Noam. 2009. "Opening Remarks + Conclusion." In *Of Minds and Language: A Dialogue with Noam Chomsky in the Basque Country*, edited by M. Piatelli-Palmarini, J. Uriagereka, and P. Salaburu, 12–43, 52–55, 379–409. Oxford: Oxford University Press.

Chomsky, Noam. 2019. "The UCLA Lectures." Lectures transcribed and edited by Robert Freidin. https://ling.auf.net/lingbuzz/005485.

Chomsky, Noam, Ángel J. Gallego, and Dennis Ott. 2019. "Generative Grammar and the Faculty of Language: Insights, Questions, and Challenges." *Catalan Journal of Linguistics*, 229–261.

Chomsky, Noam, and Morris Halle. 1968. *The Sound Pattern of English*. New York: Harper and Row.

Chomsky, Noam, Morris Halle, and Fred Lukoff. 1956. "On Accent and Juncture in English." In *For Roman Jakobson*, edited by Morris Halle, 67–80. The Hague, Netherlands: Mouton.

Chomsky, Noam, and Howard Lasnik. 1977. "Filters and Control." *Linguistic Inquiry* 8 (3): 425–504. http://www.jstor.org/stable/4177996.

Chomsky, Noam, and Howard Lasnik. 1993. "The Theory of Principles and Parameters." In *Syntax: An International Handbook of Contemporary Research*, vol. 1, edited by Joachim Jacobs et al., 506–569. Berlin: Walter de Gruyter.

Chomsky, Noam, and George Miller. 1963. "Introduction to the Formal Analysis of Natural Languages." In *Modeling and Measurement*, vol. 2 of *Handbook of Mathematical Psychology*, edited by R. Duncan Luce, Robert Bush, and Eugene Galanter, 269–321. New York: Wiley and Sons.

Chomsky, Noam, and Marcel Paul Schützenberger. 1963. "The Algebraic Theory of Context Free Languages." In *Computer Programming and Formal Systems: Studies in Logic*, edited by Paul Braffort and Dan Hirschberg, 118–161. Amsterdam, Netherlands: North-Holland.

Chung, Sandra, and Carol Georgopoulos. 1988. "Agreement with Gaps in Chamorro And." In *Agreement in Natural Languages: Approaches, Theories, and Descriptions*, edited by Michael Barlow and Charles A. Ferguson, 251–267. Stanford: Stanford University Center for the Study of Languange and Information.

Cinque, Guglielmo, and Luigi Rizzi. 2008. "The Cartography of Syntactic Structures." *Studies in Linguistics* 2:42–58.

Citko, Barbara. 2005. "On the Nature of Merge: External Merge, Internal Merge, and Parallel Merge." *Linguistic Inquiry* 36 (4): 475–496.

Cole, Peter, Gabriella Hermon, and Li-May Sung. 1990. "Principles and Parameters of Long-Distance Reflexives." *Linguistic Inquiry* 21 (1): 1–22.

Collins, Chris, and Edward Stabler. 2016. "A Formalization of Minimalist Syntax." *Syntax* 19 (1): 43–78.

Cover, Thomas M., and Joy A. Thomas. 2006. *Elements of Information Theory.* 2nd ed. New York: Wiley.

Crain, Stephen. 2012. *The Emergence of Meaning.* Cambridge: Cambridge University Press.

Culicover, Peter. 1976. *Syntax*. New York: Academic Press.

Davis, Martin. 1958. *Computability and Unsolvability.* New York: Mc-Graw-Hill.

Dell, François. 1973. *Les Règles et Les Sons*. Paris: Hermann.

Dell, François. 1981. "On the Learnability of Optional Phonological Rules." *Linguistic Inquiry* 12 (1): 31–37.

Dennett, Daniel. 1995. *Darwin's Dangerous Idea: Evolution and the Meanings of Life*. New York: Simon and Schuster.

De Rijk, Rudolphus Pieter Gerardus. 1972. "Studies in Basque Syntax: Relative Clauses." PhD dissertation, MIT.

Dougherty, Ray. 1969. "An Interpretive Theory of Pronominalization." *Foundations of Language* 5:488–519.

Dresher, B. Elan, and Jonathan D. Kaye. 1990. "A Computational Learning Model for Metrical Phonology." *Cognition* 34 (2): 137–195. https://doi.org/10.1016/0010-0277(90)90042-I.

Dunbar, Robin. 1992. "Neocortex Size as a Constraint on Group Size in Primates." *Journal of Human Evolution* 22 (6): 469–493.

Emonds, Joseph. 1970. "Roots and Structure Preserving Transformations." PhD dissertation, MIT.

Emonds, Joseph. 1976. *A Transformational Approach to English Syntax*. New York: Academic Press.

Emonds, Joseph. 1978. "The Verbal Complex V′-V in French." *Linguistic Inquiry* 9 (2): 151–175.

Everett, Daniel. 2005. "Cultural Constraints on Grammar and Cognition in Pirahã Another Look at the Design Features of Human Language." *Current Anthropology* 46 (4): 621–646. https://doi.org/10.1086/431525.

Everett, Daniel. 2017. "A Dozen Years of Misunderstanding." *Inference* 3 (2). https://inference-review.com/letter/a-dozen-years-of-misunderstanding.

Fiengo, Robert. 1974. "Semantic Conditions of Surface Structure." PhD dissertation, MIT. http://dspace.mit.edu/handle/1721.1/13018.

Fiengo, Robert, and Robert May. 1994. *Indices and Identity*. Linguistic Inquiry Monographs 24. Cambridge, MA: MIT Press.

Flynn, Suzanne, Gita Martohardjono, and Wayne O'Neil. 1998. *The Generative Study of Second Language Acquisition*. London: Lawrence Erlbaum Associates.

Fodor, Janet Dean. 1998. "Unambiguous Triggers." *Linguistic Inquiry* 29 (1): 1–36.

Fodor, Jerry. 1970. "Three Reasons for Not Deriving 'Kill' from 'Cause to Die.'" *Linguistic Inquiry* 1:429–438.

Fodor, Jerry A., and Ernie Lepore. 1998. "The Emptiness of the Lexicon: Reflections on James Pustejovsky's The Generative Lexicon." *Linguistic Inquiry* 29 (2): 269–288.

Fodor, Jerry, and Massimo Piattelli-Palmarini. 2010. *What Darwin Got Wrong*. New York: Farrar, Straus, and Giroux.

Fong, Sandiway. 1991. "The Computational Implementation of Principle-Based Parsers." In *Principle-Based Parsing*, edited by R. C. Berwick, S. P. Abney, and C. Tenny, 65–82. Studies in Linguistics and Philosophy 44. Dordrecht, Netherlands: Springer.

Fox, Danny. 2000. *Economy and Semantic Interpretation*. Cambridge, MA: MIT Press.

Fox, Danny, and David Pesetsky. 2005. "Cyclic Linearization of Syntactic Structure." *Theoretical Linguistics* 31 (1–2): 1–45.

Freidin, Robert. 1991. "Linguistic Theory and Language Acquisition: A Note on Structure-Dependence." *Behavioral and Brain Sciences* 14 (4): 618–619.

Friederici, Angela D. 2017. *Language in Our Brain: The Origins of a Uniquely Human Capacity*. Cambridge, MA: MIT Press.

Fukui, Naoki, and Yuji Takano. 1998. "Symmetry in Syntax: Merge and Demerge." *Journal of East Asian Linguistics* 7:27–86.

Gallistel, C. Randy, and Adam Philip King. 2009. *Memory and the Computational Brain: Why Cognitive Science Will Transform Neuroscience*. New York: Wiley/Blackwell.

Gardner, R. Allen, Beatrix T. Gardner, and Thomas E. Van Cantford, eds. 1989. *Teaching Sign Language to Chimpanzees*. Albany: SUNY Press.

Ginsburg, Seymour, and Barbara Partee. 1969. "A Mathematical Model of Transformational Grammars." *Information and Control* 15 (4): 297–334.

Gleitman, Lila R. 1981. "Maturational Determinants of Language Growth." *Cognition* 10 (1–3): 103–114.

Gleitman, Lila R. 1990. "The Structural Source of Verb Meanings." *Language Acquisition* 1 (1): 3–55.

Gödel, Kurt. 1934. "On Undecidable Propositions of Formal Mathematical Systems." Lecture notes taken by Stephen C. Kleene and J. Barkley Rosser. In *The Undecidable: Basic Papers on Undecidable Propositions, Unsolvable Problems, and Computable Functions*, edited by Martin Davis, 39–74. Hewlett, NY: Dover Publications.

Goodman, Nelson. 1946. "A Query on Confirmation." *Journal of Philosophy* 43 (14): 383–385.

Goodman, Nelson. 1951. *The Structure of Appearance*. Cambridge, MA: Harvard University Press.

Grano, Thomas, and Howard Lasnik. 2018. "How to Neutralize a Finite Clause Boundary: Phase Theory and the Grammar of Bound Pronouns." *Linguistic Inquiry* 49 (3): 465–499.

Grosu, Alexander. 1973. "On the Status of the So-Called Right Roof Constraint." *Language* 49 (2): 294–311.

Guimarães, Maximiliano. 2000. "In Defense of Vacuous Projections in Bare Phrase Structure." *University of Maryland Working Papers in Linguistics* 9:90–115.

Hale, Ken, and Samuel Jay Keyser. 2002. *Prolegomenon to a Theory of Argument Structure*. Cambridge, MA: MIT Press.

Halle, Morris, and Alec Marantz. 1993. "Distributed Morphology and the Pieces of Inflection." In *The View from Building 20: Essays in Linguistics in Honor of Sylvain Bromberger*, edited by K. Hale and S. J. Keyser, 111–176. Cambridge, MA: MIT Press.

Harris, Zellig. 1944. "Simultaneous Components in Phonology." *Language* 20 (4): 181–205.

Harris, Zellig. 1952. "Discourse Analysis." *Language* 28 (1): 1–30.

Harris, Zellig. 1957. "Co-Occurrence and Transformation in Linguistic Structure." Language 33 (3): 283–340.

Hauser, Marc, David Barner, and Tim O'Donnell. 2007. "Evolutionary Linguistics: A New Look at an Old Landscape." *Language Learning and Development* 3 (2): 101–132.

Hauser, Marc D., Noam Chomsky, and W. Tecumseh Fitch. 2002. "The Faculty of Language: What Is It, Who Has It, and How Did It Evolve?" *Science* 298 (5598): 1569–1579. https://doi.org/10.1126/science.298.5598.1569.

Heim, Irene. 1982. "The Semantics of Definite and Indefinite Noun Phrases." PhD dissertation, University of Massachusetts.

Heim, Irene, and Angelika Kratzer. 1998. *Semantics in Generative Grammar*. Malden, MA: Blackwell.

Heim, Irene, Howard Lasnik, and Robert May. 1991. "Reciprocity and Plurality." *Linguistic Inquiry* 22 (1): 63–102.

Higginbotham, James. 1980. "Pronouns and Bound Variables." *Linguistic Inquiry* 11 (4): 679–708.

Higginbotham, James, and Robert May. 1981. "Questions, Quantifiers and Crossing." *Linguistic Review* 1:41–80.

Hockett, Charles. 1955. *A Manual of Phonology.* Baltimore, MD: Waverly Press.

Holt, Elizabeth Jane. 1991. "Figures of Speech: An Exploration of the Use of Idiomatic Phrases in Conversation." PhD dissertation, University of York.

Horn, Laurence R. 1972. "The Semantic Properties of Logical Operators in English." PhD dissertation, UCLA.

Horn, Laurence R. 1989. *A Natural History of Negation.* Chicago: University of Chicago Press.

Hornstein, Norbert. 1995. *Logical Form: From GB to Minimalism.* Cambridge, MA: Basil, Blackwell.

Hornstein, Norbert. 2001. *Move! A Minimalist Theory of Construal.* Malden, MA: Blackwell.

Hornstein, Norbert, Howard Lasnik, and Juan Uriagereka. 2007. "The Dynamics of Islands: Speculations on the Locality of Movement." *Lingusitic Analysis* 33 (1–2): 149–75.

Hornstein, Norbert, and Jairo Nunes. 2008. "Adjunction, Labeling, and Bare Phrase Structure." *Biolinguistics* 2 (1): 57–86.

Huang, C.-T. James. 1982. "Logical Relations in Chinese and the Theory of Grammar." PhD dissertation, MIT.

Huang, C.-T. James, and C.-C. Jane Tang. 1991. "On the Local Nature of the Long-Distance Reflexive in Chinese." In *Long-Distance Anaphora*, edited by Jan Koster and Eric Reuland, 263–282. Cambridge: Cambridge University Press.

Hunter, Timothy. 2010. "Relating Movement and Adjunction in Syntax and Semantics." PhD dissertation, University of Maryland, College Park.

Iatridou, Sabine, and Ivy Sichel. 2011. "Negative DPs A-Movement, and Scope Diminishment." *Linguistic Inquiry* 42 (4): 595–629.

Jackendoff, Ray. 1969. "An Interpretive Theory of Negation." *Foundations of Language* 5 (2): 218–241.

Jackendoff, Ray. 1972. *Semantic Interpretation in Generative Grammar.* Cambridge, MA: MIT Press.

Jackendoff, Ray. 2002. *Foundations of Language: Brain, Meaning, Grammar, Evolution.* Oxford: Oxford University Press.

Jackendoff, Ray, and Steven Pinker. 2005. "The Nature of the Language Faculty and Its Implications for Evolution of Language (Reply to Fitch, Hauser, and Chomsky)." *Cognition* 97 (2): 211–225. https://doi.org/10.1016/j.cognition.2005.04.006.

Jakobson, Roman. 1960. "Linguistics and Poetics." In *Style in Language*, edited by T. Sebeok, 350–377. Cambridge, MA: MIT Press.

Jakobson, Roman, C. Gunnar M. Fant, and Morris Halle. 1952. *Preliminaries to Speech Analysis: The Distinctive Features and Their Correlates.* Cambridge, MA: MIT Press.

Jakobson, Roman, and Morris Halle. 1956. *Fundamentals of Language*. The Hague, Netherlands: Mouton.

Jespersen, Otto. 1949. *Modern English Grammar on Historical Principles*. Copenhagen: Munksgaard.

Johnson, Kyle. 2002. "Towards an Etiology of Adjunct Islands." *Nordlyd* 31 (1): 187–215.

Joshi, Aravind. 1985. "How Much Context-Sensitivity Is Necessary for Characterizing Structural Descriptions?—Tree Adjoining Grammars." In *Natural Language Processing—Theoretical, Computational and Psychological Perspectives*, edited by David Dowty, Karttunen Lauri, and Arnold Zwicky, 206–250. New York: Cambridge University Press.

Kamp, Hans. 1981. "A Theory of Truth and Semantic Representation." In *Formal Semantics—The Essential Readings*, edited by Paul Portner and Barbara Partee, 189–222. Malden, MA: Blackwell.

Karttunen, Lauri. 1968. "What Makes Definite Noun Phrases Definite?" Paper p-3781, The RAND Corporation, Santa Monica, CA.

Kayne, Richard. 1969. "The Transformational Cycle in French Syntax." PhD dissertation, MIT.

Kayne, Richard. 1975. *French Syntax: The Transformational Cycle*. Cambridge, MA: MIT Press.

Kayne, Richard. 1984. *Connectedness and Binary Branching*. Dordrecht, Netherlands: Foris.

Kayne, Richard. 1994. *The Antisymmetry of Syntax*. Cambridge, MA: MIT Press.

Kayne, Richard. 2002. "Pronouns and Their Antecedents." In *Derivation and Explanation in the Minimalist Program*, edited by S. Epstein and D. Seely, 133–166. Malden, MA: Blackwell.

Kegl, Judy, and G. Iwata. 1989. "Lenguaje de Signos Nicaraguense: A Pidgin Sheds Light on the Creole?" In *Proceedings of the Fourth Meeting of the Pacific Linguistics Conference*, edited by R. Carlson, S. DeLancey, S. Gildea, D. Payne, and A. Saxena, 266–294. Eugene: University of Oregon.

Kempson, Ruth, Tim Fernando, and Nicholas Asher, eds. 2012. *Philosophy of Linguistics*. Handbook of the Philosophy of Science. Amsterdam, Netherlands: Elsevier B.V.

Kheifets, Aaron, David Freestone, and C. R. Gallistel. 2017. "Theoretical Implications of Quantitative Properties of Interval Timing and Probability Estimation in Mouse and Rat." *Journal of the Experimental Analysis of Behavior* 108 (1): 39–72.

Kiparsky, Paul. 1973. "'Elsewhere' in Phonology." In *A Festschrift for Morris Halle*, edited by S. Anderson, 93–106. New York: Holt, Rinehart, and Winston.

Kiparsky, Paul. 2008. "On the Architecture of Pānini's Grammar." In *Sanskrit Computational Linguistics*, edited by Gérard Huet, Amba Kulkarni, and Peter Scharf, 33–94. Lecture Notes in Computer Science. Heidelberg, Germany: Springer.

Kitahara, Hisatugu. 1996. "Raising Quantifiers without Quantifier Raising." In *Minimalist Ideas: Syntactic Studies in the Minimalist Framework*, edited by W. Abraham, S. D. Epstein, H. Thráinsson, and J.-W. Zwart, 189–198. Amsterdam: John Benjamins.

Klima, Ed. 1964. "Negation in English." In *The Structure of Language*, edited by J. J. Katz and J. Fodor, 246–323. Englewood Cliffs, NJ: Prentice-Hall.

Kohl, Patrick L., Neethu Thulasi, Benjamin Rutschmann, Ebi A. George, Ingolf Steffan-Dewenter, and A. Brockmann. 2020. "Adaptive Evolution of Honeybee Dance Dialects." *Proceedings of the Royal Society B: Biological Sciences* 287 (1922): 1–9. https://doi.org/10.1098/rspb.2020.0190.

Kracht, Marcus. 2003. *The Mathematics of Language*. Studies in Generative Grammar 63. Berlin: Mouton de Gruyter.

Kratzer, Angelika. 2009. "Making a Pronoun: Fake Indexicals as Windows into the Properties of Pronouns." *Linguistic Inquiry* 40 (2): 187–237.

Kroch, Anthony S. 1989. "Reflexes of Grammar in Patterns of Language Change." *Language Variation and Change* 1 (3): 199–244. https://doi.org/10.1017/S0954394500000168.

Kroch, Anthony S. 2001. "Syntactic Change." In *The Handbook of Contemporary Syntactic Theory*, edited by M. Baltin and C. Collins, 699–730. Oxford: Blackwell.

Kuno, Susumu, and Jane J. Robinson. 1972. "Multiple Wh Questions." *Linguistic Inquiry* 3 (4): 463–487.

Labov, William. 2001. *Principles of Linguistic Change*. Vol. 2: *Social Factors*. Oxford: Blackwell.

Lakoff, George. 1971. "On Generative Semantics." In *Semantics: An Interdisciplinary Reader*. Cambridge: Cambridge University Press.

Lakoff, George. 1987. *Women, Fire, and Dangerous Things*. Chicago: University of Chicago Press.

Landgraf, Tim, Raúl Rojas, Hai Nguyen, Fabian Kriegel, and Katja Stettin. 2011. "Analysis of the Waggle Dance Motion of Honeybees for the Design of a Biomimetic Honeybee Robot." *PLOS ONE* 6 (8): 1–10.

Langacker, Ronald. 1969. "On Pronominalization and the Chain of Command." In *Modern Studies in English*, edited by D. A. Reibel and S. A. Schane, 160–186. Englewood Cliffs, NJ: Prentice-Hall.

Langendoen, D. Terence, and Paul M. Postal. 1984. *The Vastness of Natural Languages*. Oxford: Basil Blackwell.

Larson, Brooke. 2016. "The Representation of Syntactic Action at a Distance: Multidominance versus the Copy Theory." *Glossa: A Journal of General Linguistics* 1 (1): 39. https://doi.org/http://doi.org/10.5334/gjgl.15.

Larson, Richard, and Gabriel Segal. 1995. *Knowledge of Meaning: An Introduction to Semantic Theory*. Cambridge, MA: MIT Press.

Larson, Richard K. 1988. "On the Double Object Construction." *Linguistic Inquiry* 19 (3): 335–391.

Lasnik, Howard. 1972. "Analyses of Negation in English." PhD dissertation, MIT.

Lasnik, Howard. 1976. "Remarks on Coreference." *Linguistic Analysis* 2 (1): 1–22.

Lasnik, Howard. 1981. "Restricting the Theory of Transformations." In *Explanation in Linguistics*, edited by N. Hornstein and D. Lightfoot, 152–173. Harlow, UK: Longman.

Lasnik, Howard. 1989. "On Certain Substitutes for Negative Data." In *Learnability and Linguistic Theory*, edited by R. Matthews and W. Demopoulos, 89–105. Dordrecht, Netherlands: D. Reidel.

Lasnik, Howard. 1990. *Essays on Restrictiveness and Learnability.* Studies in Natural Language and Linguistic Theory 20. Dordrecht, Netherlands: Kluwer.

Lasnik, Howard. 1991. "On the Necessity of Binding Conditions." In *Principles and Parameters in Comparative Grammar*, edited by B. Freidin, 7–28. Cambridge, MA: MIT Press.

Lasnik, Howard. 1993. "Lectures on Minimalist Syntax." *Uconn Working Papers in Linguistics: Occasional Papers* 1:25–73.

Lasnik, Howard. 1995. "A Note on Pseudogapping." *MIT Working Papers in Linguistics* 27:143–163. Cambridge, MA: MIT Working Papers in Linguistics.

Lasnik, Howard. 2001. "When Can You Save a Structure by Destroying It?" In *Proceedings of the North East Linguistic Society 31*, edited by U. Strauss, vol. 2, 301–320. Amherst, MA: Graduate Linguistics Student Association.

Lasnik, Howard. 2013. "Multiple Sluicing in English?" *Syntax* 17 (1): 1–20.

Lasnik, Howard. 2018. "Two Families of Questions." In *Language, Syntax, and the Natural Sciences*, edited by A. Gallego and R. Martin, 58–76. Cambridge: Cambridge University Press.

Lasnik, Howard (with Marcela Depiante and Arthur Stepanov). 2000. *Syntactic Structures Revisited: Contemporary Lectures on Classic Transformational Theory.* Cambridge, MA: MIT Press.

Lasnik, Howard, and Robert Fiengo. 1974. "Complement Object Deletion." *Linguistic Inquiry* 5 (4): 535–571.

Lasnik, Howard, and Kenshi Funakoshi. 2011. "On the Single Copy Condition." Ms., University of Maryland, College Park.

Lasnik, Howard, and Joseph J. Kupin. 1977. "A Restrictive Theory of Transformational Grammar." *Theoretical Linguistics* 4 (1–3): 173–196.

Lasnik, Howard, and Mamoru Saito. 1984. "On the Nature of Proper Government." *Linguistic Inquiry* 15 (2): 235–289.

Lasnik, Howard, and Mamoru Saito. 1992. *Move Alpha.* Cambridge, MA: MIT Press.

Lasnik, Howard, and Tim Stowell. 1991. "Weakest Crossover." *Linguistic Inquiry* 22 (4): 687–720.

Lasnik, Howard, and Juan Uriagereka. 1988. *A Course in GB Syntax.* Cambridge, MA: MIT Press.

Lasnik, Howard, and Juan Uriagereka. 2002. "On the Poverty of the Challenge." *Linguistic Review* 19 (1–2): 147–150.

Lasnik, Howard, and Juan Uriagereka. 2005. *A Course in Minimalist Syntax.* Oxford: Blackwell.

Lebeaux, David. 1990. "Relative Clauses, Licensing and the Nature of Derivation." In *Proceedings of NELS 20*, edited by J. Carter, R. M. Déchaine, B. Phillip, and T. Sherer, 318–332. Amherst, MA: Graduate Linguistics Student Association.

Lebeaux, David. 2000. *Language Acquisition and the Form of the Grammar.* Amsterdam: John Benjamins.

Lebeaux, David. 2009. *Where Does Binding Theory Apply?* Cambridge, MA: MIT Press.

Lees, R. B. 1960. *The Grammar of English Nominalizations*. Bloomington: Indiana University Press.

Lees, R. B., and Edward S. Klima. 1963. "Rules for English Pronominalization." *Language* 39 (1): 17–28.

Legate, Julie Anne, and Charles Yang. 2002. "Empirical Re-Assessment of Stimulus Poverty Arguments." *Linguistic Review* 19 (1–2): 151–162.

Lightfoot, David. 1991. *How to Set Parameters: Arguments from Language Change*. Cambridge, MA: MIT Press, Bradford Books

Lightfoot, David. 1999. *The Development of Language: Acquisition, Change, and Evolution*. Malden, MA: Blackwell.

Lindenmayer, Aristid. 1968. "Mathematical Models for Cellular Interactions in Development I. Filaments with One-Sided Inputs." *Journal of Theoretical Biology* 18 (3): 280–299. https://doi.org/10.1016/0022-5193(68)90079-9.

Lobina, David, and Mark Brenchley. 2017. "Reply to Dan Everett's A Dozen Years of Misunderstanding." *Inference* 3 (2). https://inference-review.com/letter/a-dozen-years-of-misunderstanding.

Lodge, Donna Nemeth, and Edwin A. Leach. 1975. "Children's Acquisition of Idioms in the English Language." *Journal of Speech and Hearing Research* 18 (3): 521–529.

Longobardi, Giuseppe, and Cristina Guardiano. 2011. "The Biolinguistic Program and Historical Reconstruction." In *The Biolinguistic Enterprise New Perspectives on the Evolution and Nature of the Human Language Faculty*, edited by A. M. Di Sciullo and C. Boeckx, 266–304. Oxford: Oxford University Press.

Lou-Magnuson, Matthew, and Luca Onnis. 2018. "Social Network Limits Language Complexity." *Cognitive Science* 42 (8): 2790–2817.

Madigan, Sean, and Masahiro Yamada. 2007. "Asymmetry in Anaphoric Dependencies: A Cross-Linguistic Study of Inclusive Reference." *University of Pennsylvania Working Papers in Linguistics, Proceedings of the 30th Annual Penn Linguistics Colloquium* 13 (1): 183–195.

Mandelbrot, Benoit. 1975. *Les Objets Fractals: Forme, Hasard et Dimension*. Paris: Flammarion.

Marantz, Alec. 2005. "Generative Linguistics within the Cognitive Neuroscience of Language." *Linguistic Review* 22 (2–4): 429–445. https://doi.org/10.1515/tlir.2005.22.2-4.429.

Marcus, Mitchell. 1980. *A Theory of Syntactic Recognition for Natural Language*. Cambridge, MA: MIT Press.

May, Robert. 1977. "The Grammar of Quantification." PhD dissertation, MIT.

McCarthy, John. 1981. "A Prosodic Theory of Nonconcatenative Morphology." *Linguistic Inquiry* 12 (3): 373–418.

McCawley, James D. 1968. "The Role of Semantics in a Grammar." In *Universals in Linguistic Theory*, edited by E. Bach and R. Harms, 124–169. New York: Holt, Rinehart, and Winston.

Mehler, Jacques, Peter Jusczyk, Ghislaine Lambertz, Nilofar Halsted, Josiane Bertoncini, and Claudine Amiel-Tison. 1988. "A Precursor of Language Acquisition in Young Infants." *Cognition* 29 (2): 143–178.

Merchant, Jason. 2001. *The Syntax of Silence: Sluicing, Islands and the Theory of Ellipsis*. Oxford: Oxford University Press.

Milsark, Gary. 1974. "Existential Sentences in English." PhD dissertation, MIT.

Moro, Andrea, Marco Tettamanti, Daniela Perani, Caterina Donati, Stefano F. Cappa, and Fiorina Fazio. 2001. "Syntax and the Brain: Disentangling Grammar by Selective Anomalies." *Neuroimage* 13 (1): 110–118.

Muysken, Pieter. 1982. "Parameterizing the Notion 'Head.'" *Journal of Linguistic Research* 2 (1): 57–75.

Nespor, Marina, Mohinish Shukla, and Jacques Mehler. 2011. "Stress-Timed vs. Syllable-Timed Languages." In *Suprasegmental and Prosodic Phonology*, vol. 2 of *The Blackwell Companion to Phonology*, edited by Marc van Oostendorp, Colin J. Ewen, Elizabeth Hume, and Keren Rice, 1147–1157. Chichester, UK: Blackwell Publishing Inc.

Nevins, Andrew, David Pesetsky, and Cilene Rodrigues. 2009. "Pirahã Exceptionality: A Reassessment." *Language* 85 (2): 355–404.

Nishigauchi, Taisuke. 1998. "'Multiple Sluicing' in Japanese and the Functional Nature of Wh-Phrases." *Journal of East Asian Linguistics* 7 (2): 121–152.

Nunes, Jairo. 2004. *Linearization of Chains and Sideward Movement*. Cambridge, MA: MIT Press.

Ormazabal, Javier, Juan Uriagereka, and Myriam Uribe-Etxebarria. 1994. "Word Order and Wh-Movement: Towards a Parametric Account." Ms., University of Connecticut and University of Maryland.

Orús, Román, Roger Martin, and Juan Uriagereka. 2017. "Mathematical Foundations of Matrix Syntax." Ms., https://arxiv.org/abs/1710.00372.

Otero, Carlos. 1976. "The Dictionary in a Generative Grammar." Paper presented at the Language Theory Session of the Modern Language Association, New York.

Papoulis, Athanasios. 1984. *Probability, Random Variables, and Stochastic Processes*. New York: McGraw-Hill.

Partee, Barbara H., Alice ter Meulen, and Robert E. Wall. 1990. *Mathematical Methods in Linguistics*. Dordrecht, Netherlands: Kluwer.

Perfors, Amy, Joshua B. Tenenbaum, and Terry Regier. 2006. "Poverty of the Stimulus? A Rational Approach." In *Proceedings of the 28th Annual Conference of the Cognitive Science Society*, edited by R. Sun and N. Miyake, 136–141. n.p.: Cognitive Science Society.

Perfors, Amy, Joshua B. Tenenbaum, and Terry Regier. 2011. "The Learnability of Abstract Syntactic Principles." *Cognition* 118 (3): 306–338.

Perlmutter, David M. 1968. "Deep and Surface Structure Constraints in Syntax." PhD dissertation, MIT.

Pesetsky, David. 2000. *Phrasal Movement and Its Kin*. Cambridge, MA: MIT Press.

Piattelli-Palmarini, Massimo, ed. 1980. *Language and Learning: The Debate Between Jean Piaget and Noam Chomsky.* Cambridge, MA: Harvard University Press.

Pica, Pierre. 1987. "On the Nature of the Reflexivization Cycle." *Proceedings of the North East Linguistics Society*17 (2): 483–499.

Pietroski, Paul. 2005. *Events and Semantic Architecture.* Oxford: Oxford University Press.

Pietroski, Paul. 2008. "Minimalist Meaning, Internalist Interpretation." *Biolinguistics* 4:317–341.

Pinker, Steven. 1984. *Language Learnability and Language Development.* Cambridge, MA: Harvard University Press.

Platero, Paul. 1978. "Missing Noun Phrases in Navajo." PhD dissertation, MIT.

Plessis, Hans du. 1977. "Wh Movement in Afrikaans." *Linguistic Inquiry* 8 (4): 723–726.

Pollard, Carl, and Ivan Sag. 1992. "Anaphors in English and the Scope of Binding Theory." *Linguistic Inquiry* 23 (2): 261–303.

Pollock, Jean-Yves. 1989. "Verb Movement, Universal Grammar, and the Structure of IP." *Linguistic Inquiry* 20 (3): 365–424.

Post, Emil L. 1947. "Recursive Unsolvability of a Problem of Thue." *Journal of Symbolic Logic* 12 (1): 1–11.

Postal, Paul M. 1966a. "A Note on 'Understood Transitively.'" *International Journal of American Linguistics* 32 (1): 90–93.

Postal, Paul M. 1966b. "On So-Called 'Pronouns' I in English." In *Report of the Seventeenth Annual Round Table Meeting on Linguistics and Language Studies*, edited by Francis P. Dinneen, 177–206. Washington, DC: Georgetown University Press.

Postal, Paul M. 1970. "On the Surface Verb 'Remind.'" *Linguistic Inquiry* 1 (1): 37–120. http://www.jstor.org/stable/4177529.

Postal, Paul M. 1972. "The Best Theory." In *Goals of Linguistic Theory*, edited by Stanley Peters, 131–170. Englewood Cliffs, NJ: Prentice-Hall.

Postal, Paul M. 1974. *On Raising: One Rule of English Grammar and Its Theoretical Implications.* Cambridge, MA: MIT Press.

Prince, Alan, and Paul Smolensky. 1993. "Optimality Theory: Constraint Interaction in Generative Grammar." Ms., Brandeis University and University of Colorado at Boulder.

Prinz, Philip M. 1983. "The Development of Idiomatic Meaning in Children." *Language and Speech* 26 (3): 263–272.

Pullum, Geoffrey K., and Barbara C. Scholz. 2002. "Empirical Assessment of Stimulus Poverty Arguments." *Linguistic Review* 19 (1–2): 9–50.

Radford, Andrew. 1990. *Syntactic Theory and the Acquisition of English Syntax.* Oxford: Blackwell.

Reggia, James A., Reiner Schulz, Gerald S. Wilkinson, and Juan Uriagereka. 2001. "Conditions Enabling the Emergence of Inter-Agent Signalling in an Artificial World." *Artificial Life* 7 (1): 3–32. https://doi.org/10.1162/106454601300328007.

Reinhart, Tanya. 1976. "The Syntactic Domain of Anaphora." PhD dissertation, MIT.

Reinhart, Tanya. 1983. "Coreference and Bound Anaphora: A Restatement of the Anaphora Questions." *Linguistics and Philosophy* 6 (1): 47–88.

Reuland, Eric, Sally Chi Ho Wong, and Martin Everaert. 2020. "How the Complexity of Mandarin Zi-Ji Simplifies the Grammar." *Linguistic Inquiry* 51 (4): 799–814.

Rivero, María Luisa. 1970. "A Surface Structure Constraint on Negation in Spanish." *Language* 46 (3): 640–666.

Rizzi, Luigi. 1982. *Issues in Italian Syntax*. Studies in Generative Grammar 11. Berlin: De Gruyter Mouton.

Rizzi, Luigi. 1986. "Null Objects in Italian and the Theory of Pro." *Linguistic Inquiry* 17 (3): 501–557.

Rizzi, Luigi. 1990. *Relativized Minimality*. Cambridge, MA: MIT Press.

Rizzi, Luigi. 2001. "Relativized Minimality Effects." In *The Handbook of Contemporary Syntactic Theory*, edited by Mark Baltin and Chris Collins, 89–110. Malden, MA: Blackwell.

Roeper, Thomas, and Edwin Williams, eds. 1987. *Parameter Setting*. Studies in Theoretical Psycholinguistics. Dordrecht, Netherlands: D. Reidel.

Roeske, Tina C., Damian Kelty-Stephen, and Sebastian Wallot. 2018. "Multifractal Analysis Reveals Music-like Dynamic Structure in Songbird Rhythms." *Scientific Reports* 8:4750.

Rosenbloom, Paul C. 1950. *The Elements of Mathematical Logic*. New York: Dover Publications.

Ross, John Robert. 1967. "Constraints on Variables in Syntax." PhD dissertation, MIT. http://dspace.mit.edu/handle/1721.1/15166. [Published in 1986 as *Infinite Syntax!* Norwood, NJ: Ablex.]

Ross, John Robert. 1969. "Guess Who?" In *Papers from the 5th Regional Meeting of the Chicago Linguistic Society*, edited by Robert Binnick, Alice Davison, Georgia Green, and Jerry Morgan, 252–286. Chicago: Chicago Linguistic Society.

Rouveret, Alain, and Jean-Roger Vergnaud. 1980. "Specifying Reference to the Subject: French Causatives and Conditions on Representations." *Linguistic Inquiry* 11 (1): 97–202.

Rozenberg, Grzegorz, and Arto Salomaa. 1976. "The Mathematical Theory of L Systems." In *Advances in Information Science,* edited by Julius T. Tou, 161–206. New York: Plenum.

Runner, Jeffrey T., Rachel S. Sussman, and Michael K. Tanenhaus. 2006. "Processing Reflexives and Pronouns in Picture Noun Phrase." *Cognitive Science* 30 (2): 193–241.

Sampson, Geoffrey. 1989. "Language Acquisition: Growth or Learning?" *Philosophical Papers* 18 93): 203–240.

Saussure, Ferdinand. 1916. *Cours de Linguistique Générale*. Paris: Payot.

Schein, Barry. 2017. *'And': Conjunction Reduction Redux*. Cambridge, MA: MIT Press.

Scholz, Barbara C., and Geoffrey K. Pullum. 2007. "Tracking the Origins of Transformational Generative Grammar." *Journal of Linguistics* 43 (3): 701–723.

Searls, David B. 1992. "The Linguistics of DNA." *American Scientist* 80 (6): 579–591.

Sheehan, Michelle, Theresa Biberauer, Ian Roberts, and Anders Holmberg. 2017. *The Final-Over-Final Condition: A Syntactic Universal.* Cambridge, MA: MIT Press.

Skinner, B. F. 1957. *Verbal Behavior.* New York: Appleton-Century-Crofts.

Smolensky, Paul, and Géraldine Legendre. 2006. *The Harmonic Mind: From Neural Computation to Optimality-Theoretic Grammar.* Vol. 1: *Cognitive Architecture.* Cambridge, MA: MIT Press.

Snyder, William. 2016. "How to Set the Compounding Parameter." In *Proceedings of the 6th Conference on Generative Approaches to Language Acquisition North America (GALANA 2015)*, edited by Laurel Perkins, Rachel Dudley, Juliana Gerard, and Kasia Hitczenko, 122–130. Somerville, MA: Cascadilla Proceedings Project.

Sportiche, Dominique. 1986. "A Theory of Floating Quantifiers," *North East Linguistics Society* 17 (2): 581–594.

Stabler, Edward. 2013a. "The Epicenter of Linguistic Behavior." In *Language Down the Garden Path: The Cognitive and Biological Basis of Linguistic Structures*, edited by Montserrat Sanz, Itziar Laka, and Michael K Tanenhaus, 316–323. Oxford: Oxford University Press.

Stabler, Edward. 2013b. "Two Models of Minimalist, Incremental Syntactic Analysis." *Topics in Cognitive Science* 5 (3): 611–633. https://doi.org/10.1111/tops.12031.

Steedman, Marc. 2000. *The Syntactic Process.* Cambridge, MA: MIT Press.

Stjepanovic, Sandra. 2004. "Clitic Climbing and Restructuring with 'Finite Clause' and Infinitive Complements." *Journal of Slavic Linguistics* 12 (1–2): 173–212.

Stowell, Timothy Angus. 1981. "Origins of Phrase Structure." PhD dissertation, MIT.

Takahashi, Daiko. 1994. "Minimality of Movement." PhD dissertation, University of Connecticut, Storrs.

Tancredi, Christopher. 1992. "Deletion, Deaccenting and Presupposition." PhD dissertation, MIT.

Terzi, Arhonto. 1996. "Clitic Climbing from Finite Clauses and Tense Raising." *Probus* 8 (3): 273–296.

Tesnière, Lucien. 1959. *Éléments de Syntaxe Structurale.* Paris: Klincksieck.

Tesnière, Lucien. 2015. *Elements of Structural Syntax.* Translated by Timothy Osborne and Sylvain Kahane. Amsterdam: John Benjamins.

Thue, Axel. 1914. *Probleme über Veränderungen von Zeichenreihen nach gegebenen Regeln.* Kristiania [Oslo]: J. Dybwad.

Tomalin, Marcus. 2006. *Linguistics and the Formal Sciences: The Origins of Generative Grammar.* Cambridge: Cambridge University Press.

Townsend, David J., and Thomas G. Bever. 2001. *Sentence Comprehension: The Integration of Habits and Rules.* Cambridge, MA: MIT Press.

Travis, Lisa deMena. 1984. "Parameters and Effects of Word Order Variation." PhD dissertation, MIT.

Uriagereka, Juan. 1988. *On Government*, PhD dissertation, UConn.

Uriagereka, Juan. 1997. "Multiple Spell-Out." *Groninger Arbeiten Zur Germanistischen Linguistik* 40:109–135.

Uriagereka, Juan. 1998. *Rhyme and Reason: An Introduction to Minimalist Syntax*. Cambridge, MA: MIT Press.

Uriagereka, Juan. 1999. "Multiple Spell-Out." In *Working Minimalism*, edited by Samuel David Epstein and Norbert Hornstein, chapter 10. Cambridge, MA: MIT Press.

Uriagereka, Juan. 2008. *Syntactic Anchors: On Semantic Structuring*. Cambridge: Cambridge University Press.

Uriagereka, Juan. 2012. *Spell-Out and the Minimalist Program*. Oxford: Oxford University Press.

Uriagereka, Juan. 2018. *Biolinguistic Investigations and the Formal Language Hierarchy*. Routledge Leading Linguists. New York: Routledge.

Weir, David J., and Aravind Joshi. 1988. "Combinatory Categorial Grammars: Generative Power and Relationship to Linear Context-Free Rewriting Systems." In *Proceedings, 26th Meeting of the Association for Computational Linguistics*, 278–285. Buffalo, NY: Association for Computational Linguistics.

Wexler, Ken. 1990. "Innateness and Maturation in Linguistic Development." *Developmental Psychobiology* 23 (7): 645–660.

Williams, Edwin S. 1974. "Rule Ordering in Syntax." PhD dissertation, MIT.

Williams, Edwin S. 1981. "Transformationless Grammar." *Linguistic Inquiry* 12 (4): 645–653.

Winograd, Terry. 1976. "Towards a Procedural Understanding of Semantics." *Revue Internationale de Philosophie* 30 (117–118): 260–303.

Yang, Charles. 2013. "Ontogeny and Phylogeny of Language." *PNAS* 110 (16): 6324–6327.

Yang, Charles. 2017. "Rage Against the Machine: Evaluation Metrics in the 21st Century." *Language Acquisition* 24 (2): 100–125. https://doi.org/10.1080/10489223.2016.1274318.

Yang, Charles D. 2000. "Knowledge and Learning in Natural Language." PhD dissertation, MIT.

Zeevat, Henk. 1995. "Idiomatic Blocking and the Elsewhere Principle." In *Idioms: Structural and Psychological Perspectives*, edited by Martin Everaert, Erik-Jan van der Linden, André Schenk, and Schreuder, 301–316. London: Psychology Press.

Zuidema, Willem H. 2005. "The Major Transitions in the Evolution of Language." PhD dissertation, University of Edinburgh.

Zwicky, Arnold M. 1989. "Quicker, More Quickly, *Quicklier*." *Yearbook of Morphology* 2:139–173.

Index